LESSONS ON THE ROAD TO HOPE

A Psychiatrist's Journey

John S. Graves, M.D.

This memoir is dedicated to my beloved daughter Jessica

who is a psychotherapist.

Hope deferred makes the heart sick,

but a longing fulfilled is a tree of life.

~Proverbs 13:12

I will never view my patients as anything

other than fellow creatures in human suffering.

~Moses Maimonides (ca. 1190)

Hope is the thing with wings.

~e.e. cummings

Table of Contents

INTRODUCTION

Shortly after I retired, a woman wrote to thank me for several years of therapy. Her generous comments capture the essence of a life transformed in treatment:

"You have no agenda except getting me to care for myself. You offered me some forgiveness when I wasn't able to forgive myself. I believed in you as much as you always believed in and hoped for me."

Improved self-care. Forgiveness. A trusting relationship offering hope. These are the ingredients of what another patient called "an extraordinary friendship."

This is a memoir about my life as a psychiatrist during a period of profound changes. It is written for mental health professionals, physicians, ministers, pastoral counselors, and for those training in the helping professions. It is also addressed to anyone who is simply curious about what goes on behind the closed doors of the consultation room and how a psychiatrist manages to deal with the inevitable stresses of a busy practice. From 1962 when I first encountered chronic schizophrenics as an orderly at Marcy State Hospital in upstate New York to 2016 when I retired in Denver, the practice of psychiatry and my life as a practitioner have evolved in ways I never could have imagined.

The rich tapestries of my patients' stories have become interwoven with my own personal and professional narratives. What ties these narratives together is the *theme of emerging hope*. I have listened to thousands of stories for over half a century. Now it is time to tell my own.

Two months after I concluded my summer job at Marcy State, I experienced my first depressive episode. I was a sophomore at Wesleyan University and had just turned nineteen. Bewildered and scared by what was happening to me, my grades in pre-med courses plummeted and I changed my major to history and religion. Over the next several years I learned to manage my depressions and returned to pursue my initial vision of a life in medicine, ultimately in psychiatry.

Along the path of discovering my calling, I seriously considered careers in teaching, the ministry, and transplant surgery. Exploring these arenas, I discovered a convergence of talents for listening and empathy, an unwavering optimism regarding human change, and an interest in resolving conflicts, stimulated by those I first experienced in my own family.

My attraction to psychiatry was irresistible, with its intimate, nuanced human connections and the promise of ongoing intellectual stimulation in a field situated at the crossroads of the biological sciences, psychology, and the humanities. I came to realize that almost everything that I had learned would ultimately become relevant for my work.

I invite the reader to share the experiences of how I chose my profession, what it felt like to practice it, and what I learned from working with a diverse and challenging group of patients. As my own religious faith evolved over the years, I found ways of helping my patients utilize their own religious traditions and beliefs to augment their healing processes. To my knowledge this is the first psychiatric memoir to address these issues and to explore the benefits of using forgiveness in the process of psychotherapy.

While composing my memoir, I was surprised to find that many of my most compelling treatment cases exemplified a convergence of my own personal struggles, those of my patients, and prominent social issues of the times. In response, I decided to include chapters on listening and empathy, boundary crossings and violations, suicidal depression, and the personal vulnerabilities of physicians, gays, and bisexuals. In these chapters I utilize detailed case studies to illustrate how I worked as a therapist and how my work affected my personal life and vice versa.

As my own mood disorder evolved from a series of depressions to a form of bipolar disorder in my early forties, I experienced a frightening suicidal depression. In treatment with a skilled and empathic colleague, I came to understand that depressions in men, especially in physicians, are often encased in a cocoon of shame and denial. In my chapter "Depression, Suicide, and the Dialectic of Hope" I describe how I used my own experiences to better empathize with my patients. Mining my own struggles, I discuss how I utilized patients as co-consultants in forming one of the first outpatient therapy groups for those with bipolar disorder.

In the span of over four decades working with psychiatric patients, I have participated in remarkable changes in my field. These changes include a shift from pathological theories of mind to a "positive psychiatry" approach which emphasizes the integration of mind, body, and spirit in achieving resilience and wellness. Psychiatry, over much of its history, has been a rather isolated clinical endeavor, evoking caricatures of "shrinks," dozing analysts, and "the people in white coats who take you away." More recently, it has evolved into an interdisciplinary, highly complex branch of medicine shaped by research in multiple areas of brain function, including the neurophysiological bases of cognition, affect, behavior, and memory. In this book, I explore these innovations in detail and describe how they increased both the scope and effectiveness of my practice.

Psychiatric practice in the future will be compelled to expand its domain beyond the ailments of individuals, couples, and families. The widespread effects of climate change; pandemics such as COVID-19; social, economic, and political disruptions, and the accelerating developments of the digital age will command the attention of psychiatrists, who themselves will be dealing with a whole new set of "Acceleration Anxieties" alongside their patients. This leveling of the playing field will represent a significant challenge. It will also represent unique opportunities for increased empathy and growth on both sides of the therapeutic partnership.

Psychiatrists in the mid-twenty-first century will need to make moral choices about the extent to which they are willing to move outside the safe confines of their offices to address a broad range of social ills such as the breakdown of civil discourse, gun violence, a rampant suicide epidemic, and attacks on truth, justice, and democratic values by demagogues such as Donald Trump. We are living in an age where psychic suffering can no longer be divorced from the pervasive effects of disturbing social trends.

At the same time, the core principles of psycho-dynamic therapy, originating with Freud, Jung, Horney, and their later colleagues will, in my opinion, continue to provide an essential foundation for any practitioner who wishes to help patients undergo sustainable personality changes leading to more fulfilling and creative lives.

Most memoirs, by definition, avoid including references. It is my belief that books, like persons, have genealogies that are essential in understanding the origins of the writer's thoughts, feelings, and in my case, therapeutic interventions. As this memoir is clearly a hybrid of personal and professional genres, I have chosen to include a section on Chapter Notes which I trust will be of interest to my colleagues and to younger professionals in training.

I am aware of the fallibility of memories and of the significant differences between "historical truths" (those that can be consensually validated) and "narrative truths" (those that create unique personal meaning for the narrator). I take full responsibility for the narrative truths I describe in this memoir and trust that I have done justice to those of my patients. By disguising personal details in my clinical case studies, I have done my best to maintain confidentiality, while at the same time seeking to preserve what is unique, compelling, and psychologically salient in the therapeutic interactions I describe. In a few cases I have created composite characters to illustrate important clinical processes.

I sent requests to patients whose detailed case studies appear in this memoir and obtained written permission to publish material regarding their treatments with me, which they reviewed and approved prior to publication. I deeply appreciate their willingness to reengage and collaborate with me in the interest of bringing this work to press.

John S. Graves, M.D.
Denver, Colorado

CHAPTER 1

BORN TO LISTEN

I n a voice low and resonant, like a cello, my mother taught me to listen to others and to the "still small voice of God." She was a natural listener herself and I, born more than a decade after my brothers, was her chosen protégé. Her ability to listen had made her the confidant of many of her friends and drew them to her. She delighted in sharing their stories with me and passing along her curiosity about their feelings, conflicts, and motivations. At seven, I was unsure why, but even then I sensed the importance of the role she had entrusted to me in those after-school conversations. When my mother, whom we called "Muzz," shared stories, her empathy and concern were palpable—and the message was clear. She was dedicated to helping her friends heal from their pain and misfortune. Before she said goodnight and tucked me in we said the Lord's Prayer together, asked God to bless each member of our family, my teachers, and whichever friends most needed God's help. I drifted off to sleep with my mother humming the melody of Brahms' Lullaby.

Muzz listened to recordings of spirituals, Amazing Grace, the Robert Shaw Chorale, and popular melodies of the '50s. To this day, I can hear the uplifting sonorities of Rachmaninoff's Second Piano Con-

1

certo filling the first floor of our modest home in Delmar, a suburb of Albany, New York, where I was born in 1943. I wonder now if my mother identified with the composer's triumph over depression in writing this piece. These musical memories and our intimate prayers formed the daily bread of my childhood.

Pop's voice was more variable than my mother's: calm and reflective at times, then urgent and strident, piercing my young ears like a snare drum. From Pop, I learned to listen for subtle changes in pitch and volume and to anticipate the mood shifts they forewarned. Many of my early "conversations" with my father were designed to teach me mechanical skills for which I had little aptitude. An electrical engineer, Pop would drone on about the complexities of circuits and motors while I stifled yawns, fearful of disappointing him if I dozed off. While I quickly lost the details of his monologues, I did learn to appreciate the importance of understanding how things work.

Pop was a strict disciplinarian and he used corporal punishment as his father had with him. Sometimes his emotions got the better of him and he would lose control of his hands and the thin wooden slats with which he throttled my behind. When he was worked up, he punctuated each swat with a harsh judgment, which felt like all the fathers down the centuries were roaring in unison. I learned to go numb in the face of his anger and to disappear into a silent, black hole. The last sound in my head, my mother's pleadings from the top of the basement stairs: "Kenny... please stop."

In the spring of my kindergarten year, I jumped out of my second story bedroom window, explaining to my parents afterwards that I wanted to fly like the robin I'd watched land in an apple tree in our backyard. My Peter Pan adventure ended abruptly with fractures of my right elbow and wrist and a deep laceration on my forehead. My parents were entertaining neighbors at a party when Pop observed my "flight" from the living room window below. He rushed out to the backyard to fetch me in his arms. Our family doctor Harold Brown drove ahead to the Albany County Hospital emergency room where we met Dr. Crawford Campbell. Dr. Campbell quickly evaluated my shattered arm and asked me if I liked vanilla, chocolate or strawberry anesthesia. Strawberry, I said, and then I slept.

My recovery was complicated, requiring a second surgery and several more weeks in the hospital on my back with my arm elevated by a trapeze device with counterweights. I felt totally exposed and helpless, watching enviously as other kids with broken bones entered and left the open pediatric ward. Tethered to the trapeze tower as I was, I was terrified that I would never get to go home. Dr. Campbell, in his starched white coat and cheery smile, showed a warm attentiveness during rounds that raised my spirits. One morning he sat next to me on the bed and we discussed whether I would end up being a "southpaw" in baseball—I did. I returned home with my first lessons in good bedside manners. I'm sure I frightened my parents, but I don't recall their ever asking me about possible self-destructive elements in my flying adventure.

I do recall Dr. Campbell sawing off my cast, sparing my arm, thank God. My arm, revealed for the first time in two months, was smelly and withered. I was so weak I couldn't make a fist. Pop, refusing to accept my incapacity, used his engineering skills to devise a rehab device for me. Employing a leather glove, he attached two thick rubber bands to each of my fingertips, fixing each one in turn to a tight ring that was taped to my forearm. Twice a day he supervised my flexion and extension finger exercises until I nearly fainted with pain and exhaustion. I hated these sessions, but I loved him later for his passionate devotion to my recovery.

In my fifth and sixth years, my older brothers Tom and Charles left for college, leaving me to contend with my parents' conflicts without my brothers' affection and buffering. My parents' arguments usually took place in their bedroom, behind closed doors. I became frightened by my father's intense shouting and concerned for my mother, who said very little and often emerged in tears. I was confused about why they argued but wished I could do something to stop their fights. I imagined that if I listened to my mother's stories about herself and her friends, I would somehow be able to prevent her from becoming depressed and thus also help my father remain calm. It was a tough job for a kid my age.

I wondered if my late arrival in the family could possibly have caused my parents' fighting. For a while I imagined that I had been adopted for some mysterious reason. Watching Pop's 8mm black and white home movies and hearing my brother Charles' stories about caring for me as an infant quickly dispelled this fantasy. The backyard movies of me, my mother, my brothers Tom and Charles, and our three-legged Springer Spaniel "Silverheels" ostensibly portrayed a normal, happy family.

Pop often arrived home from work exuding tension. His job as an engineer involved designing and supervising the construction of telephone central offices in small towns in central New York. I recall his talking about "blow ups" with supervisors and colleagues and his envy of those who surpassed him in the pecking order. All of us absorbed his stress, but it seemed that my mother suffered the most. Sometimes after school, I would find her alone in her bedroom, reading the Bible or in silent prayer, seeking God's help to heal her wounds and to find a path for forgiveness. For my mother, faith was far more than a set of beliefs. Her faith defined who she was.

During their college breaks, my brothers helped nurture my listening, each in his own way. Like my mother, Tom surrounded himself with music, listening to Beethoven, Brahms, and Berlioz by the hour. I loved to imitate him as he conducted and hummed along with the 78 rpm recordings of their great symphonies booming from the mono speakers in his bedroom. Beginning at age six he taught me to play on his wheezy antique pump organ with its twelve stops mimicking various wind and stringed instruments. I created my first tunes with Tom holding me between his legs as I stomped on the pedals and fingered the ivories. These happy interludes provided my first lessons in pitch, rhythm, and melody and generated my lifelong interest in music and keyboard instruments. Charles, who was two years younger than Tom, introduced me to chess, prompting me wordlessly as I struggled to think three moves in advance. If I reached to make an inopportune

4

move, he would raise an eyebrow. With shrewder moves, a faint smile would enlighten his face and, I am certain, mine as well. As we played chess, I imbibed the rudiments of non-verbal communication and thinking ahead. What I remember most about Charles was his consistent devotion to my wellbeing.

My parents, sensing my budding interest in music, bought a used upright piano when I was six and had it moved into my bedroom a few years later. After a few months I was begging for lessons. They found a congenial teacher in Mr. Morris, who taught at the Albany Conservatory. Walking into this ivy-covered stone building off State Street, I was enveloped by an impressive polyphony of pianos, flutes, and violins. There I discovered a safe oasis of melodies to offset the dissonance in my family. Mr. Morris was astute in allowing me to pick my own pieces, work at my own pace, and spared me the experiences of nail-biting recitals. I learned that listening to what I was playing was as important as any techniques I could learn. I enjoyed my lessons and Mr. Morris' relaxed permissiveness for seven years.

When I wasn't practicing piano, I roamed the neighborhood after school. My buddy Roger and I often put our ears to the train tracks, waiting for the massive Delaware and Hudson steam engines to come clanging and snorting through our neighborhood. We could feel the vibrations on the tracks long before the horn bellowed its ear-splitting, mournful warnings. The D & H engineers waved to us as the locomotive's gigantic iron wheels crushed the pennies we had carefully placed on the tracks. Feeling a connection with such power was truly exhilarating. A decade later these behemoths vanished forever, eclipsed by the age of diesel.

When I was ten, I read an edition of *Robin Hood* including the vivid color illustrations by N.C. Wyeth. I was inspired to join a neighborhood gang, featuring me as Little John, my swarthy friend Art as Robin, Paul as a portly Friar Tuck, and Mike as Alan-A-Dale. We held archery contests in our own Sherwood Forest, engaged in stick-sword fighting, where we won bloody battles against the Sheriff of Nottingham and his boys from across the tracks, and robbed the rich to feed the poor. Our parents gave us free run of the woods and trusted us to be responsible and stay safe. I grew in confidence with these adventures, a welcome distraction from the periodic storms at home.

With these same friends, I advanced from Cubs to Boy Scouts and, with Pop's concerted support, attained the rank of Eagle. When I was fourteen, I traveled with a dozen other scouts around the U.S. in a three-car caravan, exploring Mount Rushmore, the Badlands, Yellowstone, Yosemite, L.A., and the Philmont Scout Ranch in New Mexico where we met hundreds of boys from all over America. My involvement with Scouting gave me a lifelong appreciation for discipline, teamwork, a love of outdoor adventures, community service, and the value of supportive men friends.

Pop loved to fish and in the fall often took me to our cottage on Chaumont Bay on the eastern end of Lake Ontario. We drove north, just the two of us, for five hours in our green '50 Studebaker bulletnose convertible. Fishing days usually started out in typical Pop style. "Time to get up—half the day's shot," he'd shout at 5:30 a.m. We gobbled down our Shredded Wheat and burnt toast with strawberry jam and hustled up the shore to cast minnows and crayfish out over the limestone banks where feisty smallmouth bass were eager for breakfast.

Once we'd been on the water for a while, Pop was transformed. He became relaxed, jovial, and reflective. Apart from the fishing stories from his childhood on the Indian River near "little Philadelphia," we barely spoke, tuning in to the sounds of the waves and the shrill cries of seagulls swooping down to snatch our cast minnows before they hit the water. Pop's contented whistling increased as the rising sun warmed our faces. By nine o'clock, we had cleaned our heavy stringer of bass and returned triumphantly to the cottage.

In the afternoon, we listened to the World Series on the radio, always rooting for the underdog. Between innings, Pop taught me to skip thin pieces of limestone over the water's surface. In the evenings, soothed by our time on the water, Pop strummed his ukulele or blew "I've Been Working on the Railroad" on his harmonica as we sat in front of the glowing Franklin stove, the only source of heat in our drafty cottage. I felt closer and safer with him at those times and knew that he loved me.

When I was in my early teens Pop made genuine attempts to make up for his early harsh discipline. We took a week-long road trip to visit a family friend in Michigan and to fly fish the legendary Au Sable River. As we talked during this trip, I sensed that he was trying hard to provide me with the intimacy and affection he never got from his father who died when he was fourteen. Later in therapy I developed a keen sense of empathy for how challenging fathering without a positive male role model must have been for him.

My parents' arguments became increasingly frequent in the late 1950s. A glance at my mother's VW Beetle revealed peace signs while Pop's Ford Station wagon sported twin American flags, trumpeting his conservative brand of patriotism. My mother often reverted to her soft southern drawl, hinting at her Tar Heel origins in Chapel Hill, while Pop spoke in the short, clipped manner of his Yankee farming community origins in Adams Center, New York.

Muzz was no match for Pop and often retreated from his tirades. I usually followed suit and sought the solace of my bedroom, wishing I could protect her, but afraid to take the brunt of my father's anger. As I grew older, I found I could soothe myself by playing on the piano or returning to my Robin Hood haunts in the woods, where the rhythmic, cheerful sounds of birds and crickets restored my equilibrium.

As I improved on the piano, I discovered that I could mold my improvisations to fit my moods and sort out my feelings. My piano became my best friend for a while, a kind and dependable alter ego. With it, I found I could summon tender longings for peace or explode with all the ferocity of pitched battle. As I listened to my playing, I realized I had it within my power to create a whole universe of my own, a safe haven of sound.

At first, I assumed my mother's depression was a result of my father's outbursts. Later, I learned that my mother's mother had depressions as well. When Muzz became depressed, I initially felt help-less. I was drawn in by her need for companionship and felt that my presence was comforting for her, but I lacked the words to console her. Pop, whose irritability seemed to parallel my mother's depressions, would say, "Don't upset your mother." This felt like a warning, so I sat quietly with her, absorbing the dark ambience of her mood. I was old enough to wonder if there were other causes for her depression. My friends' mothers seemed breezy and cheerful most of the time. They must possess some special ingredient, I mused.

When I was eight, Muzz suffered an unusually severe depressive episode. Dr. Brown sent her to Sarasota, Florida, for a six-week "sun cure." While I missed her dearly, I also felt relieved that the ominous cloud surrounding her had left our home. While she was away, I felt empty, missing our nighttime prayers and her warm hugs. I wondered where God went during her depressions and how the sun cure worked. She returned home, tanned, relaxed, and full of energy. I noticed, for the first time, that her hair had turned almost completely white.

In 1954, Muzz took me to hear the Reverend Billy Graham preach during one of his evangelical "Crusades" in Albany. Rev. Graham's charismatic presence filled the large auditorium, and he im-plored the audience to "accept Jesus Christ as your personal Lord and Savior." I watched in amazement as my mother walked up to the stage with dozens of others, fell on her knees, and experienced a "personal conversion." Escorted by Graham's associates, she returned to her seat next to me, overwhelmed with tears of joy. I was confused and awe-stricken by what I had just seen. All I knew was that Something Power-ful had transformed her.

Two weeks later, two of Graham's lieutenants visited our home on a follow-up mission, apparently to solidify my mother's conversion. Following a long conversation, my mother knelt once again on our liv-ing room rug and surrendered in prayer. Graham's men then turned their attention to me and asked, "Son, are you ready to follow in your mother's footsteps?" Their question felt "yucky," and I resisted being coerced to do something I neither understood nor wanted. My mother must have sensed my discomfort, because she never allowed Graham's men to pester me, or her, at home again. I struggled to make sense of the contrast between my mother's intimate prayers with me and this pushy, public evangelism. Pop remained skeptical about these developments but somehow tolerated my mother's newfound fervor. He must have sensed how important faith was for her stability.

Around this time, my parents began putting me on the train to visit my mother's parents in Syracuse. My grandfather was a professor of economics at Syracuse University and the dean of the School of Business Administration, where he specialized in railway transportation. I was thrilled by the freedom and autonomy of riding alone from Albany to Syracuse and I adopted Gramps' enthusiasm for the New York Central Railroad. I eagerly explored the length of the train—from engine to dining car—braving the windy, raucous connections between passenger cars.

Conductors in crisp blue uniforms eyed me with stern curiosity. "Are you sure you know where you are going, young fella?" they would ask.

"Yep," I'd reply proudly. "I'm going to see my grandfather in Syracuse. He knows all about trains."

Gramps was always there to meet me at the station, dapper in his three-piece gray business suit, accented with a gold watch fob, and elegantly shaped gray felt hat. His dignified bearing and warm civility was a welcome relief from the tensions at home.

Gramps had a blue velvet armchair in the living room from which he loved to hold forth on all manner of topics. Raised on a farm near High Point, North Carolina, he graduated from Trinity College (now Duke University) with studies in classical Greek, Latin, history, and economics. He never missed an opportunity to teach me the value of advanced education and a lifetime of learning. He encouraged me to rummage through his floor-to-ceiling library, where I found books on every imaginable subject. He was a model for civic engagement, volunteering his time to highway and railroad commissions and frequently testifying before the State Legislature.

Sitting beside me, he told me bedtime stories from his youth in High Point—I remember one about his catching eels from irrigation ditches with sand in his bare hands—and sang songs he'd learned from Rufus, a poor Negro sharecropper, about cooking possum meat on his family's farm: "Possum meat am good to eat...carve him to the bone." Later as a history major in college, I came to appreciate this poignant glimpse of impoverished African-American life in the Reconstruction period in rural North Carolina. Gramps' father Solomon, a farmer, had served briefly in Robert E. Lee's Confederate Army. I loved my grandfather's warm earthiness during these bedtime stories—such a marked contrast to his erudition.

My memories of Granner are much less vivid. What I do recall is a slender, immaculately dressed woman who seemed quite satisfied to remain in the role of supporting actress enhancing her husband's academic career. My mother spoke lovingly and sometimes tearfully of her own mother, whose love of Shakespeare's sonnets, the poetry of Wordsworth and Dickinson, and whose pleasure of discovering word derivations and humble religious faith were undoubtedly passed on to me. When I was five, Granner had a series of strokes and was subsequently admitted to a nursing facility where she died two years later from complications of vascular dementia. I had a vague sense of her increasing frailty, slowly disappearing into an anonymous fog. Following her death, my mother became listless, moody, and withdrawn and I felt her slip away in what I later learned was her worst depression.

Gramps outlived his wife by seven years and died from a stroke at age 87 when I was fourteen. Like many children of this period, I was protected by my parents from any involvement in his funeral. Instead, we grieved in silence, barely acknowledging the gaping hole Gramps' and Granner's deaths left in the fabric of our family. This same year, my family moved from Delmar to New Hartford, a suburb of Utica. Within a few short months, I had lost all of my friends, my classmates, and my grandfather. I dealt with these losses by single-mindedly pursuing studies as a high school freshman, competing with my brothers who had been first and second in their classes.

For two summers between my thirteenth and fifteenth years, I worked ten hours per day on a large dairy farm on Chaumont Bay, Lake Ontario. Col. Clough Gee, who had served under General Patton in WWII, continued to bark out orders to all of his farmhands. I was a loyal soldier for Colonel Gee, lifting eighty-pound hay bales onto a wooden wagon and treading silage to feed his herd of 120 head of milk "keows" as they were called in the upstate dialect. My co-workers, Glen and Hank, were tenant farmers who had never traveled outside Jefferson County. Hank's constant, creative variations on the F-word pierced the hot, humid air nonstop. He and Glen laughed uproariously when I described how my first carefully-fashioned hay load collapsed with me on it, tossing me on the ground, embarrassed and frustrated. For a brief moment, I screamed at the top of my lungs at the Colonel, who was stone deaf without his hearing aids and happily bouncing down the row on his tractor, oblivious to my plight.

I got better at hay-loading as the summer progressed and was promoted to treading alfalfa silage two hours at a time. Emerging from the suffocating silo, green-tinged and drenched with sweat, I inhaled deeply and gazed in relief as the whitecaps broke over the limestone shoals out on the bay. I was bored to tears these two summers, which were designed by my father to "build character." For my character-building efforts, I received $100 cash at the end of each August.

During my teen years, my listening apprenticeship expanded. I participated in Saint Stephen's Episcopal Church choir and studied pipe organ. Alone in the organ loft, I opened all the stops and whooped along with the gut-trembling *fortissimo* from my augmented versions of Bach fugues. I joined the *acapella* choir and was thrilled with the interweaving of all the vocal parts as I sang in my maturing baritone register. At home, I listened to choral music by the hour as I did my homework. I can still hear our rector's voice as he taught us the melody and lyrics of Christmas hymns such as "Greensleeves" and "In the Bleak Midwinter."

Judy, the rector's daughter and my first love, gave me a copy of Pasternak's *Doctor Zhivago* as a Christmas present during my sophomore year. The romantic intrigues of this young physician caught up in the grand sweep of the Russian Revolution riveted my attention and, for the first time since my flight out the window, I imagined becoming a doctor. Tumescent fantasies about Yuri and Nurse Lara's love affair mingled with idealistic images of treating the wounded on the snow-swept steppes of the Caucasus. Every decade or so, I return to this novel and marvel, as I did at age fifteen, at Pasternak's poetic visions of hope in the midst of war's devastation: "Snow swept the world from end to end. A candle burned on the table. A candle burned" (1).

While my relationship with Judy lasted less than a year, I kept in close touch with her father, whom I admired for his sermons and musicianship. His short sermons were memorable, often laced with subtle humor and wit. I smiled inwardly as he relished swigging down what remained of the Communion wine.

As I progressed through high school, my parents frequently sought his counsel regarding important decisions. During my junior year the tension in their relationship worsened, and I could see that Muzz was rapidly descending into another depression. Though they never spoke of it in my presence, I felt certain they were headed for a divorce. Desperate, I called Rev. Schmidgall to ask if he could counsel them as a couple. He agreed to do this and their relationship improved after a few months. Much to my relief, the palpable tension in our household subsided. While my father didn't mention a thing about my intervention, my mother thanked me several times.

By this time, Tom and Charles had completed their graduate programs at Yale Architecture School and Princeton Seminary after which they each got married. On the Strong Vocational Interest Test, I scored high on abstract reasoning and community service and very low on mechanical ability. Teaching, social work, the ministry, and medicine were suggested as possible careers. I felt some affinity for the ministry, but also some doubts about leading a parish.

Early in my senior year, I drove Muzz to a doctor's appointment. I was surprised when her internist, Dr. Willis, entered the waiting room and beckoned me to join him in his office. Dr. Willis asked me if I had ever considered a career in medicine. I thought back to Dr. Campbell and Dr. Zhivago and, without hesitation, told him I was considering enrolling in pre-med classes in college and had recently applied for early admission to Wesleyan. He was enthused by my response and suggested that I consider working as a hospital orderly to get a feeling for the daily life and responsibilities of a doctor. Driving home, I felt energized with my new sense of direction.

In the fall of my junior year, I attended a choral concert in the New Harford High School Auditorium, featuring the Chantettes, a talented girl's quartet. Ellen Guckemus' soothing soprano voice captivated me and within a month, we were "going steady." We attended the Junior Prom in the spring of 1960 and I met many members of her extended, fun-loving family, who accepted me as one of their own. Our parents became close friends and I continued to date Ellen throughout my college years.

In June 1961, I graduated first in my high school class with honors in science. I concluded my valedictory address with a sonnet praying for an end to the Cold War with Russia. Several of my classmates' notes in my yearbook mentioned my being a kind and compassionate advocate for others. The New Harford swim team, which I had joined as a freshman freestyler, set a Central New York record of 37 straight victories. Shortly after my graduation, I was named "Optimist Boy of the Month."

In my senior year I had become fascinated with the nature of conflicts and how people were healed. Following the death of C.G. Jung, I read an account of his experiences as an analyst. The Swiss psychiatrist had built a remarkable career by synthesizing the findings of medical science with anthropology, comparative religion, theology, and universal themes in art. I was intrigued by Jung's self-styled mystical faith and the broad scope of his intellect. As a healer, he seemed to understand, better than anyone, our deep psychological need for a spiritual connection. Over the next few years I immersed myself in Jung, who spoke directly to my growing spiritual awareness. I wondered what it would be like to be a psychiatrist.

13

Above left: *Maternal grandfather, Prof. Charles Lee Raper, economist and Dean, Syracuse University School of Business Administration, ca. 1950.* **Above right:** *Maternal grandmother, Henrietta F. Raper, lover of literature and poetry. Below: Paternal grandparents: Silas Freeman Graves, school superintendent, and Ada Sloat Graves, school teacher, with my aunt Agnes Graves, Adams Center, New York, ca.1900.*

Me, age 9 months, with "Silverheels," in Delmar, New York, 1944.

My parents, Mary Lee and Ken, ca. 1948.

Me, age 5, with parents, brothers Tom (top) and Charles (right), 1948.

CHAPTER 2

THE MAKING OF
A WOUNDED HEALER

When my parents dropped me off to begin my freshman year at Wesleyan I felt confident in my academic abilities and had a clear sense that I would end up pursuing a career in medicine or one of the other helping professions. I had no reason to suspect that either my confidence or my career vision would be challenged. I worked hard in my pre-med classes, competing with classmates who had graduated from many of the best private schools in the country. I joined the Eclectic Fraternity (Socratic Literary Society) and managed to complete my first year with solid B's in chemistry and biology. During college, I continued to date Ellen, who was attending Potsdam State Teacher's College.

I planned to follow Dr. Willis' advice to gain work experience in a general hospital. But when an opportunity arose to work as an orderly at Marcy State, an upstate New York mental hospital north of Utica, my curiosity about psychiatry prevailed. I was enthusiastic about the job, eager to test my mettle in a clinical setting and to learn the nuts and bolts of psychiatry. As an orderly, I supervised group activities and assisted in the physical care of adults with chronic schizophrenia, manic depressive illness, and a variety of dementias. Marcy's lost souls were

16

warehoused on separate men's and women's units, often over-medicated and given electro-convulsive therapy (ECT) without muscle relaxants.

One of my tasks during the ECT was to hold down the patient's arms and legs as they convulsed. Nauseated and horrified by what I was witnessing, it was hard to escape the impression that treatment was anything other than a form of punishment. Institutionalization and the side effects of treatments often eclipsed the essential humanity of those I served. Many of these patients were to languish in the hospital for the rest of their lives with very little individual attention or psychotherapy.

On a back ward for "The Disturbed," I bathed and cut the fungus-infested toenails of men with hollowed out foreheads bearing unmistakable evidence of prefrontal lobotomies performed a decade earlier. Their drab hospital gowns, leather ankle shackles, shuffling gaits, incoherent mumblings, and vacant stares are as vivid for me today as they were in the summer of 1962. Towards the end of the summer I met with the hospital director to protest what I considered to be their inhumane treatment and living conditions. Dr. Bigelow listened politely, thanked me for voicing my concerns, and dismissed me without further comment.

Overwhelmed, disillusioned, and outraged by my experiences, I wished I could have shared them with my parents, but didn't want to burden them with my distress. As there were no physicians in my extended family to help me gain a perspective, I kept my experiences to myself, hoping that further science and psychology studies would somehow help me understand what I had seen and how it had affected me.

Later that year, Ken Kesey's novel *One Flew Over the Cuckoo's Nest* (1) was published, and the outrage it triggered across the country seemed to mirror my own. Psychiatry was barely emerging from the Dark Ages when, eight years later, Neil Armstrong walked on the moon and I began my first psychiatry rotation in medical school. It would take another ten years before the neurosciences would begin to match the sophistication of astrophysics.

I returned to Wesleyan as a sophomore that fall to continue my pre-med studies, rattled and haunted by my experiences at Marcy State and questioning my decision to pursue medicine as a career. Within two months I was floundering. It began with a vague fatigue and the sensation of slowly sinking in quicksand. I felt dazed and started sleeping nine to ten hours per day. Hauling myself out of bed for my eight o'clock German classes required a Herculean effort. Breakfast tasted like cardboard. My retention of new vocabulary was atrocious, and I stuttered when called on in class to translate the verbs that piled up at the end of sentences, guttural, grotesque, and incomprehensible. In afternoon physics lab, I struggled with directions for setting up the equipment and was chagrined by my bench partner's obvious frustration.

My calculus professor wrote lengthy differential equations on three blackboards, speaking smugly about "elegant proofs" that were "intuitively obvious." I resented his comments, as nothing he was writing made sense to me. My brain was stuck in mental molasses. Soon, I started skipping classes, confining myself to my room except for meals. I was afraid to speak with my friends about my altered state for fear they would laugh at me. I felt doomed and I didn't have a clue what was happening.

Finally, I checked myself into the campus infirmary feeling weak and depleted. Multiple blood tests and a chest X-ray revealed nothing, and I was discharged three days later with the presumptive diagnosis of mononucleosis. It's hard to describe the pervasive impotence I felt. Whatever it involved, I was too embarrassed to speak about it with my doctor, my parents, or my roommate who was also pre-med and doing brilliantly in his courses. I felt dead, encased in a cocoon of shame. After the Christmas break I returned to campus to find an envelope from the Wesleyan Registrar summarizing the mess I was too embarrassed to articulate. I had flat out flunked calculus and had gotten a C minus in physics. I had never failed at anything before. The Optimist Boy of the Month was nowhere to be seen.

I met with Dean Barlow to discuss changing my major. He was surprised by my sudden decline in performance and asked me to explain how I understood it. In my shame, I was at a loss to say much except that I felt "burned out." It was probably a virus, "sophomore slump," or a touch of homesickness, he offered. I sensed that none of these phenomena did justice to my experience, but I lacked the perspective to offer alternative explanations. I don't believe the possibility of a clinical depression ever came up. We discussed changing major fields and I chose history, combined with religious studies, following in my brother Charles' footsteps. By mid-January, I had enrolled in two American History courses, the History of Christianity, and Abnormal Psychology.

As spring returned to Middletown, my spirits gradually lifted and I began to enjoy my classes and assignments. I joined the Glee Club and discovered a piano in the basement of the music department which I played in the evenings. I picked up some Beethoven and Mozart sonata scores and in practicing, eked out my own form of recovery, enhanced by beginning lessons with Professor Ray Rendall. Within a month, after reading Freud's classic paper on "Mourning and Melancholia (2)." I realized I had suffered a clinical depression, not unlike the episodes I had observed in my mother. My symptoms, much to my relief, had names and meaning. *I was not alone.* Learning about my diagnosis, while frightening, enabled me to wrest some order out of the chaos I had emerged from. I no longer felt like Igor, the bug on the wall from Kafka's novella *Metamorphosis.* For the first time in months, I could imagine a future. Dropping pre-med provided an opportunity for me to embark, through my studies and piano practice, on a road to self-discovery and healing.

In the early 1960s Wesleyan was known for its small student body (1,200 male undergraduates), commitment to developing critical thinking, and a politically liberal faculty. Several faculty members, notably in the religion department, were engaged in the burgeoning civil rights movement. One of my religion professors, John Maguire, was a personal friend of Martin Luther King, Jr. and had been a Freedom Rider with him. Although his course dealt with the Protestant Reformation, many of our discussions afterward focused on his profound admiration for King's capacity to combine the non-violent teachings of Jesus and Gandhi in forging the civil rights movement.

Another professor, David Swift, who taught our Old Testament course, compared King to the prophet Amos, whose lines he quoted repeatedly in his sermons: "Let justice roll down like waters and righteousness like an ever-flowing stream." (Amos 5:24) During my time at Wesleyan, Rev. King preached in our campus chapel once and another time to an overflow crowd in the College Field House. Hearing this charismatic preacher was transformative for me. I began to ask what it meant to be a follower of Jesus and to what extent I would become involved in "The Movement."

Up to this point, my experience with political and social activism had been non-existent. I arrived on campus with a framed print of President Eisenhower by Norman Rockwell and viewed myself as a moderate Republican. By contrast, several of my friends and classmates had been active in liberal causes including voter registration in the southern states. Some were actively involved with SNCC (Student Non-Violent Coordinating Committee) and FOR (Fellowship of Reconciliation) in the Deep South. I yearned to do something that would make a difference in the fight for racial justice but had no idea how to plug in.

In the spring of 1963 I traveled with the Wesleyan Glee Club to perform at a Presbyterian church in Brooklyn. I met the minister after our concert and was impressed by his description of the church's summer outreach program to poor black kids in the community. I signed on as a volunteer in the program for the summer and found myself, for the first time, living in a ghetto and organizing recreation activities in the streets surrounding the church. During the daytime, we cordoned off a whole block in order to play basketball, stickball, and hopscotch with the neighborhood children. In the oppressive late afternoon heat the corner fire hydrants were opened and kids splashed around, shouting with delight. Inside the parish hall, other volunteers conducted Bible School and prayer meetings.

That August, we watched on black and white TV as Rev. King gave his "I Have a Dream" speech in front of the Lincoln Memorial. I wondered how many of the kids I'd played with that day would experience a piece of the dream. I became acutely aware that my time in the ghetto was limited to three months in a clean, air-conditioned parish house, while the kids I supervised returned home every evening to sweltering, crowded walk-ups with lead paint chipping off the walls. I was stunned by how the mere color of my skin provided me with opportunities and privileges the kids I supervised could only dream of.

Returning for classes in the fall of 1963, I presented an essay entitled "Service" to my Eclectic Fraternity brothers. I concluded by saying that I felt it was I who had been served by the community of children I supervised. My summer on the streets of Brooklyn opened my eyes to the injustices of racial segregation and poverty. That November President Kennedy was assassinated just a few months after he had given a speech advocating for a national Civil Rights Act.

In the early 1964 lead-up to the Mississippi "Freedom Summer" I seriously considered going south to participate in voter registration along with several of my classmates. When I floated this idea with my parents, Pop, without missing a beat, warned, "Go down there and you'll get killed." Even at age twenty I wasn't independent enough to disobey what felt like an ironclad prohibition. So I stayed in Middletown, joined the NAACP, and did voter registration in the black neighborhoods near the campus.

In the spring of 1964 a black and two white college volunteers were reported missing. Two months later the decaying bodies of James Chaney, Michael Schwerner, and Andrew Goodman were discovered buried in an earthen dam in Mississippi, brutally murdered by white racists. Reading about their tragic deaths, I thought: *These men were making history,* while I was observing on the sidelines, reading history. I envied those who had the courage to risk their lives in the Movement, but I needed more time to ground myself before I took risks in helping others.

During the Freedom Summer, I lived in Northfield, Massachusetts, where I co-taught a course on Comparative Religion with Prof J. Leslie Dunstan at the Mount Herman School. The ten students who took our seminar were gifted college-bound Jews, Catholics, and Protestants from northeastern urban areas. Our class discussions were intense and provocative and helped me clarify the uniqueness of my own Christian beliefs. I began to question the relevance and importance of Christian dogmas such as the virgin birth, the Holy Trinity, and the physical resurrection. I enjoyed my initial experiences of co-teaching but was not convinced it was the best fit for me.

Returning to Wesleyan for my senior year I read Nikos Kazantzakis' *The Last Temptation of Christ* (3). This compelling fictional account of Jesus' life described him with all the human passions, sexual urges, jealousies, frustrations, and anger one would expect in a young Jewish carpenter of his time. During my college religion courses I had become increasingly uncomfortable with Christian writings which held up self-denial and suffering for others as the highest pathway to salvation.

Jesus, in Kazantzakis' portrayal, is torn between submitting to his Father's will to be sacrificed for the sins of others and experiencing the joys of family life. Hanging on the cross, delirious and near death, he dreams that he is married to Mary Magdalene and that they have conceived a son. Reading this novel transformed my understanding of what it meant to be a Christian. I could use the life of this Jewish teacher as a very human model, without giving up my own natural human longings for sexual intimacy and having a family of my own.

Within a few months I was engaged to Ellen and graduated from Wesleyan in 1965 with a B.A. in history and religion. Ellen and I

21

planned to be married in late June of 1965 in a local Catholic church ceremony in New Hartford, where both sets of parents lived. On the morning of our wedding Pop lingered at the kitchen table and indicated he had something important to tell me. There was a curious expression on his face, a mixture of bemusement and solemnity, that I had never seen before. I felt the tension build up in my neck and buttocks as he began to speak. As best as I can recall, this is what he said:

"You may have wondered why you are so much younger than your brothers Tom and Charles....Here's the answer: Your mom and I were at a New Year's Eve party in Albany. We had a grand ol' time and a lot to drink. You were the result of the "second martini."

On the morning of my wedding, Pop had told me, basically, that I was a mistake, an unplanned child. I was shocked and speechless, unable to respond to what I had just heard. I retreated to my bedroom to get dressed in my new dark blue three-piece suit. I did the mental calculations. December 31 to August 31...that's eight months. My mother had told me I was born three weeks early, a "preemie" of only five pounds, seven ounces. I may have been a mistake, but at least I got off to a head start.

Within minutes, my best man and roommate from college, Bob Bast, appeared to offer me support for the upcoming ceremony. I never shared what I had just learned from Pop. Instead, I gave Bob a forty-five minute lecture on everything I had learned about the ancient Inca civilization, which had developed an advanced empire seven centuries earlier, thousands of miles south of upstate New York. With my temporal and geographical retreat, I buried all considerations of my accidental origins. Bob listened politely and we took off for the little Roman Catholic Church where Ellen and I were married.

At the reception I gave an awkward and rambling speech about how grateful I was for all the love and support my parents and family had given me. As I spoke I thought: *This is all very surreal. Is this really happening? If I am a mistake, what does this mean about who I am, who I will become and the decisions I am making?* It would be another twenty years before I understood the seismic transformations taking place within me on that day.

After a brief honeymoon in Boothbay Harbor, Maine, Ellen and I spent the summer of 1965 in Arequipa, Peru, where we volunteered for two months teaching English and supervising recreational activities in a Catholic School for blind children. Our swarthy young charges, eyes dimmed by corneal scarring, gleefully chased their soccer balls around, keying to their location by the jingling of inserted Coke bottle caps. In the *Cordillera Blanca* to the west, the conical summit of El Misti dominated the town.

We returned to New York were I pursued graduate studies at Union Theological Seminary and Ellen taught elementary school in White Plains. In choosing Union, my most significant model was my brother Charles, who worked briefly as an ordained Presbyterian minister and subsequently earned his doctorate in church history and theology following extended studies at Oxford and the University of Basel. Before the advent of email, we communicated for many years about his evolving career via handwritten letters.

My choice of Union Seminary involved earlier family determinants reaching back into the nineteenth century. My mother's avid Biblical and Hebrew studies and multiple trips to Israel undoubtedly derived from many summers spent in her youth in Paterson, New Jersey where her maternal grandparents, William and Mary Williams, staunch Presbyterians, held regular Bible study sessions in their home.

On my father's side, my great grandfather was a Methodist clergyman and circuit rider in upstate New York. His half-brother did missionary work with the Shoshone Amerindian people in Nevada and taught in a mission school in Puerto Rico. In beginning my post graduate studies at Union, I was simply doing what came naturally.

At Union I took courses in the Bachelor of Divinity curriculum as well as in their newly-created program in Psychiatry and Religion, designed for young men and women who, like myself, were psychologically-minded and interested in human services and counseling, but unclear about their ultimate career paths.

Professor Paul Lehman, a specialist in Christian ethics, taught our course in Systematic Theology in which we read *The Institutes of the Christian Religion* by John Calvin(4), whose writings formed the core beliefs of the modern Presbyterian denomination. We were given the assignment of writing a journal, describing our personal reactions to each section of this two volume *magnum opus*. As my weekly journal entries progressed, they became shorter and more polemical.

Calvin drew heavily on his theology from Saint Augustine and Saint Paul, both of whom viewed the flesh and carnal desire as the enemy of the spirit. I found it difficult to accept Calvin's concept of God as a distant sovereign who lorded over humans whom he viewed as inherently depraved and kept in suspense as to whether they were among the Elect or condemned to roast in Hell. The doctrine of predestination struck me as cruel, capricious, and diametrically opposed to Jesus' teachings about forgiveness and the equality of all humans in the eyes of God.

For me, there was too much sin and too little joy in this version of the Christian faith. For my final paper I wrote a scathing manifesto based on the contents of the Apostle's Creed in which I dispensed with the virgin birth, the Resurrection, and the Trinity. Professor Lehman was not pleased with my diatribe and gave me an F on my paper. My theological rebellion was on the leading edge of my decision to leave Union and to return to my goal, abandoned four years previously, of becoming a doctor.

Since there were limited clinical experiences in the psychiatry and religion program, I created a chaplain internship at Saint Luke's Hospital, an Episcopal institution across town. In this capacity I made rounds with the hospital chaplain on several medical and surgical units. I was assigned to follow a group of male cancer patients who shared an eight-bed open unit. Several of these men had terminal illnesses and needed solace and hope via Holy Communion and prayer. As I listened to their stories, I heard them demand, like Job, an answer from God: *Why me?* "The Lord giveth, the Lord taketh away" was not exactly a message of reassurance. I struggled to help them with prayer and Biblical healing parables, but often doubted the usefulness of my efforts.

My chaplain supervisor stressed the importance of hope and "being present as a companion in Christ." Being present in this way required a depth of faith and acceptance of mortality that exceeded my capacity as a twenty-three year old. I had doubts about the existence of life after death and found it difficult to support my terminal patient's hopes of joining their loved ones in heaven. I wondered how I could offer hope if I didn't really understand their illnesses and prognoses. I found myself reading more and more of my patient's charts, especially the oncology notes, hoping to glean some sense of certainty and hope that would sustain my efforts. What I found was an entirely new language related to organ functions, laboratory tests, and X-ray reports describing tumor size, location, and metastasis. I would have to learn this language if I was to help save their lives.

Saving lives seemed infinitely more relevant than saving souls. If I could save lives, perhaps I could conquer death itself. I felt that the white coat of the physician offered more hope and promise than the white collar of the cleric. By the spring of 1966 I made my decision: I would leave Union, finish my pre-med studies at Columbia, and apply to medical school. My plans were complicated by what I learned from the draft lottery: I was reclassified 1-A, having drawn number 11 out of 365 in the draft lottery, which meant I was very likely to be sent to fight in Vietnam in a war which I strenuously opposed. As a pre-medical student, I had lost my graduate training status. I learned that I had to pass an exam similar to the Graduate Record Exam in order to extend my student deferment. Sweating through this test like none I had ever taken, I was immensely relieved when I learned I had passed. I began the arduous process of reviewing all my basic science courses for the Medical College Admission Tests (MCATs).

I did well on the MCATS and thoroughly enjoyed my classes in cytology, calculus, medical anthropology, and physics at Columbia. Organic Chemistry was another story altogether. I took a summer class which compressed a whole year's material into ten weeks, with an exam every Monday morning. Working at the limits of rote memory, I managed to eke out a C+. My faculty advisor said he doubted I would make it into medical school, given my mediocre performance. I took his skepticism as a challenge and promptly began the application process.

I considered applying to McGill University in Montreal to escape the draft, but reconsidered when I discovered that their science prerequisites exceeded what I had taken. Among the top medical schools in the East, a new one caught my attention: Albert Einstein College of Medicine (AECOM) in the Bronx. I learned that AECOM was accepting several students who had previously been in other occupations and had fewer science prerequisites. I interviewed at Einstein, Case Western Reserve, and Rochester. As the Vietnam War was heating up, I decided to take the first school that accepted me. When the letter came from Einstein I was ecstatic.

AECOM was founded in the early 1950s as part of Yeshiva University by Jewish physicians who had experienced anti-Semitism which precluded their advancement in numerous American medical school faculties. Albert Einstein gave his name and summoned financial support for the fledgling school and was present at its dedication in 1955 a few months before his death. When I applied, AECOM already had a reputation for cutting-edge neuroscience research, a renowned faculty, and a strong commitment to social justice, all of which appealed to me. I began classes there in September 1967 just three months after Israel's Six Day War with Egypt.

My entering class of 105 students included about 20 Christians, 20 women, 85 men, and a dedicated majority of Jewish students mostly from large urban areas along the northeastern corridor. About a third of our class was Orthodox, easily distinguished by their somber attire and tendency to sit together in the large lecture halls and cafeteria. A number of my classmates had worked previously as teachers, journalists, social workers, or in scientific research. I noticed that several of them vanished from campus with their laundry on Friday afternoons to join their families in Manhattan, Brooklyn, or Queens for Sabbath meals. The intensity of their faith and family connections impressed me.

Moving from a Protestant seminary to a predominantly Jewish medical school was a real culture shock. I was inundated with Yiddish phrases, loud and animated disagreements, and discovered a whole new vegetarian cuisine served in the cafeteria on dairy days. My college German helped somewhat with Yiddish and I soon found myself sprinkling my conversation with my newly-found idioms. I ate blintzes, latkes, enjoyed lox and bagels for the first time, and broke my longstanding anti-beet resolution with a bowl of Rappaport's best borscht.

By the fourth year, a few classmates wondered if my last name had been anglicized. Surely they were kidding. I was surprised to recognize how much I had assimilated. In my eagerness to absorb a whole new culture and master the demanding health science curriculum, I drifted away from prayer and church attendance. I made friends with several classmates whose Reform Judaism, prioritizing ethical behavior over doctrine, felt much closer to the pared-down Christianity I was then espousing.

Our basic science faculty were outstanding contributors in their fields, several having authored texts in the subjects they taught. Many spoke with the eastern European accents of the Ashkenazi. I was immediately impressed with their combination of scientific rigor and human compassion. Some faculty of Sephardic origin embodied the ethical ideals of Maimonides, the twelfth century physician-philosopher from Spain whose mantra I have repeated throughout my training and practice: "I will never view my patients as anything other than fellow creatures in human suffering" (5). Many professors were outspoken civil rights advocates and ardent opponents of the Vietnam War. On the other hand, I knew more conservative Israeli classmates who had gone home to serve as medics in the Six Day War. I admired my classmates' dedication to their studies and their seemingly endless capacity for spirited arguments regarding medical, political, and social issues.

From the moment I started my first surgical rotation early in my third year, I was attracted to the life-saving dramas, imperative for decisiveness, quick manual dexterity, and the artful joining of aggression and healing which this specialty involves. While at Columbia, I had donated blood for the wife of a cab driver who was scheduled to undergo major surgery. I was able to obtain permission from her surgeon to observe him in the OR. At one point when the surgical field became inundated with blood, I fainted. I came to with an OR nurse reviving me with smelling salts and returned to watch the remainder of the operation. I later learned that my fainting was a common physiologic reaction in the uninitiated.

In my third year, I was assigned to Einstein's Montefiore Hospital surgical team, scrubbing in on several abdominal surgeries per week during my three month rotation. I worked hard, practicing my surgical knots until late at night. These repetitive movements, like scales and arpeggios on the piano, softened the anxiety I felt with patients experiencing serious post-op complications. My professors quickly noted my enthusiasm and allowed me to do skin closures following hernia repairs, and other common abdominal procedures. I followed my patients carefully to ensure proper wound healing and they complimented me on my efforts.

At the same time, slivers of doubt began to work under my skin. I noticed that surgery residents objectified their patients by calling them "hernias" and "gallbladders," rather than by their names. I winced as they threaded down nasogastric tubes with scant explanation or sensitivity to their patient's discomfort, vowing to be more careful and sensitive when called upon to follow their lead. What I viewed initially as callousness, I came to see as their means of coping with their own and their patient's emotional vulnerabilities.

In the O.R., I watched as the polished bedside manners of surgeons occasionally morphed into temper tantrums when handed the wrong instrument or if their sterile field became contaminated. I was shocked when they threw instruments and gloves on the floor and stormed out of the operating theatre, necessitating delays for rescrubbing. While these experiences gave me pause, I scuttled my doubts about the field and pushed ahead, signing up for a summer elective in transplant surgery between my third and fourth year.

The director of the thoracic surgery division at Montefiore Hospital, Dr. Frank Veith, was a pioneer in lung transplantation, having performed the second transplant in the world. Although the operation was successful, his patient died from complications of donor tissue rejection, a common occurrence in those days. Our surgical lab investigations focused on how best to preserve donor lung tissue in the brief period between harvest and insertion in the canine recipients. My task was to assist in lung transplant surgery on dogs and to compare the effects of perfusion of the un-inflated lung with a saline solution versus simply keeping the lung ventilated mechanically without the saline perfusion.

I worked closely in the lab with Israel Colon, a surgical technician and former champion bodybuilder and Dr. Sashi Sinha, from a Brahmin family in India. "Izzy's" pulmonary artery connections were superb, rarely leaking a drop after I released the clamps. Dr. Sinha was smooth, unflappable, and displayed the aristocratic carriage of someone used to visiting his rural patients astride an elephant, receiving all the respect of royalty. I slept several nights on the lab floor on an air mattress, providing post-op care for Labradors and Pointers as they struggled to accept their new lungs and me, with my fond but short-lived attachments to them. If there is a canine heaven, I'm sure many of their souls are resting there.

Later that summer, Dr. Veith performed another lung transplant on a patient with advanced silicosis. The patient initially did well in the pulmonary ICU on high doses of steroids to suppress tissue rejection. Our lab team followed his medical updates with rapt attention, hoping for a better outcome. Two weeks later, he died from bacterial pneumonia related to his immunosuppression. It was clear that further progress in lung transplantation would have to await development of more effective means of combatting the tissue-rejection process.

Meanwhile, my colleagues and I tabulated the data from our perfusion and ventilation cohorts. There was a trend favoring ventilation but it appeared that our sample size was rather small to reach definitive conclusions. I was surprised to learn that our research had been already accepted for publication in one of the top thoracic surgery journals. Hearing this, I meditated on the pros and cons of the imperative to "publish or perish."

In the rapidly expanding arena of transplant surgery in the late 60s, competition was fierce. While surgeons could often effect dramatic cures with a single operation, their relationships with their patients tended to be brief and more superficial. My more introverted and contemplative style didn't seem to fit into this specialty or with the temperament of many of its practitioners. I began my fourth year open to considering other specialty options.

Of all my other clinical rotations, I was most impressed with those in neurology and psychiatry. Einstein's future dean, Dominic Purpura, a superb, witty teacher (Eric Kandel called him the "Woody Allen of neurobiology,") was chair of the neuroscience division which had provided us with an outstanding grounding in neuroanatomy and neurophysiology. Prior to joining Einstein's faculty, Dr. Purpura worked at Columbia researching synaptic neurotransmission, collaborating with Kandel, who later won the Nobel Prize for his research on the neuroanatomical basis of memory. Our neurology clinical faculty included Oliver Sacks, Elliot Gross, and Labe Scheinberg, all of whom were brilliant and entertaining clinician-teachers.

My one reservation regarding neurology was that, in 1970, it remained primarily a diagnostic specialty with few definitive treatments available. When Oliver Sacks and other clinicians began to treat Parkinson's Disease with L-Dopa, many patients literally "came alive" for the first time in years, liberated from the prison of frozen muscular activity related to their dopamine deficiency. Otherwise, patients with other major neurological disorders and cerebral vascular disease complicated by strokes could only be treated symptomatically and faced years of disability and drastically shortened lifespans.

My final rotation in psychiatry proved to be the most stimulating and gratifying of all my clinical work at Einstein. It was as if I had saved the best for last. The combination of a friendly, personally involved faculty, excellent supervision of treatment cases, and the opportunity to integrate what I had learned from previous clerkships made for an exhilarating experience.

During my three-month clerkship in the outpatient clinic of Jacobi Hospital, I saw a number of patients for short-term dynamic psychotherapy. My first case involved working with a psychology graduate student, Sarah, who was depressed and anxious in the aftermath of breaking up with her boyfriend. The closeness of our ages and a feeling of collegiality, along with sensitive supervision with Dr. Joel Kovel, combined to produce a successful therapy outcome. There were times when Sarah empathized with my tentativeness as a beginning therapist. She was open about sharing with me which of my interventions were helpful and which were not. I couldn't have asked for a better match. Dr. Kovel's supervision was both stimulating and empathic.

Initially trained as an analyst, Dr. Kovel embraced a humanistic approach to therapy. As a Marxist, the top-down hierarchical approach of classical analysis was abhorrent to him. He encouraged me to be authentic, use judicious self-disclosure, and to avoid getting blinded by analytic dogmatism or rigid diagnostic categories. Sarah was a totally unique individual in her style of mourning. My job as a student doctor was, as Voltaire said, not to get in the way of a natural healing process. Dr. Kovel communicated the wisdom of Maimonides and encouraged me to see myself on a par with my patients in all the human predicaments of change, loss, physical and mental pain, helplessness, and the inevitability of death. It was he who first introduced me to Maimonides' late twelfth century classic *Guide for the Perplexed* (5).

Dr. Kovel's field of observation extended far beyond the mental processes of his patients to an in-depth analysis of social ills. The same year I worked with him in supervision, he published a controversial volume entitled *White Racism: A Psychohistory* (6). He concluded that the phenomenon of white racism arose from a pervasive and unconscious need to devalue and destroy all that is abhorrent and disgusting in ourselves. He saw the black population in the United States as tragic containers for white people's deepest shame and guilt involving 400 years of slavery. I am indebted to the late Dr. Kovel for conveying the importance of viewing all of my patients in the complex matrix of their social, ethnic, and religious contexts.

Ed Hornick, a former neurosurgeon-turned analyst, was a brilliant, eccentric, and arresting presence in the department. With his cape, single earring, broad forehead, and mischievous darting gaze, he was a veritable reincarnation of Franz Liszt and equally charming with his female admirers. Dr. Hornick's contribution to my training took place largely on an emotional level. He directed the inpatient unit at Bronx State Hospital where we treated a variety of patients with chronic mental illness, depression, and addictions. In our case conferences and at Grand Rounds, he had a unique capacity to empathize with our feelings of fear and fascination stimulated by entering into the often chaotic worlds of psychosis and the unhinged pursuits of mind-altering chemicals.

At the end of our rotation he invited our clerkship group and our spouses to his lavishly decorated brownstone in Manhattan's Upper East Side, featuring a double-decker wrought iron-framed purple upholstered couch. There he entertained us with descriptions of his practice as an analyst. Neurosurgeons have to worry about a misplaced scalpel destroying vital functions, movement, memory, or speech. Analysts, who perform equally delicate interpretations, must beware that their zeal to affect a "cure" for neurosis can potentially unleash powerfully destructive forces. Dr. Hornick stressed that we must employ our interventions with utmost care and tact, always respecting our patient's limitations and autonomy.

These two insightful mentors were invaluable in helping me consolidate my decision to become a psychiatrist. The experience of working with them and other sensitive faculty provided what was missing nine years previously at Marcy State: an empathic understanding of my experiences facing those with serious mental illness. I emerged from my psychiatry clerkship feeling at home and validated by faculty and classmate-colleagues. These experiences enabled me to let go of my earlier doubts and to forge ahead with psychiatric training.

I felt that a career in psychiatry would allow me to form deeper, more meaningful connections with my patients in a joint effort to bring about lasting change. Psychiatry combined the infinite complexity of brain science with all the humanistic sensibilities of music, literature, philosophy, and the arts in a way that was impossible to resist. In early May of 1971, I was surprised when I received a letter from the Dean's office congratulating me on being elected to Alpha Omega Alpha, the medical honor society. Because Ellen and I were expecting a child, we decided to skip graduation and move to San Francisco in mid-May in order to prepare our apartment for our new arrival whose debut was scheduled shortly before the start of my internship. I recited the Medical Oath of Geneva in Dean Lazar's office with the Dean and Ellen as my witnesses.

We said goodbye to our friends, stuffed our faded green '67 Volkswagen Fastback with our belongings, and headed west out of the Bronx, full of excitement and anticipation. Within a six-week period, we moved three thousand miles away from our families and friends, became new parents of our baby girl Jessica, and I embarked on my career as an intern in medicine and psychiatry at Mount Zion Hospital.

Top: *College graduation photo, Wesleyan University, Middletown, Connecticut, 1965.*

Below: *Ellen Graves, first wife, in New York, 1970.*

CHAPTER 3

TRAINING AND
EARLY PRACTICE YEARS

When I began my rotating medical internship at Mount Zion Hospital in July 1971, our daughter Jessica was just two weeks old. Her mother and I had worked hard to prepare our three story walk-up near Golden Gate Park for our new arrival. I chose Mount Zion, a Jewish community hospital, for its relatively "easy" on-call schedule of every third night which I hoped would allow me to be a bit more available as a husband and father. Still, my 70-80 hours per week schedule left me exhausted much of the time. The on-call rooms were often chilly and I struggled to fall back asleep after being awakened at 2:00 a.m. to restart IVs or work-up new admissions. The sounds of a surgery resident enjoying his favorite nurse in the next room penetrated the thin walls. At these times, I longed to be home with my wife and baby girl.

Mount Zion's psychiatry department was chaired by Dr. Robert Wallerstein, whose psychoanalytic approach and leadership provided a clear focus for our clinical activities. As Dr. Wallerstein was a close friend and colleague of Erik Erikson, we had the privilege of interacting with him at Grand Rounds on several occasions as he described his fascinating black and white films of children in play sessions demonstrating gender differences in normal development. These discussions stimulated my life-long interest in early childhood issues and how they affected adult coping mechanisms.

As part of my internship, I served for two months in Oakland's Alameda County Hospital emergency room. There I learned to identify who was really sick and how to make quick decisions. One August evening a band of Hell's Angels came careening into the ER after a rumble with a rival gang. They were drunk, agitated, and bleeding from a knife fight. The man I was assigned to treat at first reminded me of Queequeg—tattooed all over and snoring off his Jack Daniels. As I began to sew up the lacerations on his forearm, he exploded off his gurney, cussing and swinging at me, scattering the sterile instrument tray and its contents like pick-up sticks on the floor. I jumped back and before I could catch my breath, a policeman materialized, subdued and handcuffed my assailant, and hustled him out of sight.

From my late 60s anti-war demonstrations, I had come to view policemen as baton-wielding bullies who protected the military-industrial complex. A few minutes later, Officer Sullivan returned with a smile on his face and asked, "Doc, you OK?" I assured him I was just a bit shaken up (a little stoicism never hurt) and thanked him for his rapid intervention. After that night, I viewed the Boys in Blue as my allies.

My next exposure to the Bay Area's counter-culture was of a different sort. I volunteered to work a few hours per month at the Haight-Ashbury Free Clinic, treating the casualties of bad LSD trips, the infectious aftereffects of free love, and failed attempts to leap off the Golden Gate Bridge. One evening I visited a commune on the third floor of a condemned brick warehouse off Market Street. The entire room was filled with a marijuana haze and a dozen or so colored tents with young tattered occupants, strumming guitars and hanging out. A handful of one to three-year-olds provided the evening's entertainment, squealing and scampering about in unabashed nakedness. My job was to screen their parents for sexually transmitted diseases and a variety of skin ailments. A young public health nurse accompanied me as we took urine samples and she did pelvic exams in a makeshift examining room screened off with plastic tarps.

Our young patients were grateful for our services, and I for an opportunity to do follow-ups at the clinic where I could speak with them more confidentially. What I heard involved numerous tales of disillusionment and sadness. The Summer of Love had ended three years before with psychedelics being replaced by narcotics and other addictive substances. My patients' brothers, fathers, and uncles were being flown back from Vietnam physically and emotionally maimed, or in body bags. I choked up listening to their stories.

During the spring of 1972, I became a Conscientious Objector (C.O.) based on my religious beliefs and the Medical Oath of Geneva which explicitly stated: "I will maintain the utmost respect for human life…even under threat, I will not use my medical knowledge contrary to the laws of humanity" (1). This oath had been written as an explicit response to Nazi Germany's use of doctors in support of the Holocaust.

I flew back to Utica, New York to present my case to my draft board. Within two weeks they informed me that I had been reclassified as a C.O. That evening as Ellen and I celebrated with a glass of wine, little brown-eyed Jessica pulled herself up from the floor, grasped the coffee table, and gleefully gyrated to the sounds of Cat Stevens' "Moonshadow."

In late June 1972 we drove to Denver to start my residency training at the University of Colorado Department of Psychiatry. Denver was still a cow town in those days—its tallest building was a mere 23 stories. On our first night we stayed in a motel in north Denver, with eighteen-wheelers coming and going. Doors above us creaked open and slammed shut all night. I'm sure it was a brothel. A few weeks later, I watched as a purse-snatcher fled a grocery store down a side alley with an onlooker in hot pursuit. On Colorado Boulevard, Shotgun Willie's hawked nightly strip shows. The Wild West was alive and well.

We were welcomed to the program by Drs. Brandt and Eleanor Steele, who held a lively potluck dinner for first-year residents and their spouses/lovers in their sprawling ranch home, with its large fireplace surrounded by books, leather couches, and oversized chairs. Our charming hosts greeted each of us warmly, asked how we had come to Denver, and immediately treated us as junior colleagues. As the evening drew to a close I knew I had made a good choice to begin my training in Denver.

In my first year, I was assigned to treat a challenging couple in the clinic. Theirs was a match made in hell. He was a hefty schizoid gentleman fond of sulking and picking fights when people got too close. When on the spot, he retreated behind his unruly red beard and denim coveralls. She was petite, flamboyant, and dressed to the nines— and perpetually frustrated by what she viewed as his deliberate emotional stinginess. Sessions often started with her litany of complaints from the previous week, to which he responded by focusing his gaze somewhere in the vicinity of Pluto. Feeling abandoned, she pushed the fortissimo button, badgering him until he shouted, "Would you just shut the f… up!!"

At this point, Professor Rene Spitz knocked on the door, annoyed by the commotion, and in his thick Hungarian accent queried, *Zis ist psycho-therapie?* This was my cue to end the session and call my supervisor, who asked, "Have you thought of referring each of them for individual therapy? They don't seem to have the ego strength to benefit from couples work."

Right. It seemed none of my couples in the clinic were mature enough for couples therapy. Many were borderline psychotic, addicted, impulsively angry, or given to "letting it all hang out," reinforcing the cultural meme of the early 70s. Listening empathically and offering nonjudgmental interpretations just didn't cut it. If anything, it seemed to make things worse. My thin quiver of therapeutic arrows included psychodynamic, transactional, and teaching communications skills.

None of my courses or readings indicated which type of therapy constituted the best practice for treating couples with varying degrees of maturity. Should I try one type of therapy and then institute another, like switching antibiotics when the blood culture showed resistant organisms? The organizing principle of "treating the relationship" rather than individuals sounded great, but how did one actually *implement* it? That would have to wait for over twenty years until Judith Wallerstein and Sandra Blakeslee published their now classic study, *The Good Marriage,* on how healthy couples manage conflict (2).

I was impressed by the assemblage of impressive intellect and stellar analytic lineages among our faculty, but it wasn't long before I began to feel hemmed in by orthodoxy. Freud's theory of the mind and René Spitz's theories of child development were preeminent in our readings, supervision, and clinical case conferences. Dr. Spitz had the additional cachet of having been analyzed by Freud himself. He always took "his" seat in the front row of the Colorado Psychiatric Hospital auditorium next to Dr. Herbert Gaskell, our soft-spoken, magisterially aloof Chairman. A reverent silence fell upon the room when Disciple Spitz offered erudite commentaries on the Grand Rounds speaker's address. Few dared to preempt him in posing the first question. Tightly clustered cadres of senior faculty and tweedy training analysts shared the first and second rows. Assorted junior faculty occupied the third row, leaving us residents, social workers, psychologists, and sundry occupants from the community to fill in the top seats. "Discussions" were mostly laudatory, polite, and deferential.

I missed the excitement of rounds at Einstein where general surgeons, internists, and radiologists engaged in friendly cockfights over the meaning of X-ray and laboratory findings. It was as if a microcosm of late nineteenth century Vienna had been transplanted to this frontier town on the edge of the Rockies.

In case conferences I began to question the party line. When one of my treatment cases, a young law student, got worse under the tutelage of a rigid supervisor, I fired my supervisor and transferred to a more open-minded faculty member who supported my more eclectic approaches to therapy. As a result, both I and my patient improved. I discovered the importance of developing flexible theories of mind more congruent with my patient's lived experiences.

I became frustrated when another analytic supervisor told me to remove a small framed photo of my wife and daughter from my office desk, saying that it revealed too much about me. I ended up hiding it during my supervision sessions and otherwise keeping it out on my desk. These and several other experiences confirmed Janet Malcolm's later critique of analytic training as embodying a quasi-religious type of dogmatism. After graduating from the program in 1975 I had long conversations with classmates who had joined the Denver Institute for Psychoanalysis as candidates. Some of them were mired in training analyses of six to ten years' duration with no end in sight. Hearing this validated my decision not to matriculate as an analytic candidate.

With the above exceptions, my other clinical supervisors and case conferences were generally helpful, but I soon discovered that working with chronically depressed, anxious, and disorganized patients could be overwhelming at times. I became anxious and irritable at home and developed chronic insomnia. Over-identifying with my patients' mood states, I struggled to compartmentalize them and relate more affectionately with my wife or play with our three-year-old daughter.

I became needy and demanding at home and struggled to find ways of nourishing and centering myself. What if my patients' depression was contagious and I developed another episode? Sometimes the only way I could settle down was by soaking for up to an hour in a bathtub of steaming hot water. Fortunately, one of my supervisors recognized my high stress level and referred me to Dr. Homer Olsen, a young faculty member in our department.

My treatment experience with Homer provided a helpful intro-duction to therapy and also gave me tools to handle the stress of my new occupation. He empathized with the chaotic affect states induced by my patients and helped me step back and empathize with myself. He was also able to normalize my experiences as a psychiatry trainee, which reduced my fears of contagion. Recognizing that I was thin-skinned emotionally, he encouraged me to be a little *less empathic* at times, saying, "Sometimes you just have to duck a little and let this stuff go over your head." His one-liners stuck with me over the years and I found myself using them frequently as I supervised residents and other mental health professionals.

Homer also made a point of supporting my strengths and inter-ests in classical music, writing, and outdoor recreational activities such as skiing, hiking, and fly fishing. I bought an upright piano and once again found a soothing and organizing outlet in playing the classical repertoire. In the last year of my residency I wrote and published an article entitled "Becoming a Psychiatrist: Or, Adolescence Revisited" in which I described the emotional storms triggered by my work with severely disturbed patients (3). My writing helped me gain some per-spective on the intense inner turmoil I had experienced as a trainee. Homer's focus on positive adaptations, rather than excavating internal conflicts, was both refreshing and helpful. In him I found a fine model to emulate in the years to come.

By the time I finished my therapy with Homer, I had managed to cobble together a good portion of my family's psychiatric history, which included multiple members with depression, a suicide in a second cousin, a great aunt with schizophrenia, and explosive episodes in my father. Both of my older brothers had been depressed and one required a brief hospital treatment. Fortunately, my brothers and mother each had good experi-ences with their treatments. I imagined that, if I could master psychiatry, I might find the means to reduce our family's conflicts and create a close-knit, warm, and loving family. This was a utopian dream destined to fail; nevertheless, I pursued it for several years.

Many of us in the residency program bonded together around the intense experiences of our ongoing patient contacts, feelings of vulnerability in supervision, and the wild rides of personal therapy and analysis. We enjoyed potluck suppers and Thanksgiving meals together and forged friendships that, for me, have lasted nearly fifty years. My classmate Geoff Heron and I bonded immediately around our mutual interests in hiking, mountain climbing, skiing, and fishing. We eventually climbed over thirty of Colorado's "Fourteeners" together. On our way to and from these outings we spoke in detail about challenging cases and what it was like to treat them.

In our residency class of fifteen, nearly all of us entered psychoanalysis at some point during our training. I had hoped to continue with Homer for analysis but he was totally booked. I was referred to another analyst and in 1973 began what turned out to be a five-and-a-half-year surgical dissection of my unconscious.

The prevailing theory when I entered analysis was that neurotic conflicts could be divided into "pre-Oedipal" (up to age four) and "Oedipal" when I was supposedly in competition with my father for my mother's love. "Pre-oedipal" issues were viewed condescendingly as not benefitting from classical analytic techniques with the patient free-associating on the couch.

My issues were definitely more "pre-Oedipal" than Oedipal. The last thing I wanted was to sleep with my mother. What I needed as a little boy was my father's support in escaping the pull of her depressed moods. My father, with his own anxieties and hot temper, was ill-equipped to help me with this. By the third year on the couch, I was becoming more and more like my father: moody, irritable, and truculent.

In my fourth year of analysis, I had a vivid dream which summed up my experiences of treatment:

I was lying fully awake on my stomach strapped to an operating table in four-point restraints in an amphitheater surrounded by medical students in medieval clothing. Half of the space was illuminated by intense bright light; the other half was in total darkness. A masked surgeon was making an excruciatingly painful, slow, longitudinal incision from my head down to my tailbone along the line demarcating light and shadow. I had the impulse to scream but nothing came out. I awoke horrified.

I honestly don't remember a word of what my analyst said when I reported the dream. I probably tuned him out as soon as I sensed that he was missing the point. My dream portrayed my experience of him using an excruciating, outmoded, rigid, and terrifying form of "therapy." My neediness and irritability at home reflected his almost exclusive focus on unleashing dark forces without providing me with the tools to contain, understand, and control them.

My analysis was clearly promoting a destructive regression, the likes of which I had never experienced before. I was depressed for long periods and caught in a vortex of dreams and fantasies without acquiring the capacity to verbalize what was happening to me. I tried to sandbag myself and my family from the rising torrents but it felt like a losing battle. Although I gained some understanding about my family of origin and its impact on my development, few of these insights helped me become a better husband, father, or therapist.

I said and did some things that frightened my analyst and Ellen. He finally recommended that I sit up and reduce our sessions from four to two times per week. This resulted in almost immediate relief. Now I could see his dark brown eyes, receding hairline, and furrowed brow deep in concentration as I spoke. The man I had experienced as a robotic interpreter became a real person who actually seemed interested in me *in the present*. I entertained the possibility of his being considerate, even kind. He loosened up and told me a couple of bad jokes.

We focused on current problem-solving, including starting a private practice and my oldest brother's recent hospitalization for depression. Somehow I managed to develop a real enough relationship with him to regroup and to crawl out of my dark pit. Within a few months of ending analysis, my depression began to lift. It had gone on for almost four years, without his ever recommending that I take an antidepressant.

I quit treatment knowing I would need more, but for now I had had enough of the wrong kind. I vowed that I would do more careful research before choosing my next therapist. One of the most difficult and confusing things about this whole affair was that I had developed severe doubts about the usefulness of the very type of treatment I had been trained to practice. I would have to develop a different set of skills if I was to be helpful for my patients.

By the time I finished analysis in 1979 I had completed two consecutive staff psychiatrist positions of eighteen months each, first at Fort Logan Mental Health Center (inpatient) and second at Arapahoe Mental Health Center (outpatient). By then I had gotten enough referrals to leave my position at the Arapahoe MHC and take the leap into full-time private practice.

One of my first private patients was a thirty-year-old single depressed woman I had begun to treat as a third-year resident. While I continued to use analytic concepts such as transference (what she projected onto me from her past caretakers), I was determined, in the aftermath of my painful analytic experiences, to shift the focus more onto her current life struggles.

I stopped trying to be a "blank screen" for her and took the risk of being more authentic and honest. For example, I said, "Patricia, as you were telling me how your boyfriend was an hour late for dinner last night, I began to feel frustrated. I'm wondering if that's similar to what *you* felt."

As I became increasingly comfortable with being more transparent, Patricia progressed. At the same time, I remained cautious about self-disclosure unless I felt it served my patients' treatment needs, as opposed to my own. Patricia became engaged to her boyfriend and invited me to their wedding, an invitation my analytic supervisors would have forbidden me to accept. By this time, I had found an open-minded consultant in an analytically-trained pediatrician, Dave Metcalf, who agreed that it was appropriate for me to go, provided I didn't disclose my relationship to anyone at the wedding.

I sat in the back row of the large suburban church and nodded as she walked down the aisle on her favorite uncle's arm. She met my gaze and responded with a bright smile, as if to say *I knew you'd come.* I left the sanctuary shortly after the ceremony ended. As I descended the steps in the warm June sunlight, I paused to savor a priceless moment.

My discovery of the value of becoming more authentic as a therapist was enhanced by my voracious reading habits. For a number of years, I had been reading Russian fiction and the existentialist literature, including Tolstoy's *The Death of Ivan Ilych, Anna Karenina,* Camus' *The Stranger,* Sartre's *No Exit,* and Archibald MacLeish's dramatic portrayal of Job, in *JB*. All of these works, in different ways, plumbed the vast interior landscape of universal human concerns about meaninglessness, freedom, isolation and the inevitability of death.

When Irvin Yalom's new book *Existential Psychotherapy* came out in 1980, I pounced on it. Here, finally, was a profound and moving description of treating humans who struggled with basic, universal dilemmas (4). Yalom's approach advocated an entirely new way of listening, hearing, and *being present* with my patients' pain and anxieties. I could jettison orthodoxy, be authentic and spontaneous, use my own internal dialogue and dilemmas to formulate responses, readily admit my foibles, and continue to help my patients in their search for meaning. I began to see that forming a genuine human relationship in therapy was more essential for lasting change than any specialized technique I could master.

With the increased energy I experienced by leaving analysis, I plunged into full-time practice. I gave a number of lectures on bereavement related to what I had learned after the suicide deaths of a colleague from the residency and one from medical school (see chapter on depression and suicide). I was invited by Dr. Laura Dodson, a prominent Jungian analyst, to participate on a panel discussing the differences between Jung's and Freud's approach to therapy and analysis. Two individuals from the audience called me for appointments, saying they were intrigued by my presentation.

Within the next six months, Dr. Dodson referred me several interesting patients. A few others called me after reading hospital newsletters in which I had published articles on bereavement. By 1980, patients started referring their friends. I suddenly had all the patients I could handle and was obliged to master the art of graciously turning down referrals and passing them along to my colleagues. My income rose dramatically that year and I decided to incorporate my practice in the state of Colorado. I celebrated these successes by purchasing a Steinway baby grand piano and beginning piano lessons. At age thirty-seven, sixteen years after I graduated from college, my career was fully launched.

By age forty, I was working fifty-hour weeks, seeing a mixture of outpatients and inpatients in three different Denver hospitals, consulting for Denver Catholic Community Services and Bethesda Hospital, and beginning to write articles and give professional workshops on bereavement.

While we enjoyed family activities in camping, hiking, and skiing, I realized that my wife and I had grown apart emotionally over the ten years of my rigorous training and the demands of my early practice. We had both been in intensive therapy and/or analysis for several years. While our treatments had provided significant insights, they also were accompanied by an increase in our conflicts.

I don't wish to imply that the treatments drove us apart. It is more likely that they led to more uncensored arguments and exposed the solid cores of our incompatibilities. It was also during this period that I began to develop early symptoms of hypomania which included increased insomnia, irritability, racing thoughts, increased energy and libido, and brief periods of dissociation.

The result of this was that my first wife and I separated in June 1983 and were divorced in 1984. During the next year and a half I immersed myself in my practice to maintain my focus and self-esteem, while inundated with despair and grief about the failure of my marriage and the understandable withdrawal of my daughter's affections. I rented a house within a mile of my ex-wife's so I could be close to my daughter and struggled with how to be a good divorced father for her.

It was during this time that I began dating my future second wife, Nancy, who worked as a psychiatric nurse. We lived together for a brief period and were married in May 1986 in a civil ceremony, exchanging our own written vows before our close friends and family. Within a short period I had become a stepfather of two young girls, Kristin and Jesse Lynn and was elected President of the Medical Staff at Bethesda Hospital. My daughter Jessica stayed with us in our new home every other weekend and one night per week. Through our love of hiking and skiing we slowly rebuilt our relationship, which had been shaken by the divorce.

Several months later, my brother Charles flew over from Switzerland for a week-long visit. He had been consistently supportive of my new relationship and I welcomed the opportunity to see him in my new home.

During his visit, Charles and I took long walks around a park in Lakewood, one of Denver's western suburbs. Encircling the large pond as scores of Canada geese and mallards took off and landed, we shared experiences about our parents, our marriages, and our experiences with Pop's beatings. I learned that Charles and Tom had actually suffered more severe discipline than I had. Charles revealed in calm, measured tones a story of immense sadness.

When he finished speaking, I trembled with a mixture of grief and excitement. For the first time, someone in my family, *my own brother*, was available to understand, empathize, and help me articulate my own story. His story was unique but in many ways similar to mine. I felt immensely validated.

"You've been very strong to overcome these painful events. It must have been very hard for you to handle Pop's outbursts and Muzz's depressions without your brothers there to buffer you. At least I had Tom to turn to."

Our long conversation came to a close. As we walked in silence to my car, I became aware that my gait was more steady and purposeful. *I felt more comfortable with just being me.*

The next week, having driven Charles to the airport for his flight back to Geneva, I returned to the same park to meditate on our conversation. A wet spring snowstorm had left the tree branches glistening with ice. Suddenly a stiff breeze stirred up whitecaps on the pond and crystals from the trees tinkled to the ground. As I zipped up

my parka, my pace quickened. I was breaking into a run, when suddenly from the depths of my being, I cried out to the bright western sky:
I AM <u>NOT</u> A MISTAKE!!

Left: *With my brother Charles, resting on a hike above Boulder, Colorado, 1985.*

Right: *With my second wife, Nancy Bell (left), stepdaughters Jesse Lynn (top), Kristin (bottom Center) and daughter Jessica (bottom right), Denver, Colorado, 1986*

Left: *(From left to right), My father, me, Tom, mother, and Charles in Severna Park, Maryland, ca.1988.*

CHAPTER 4

MANAGING THE STRESSES
OF PRACTICE

When I decided to become a psychiatrist in my fourth year of medical school I never anticipated how pervasively my career would affect my personal and family life. Most of the time, I felt energized and grateful for the privilege of witnessing my patients' growth, personal triumphs, and increased sense of hope. However, there were also periods when the convergence of my patients' sad stories, traumatic memories, losses, and psychotic processes pushed me to the limits of my endurance, exacerbating my mood disorder and increasing the conflicts I experienced in my two marriages, each of which ended in divorce. In my life as a psychiatrist I've engaged in an ongoing struggle to find a balance between my work, personal relationships, and recreational activities. My commitment to maintaining nourishing personal and professional relationships has enabled me to manage and moderate the inevitable stresses of practice and its effects on my life.

Over the years, my practice focused primarily on providing outpatient psycho-dynamic therapy and medications for adults, adolescents, couples, and group therapy for bipolar patients and men. I always preferred the autonomy and lack of administrative intrusions in my private office practice and found a stimulating and welcome variety in my consultation activities in both public and private settings. By limiting my hospital cases and minimizing work with those who had severe personality disorders, I managed to keep my stress at tolerable levels most of the time.

In addition to clinical and consultation activities, I enjoyed supervising third and fourth-year psychiatric residents at the University of Colorado Health Sciences Center for over thirty-five years. Many of the young men and women I supervised were taking elective courses in psychodynamic therapy. My supervision activities provided a welcome stimulus for keeping up with new developments in brain science and psychotherapy techniques. As a supervisor, I became increasingly focused on sharing my personal experiences as a therapist to help trainees manage the stresses of practice, decrease burnout, and nourish themselves. My discussions with residents often focused on the value of being "good enough" in our multiple roles as physician, spouse, parent, and friend.

At the height of my practice I saw between eighty and one hundred outpatients per month with two thirds involved in psychodynamic or cognitive behavioral therapy and the remaining one third focused on medication maintenance and supportive therapy. Many of my patients had chronic depressions, bipolar disorder, or anxiety disorders and had done intensive therapy with me at the outset of their treatments. My long-term patients often came to view me much as they would a family doctor, since I had guided many of them through marriage, beginning parenthood, major illnesses, divorces, and the losses of parents, jobs, and friends. I also enjoyed doing home, nursing home, and hospice visits when they developed severe or terminal illnesses.

Patients who had personality disorders sometimes targeted me with their rage and disillusionment, as if I were their parent or spouse. As their therapist, I served as a "container" for their feelings while helping them find new ways of understanding what they experienced and expressing their feelings in ways that were less destructive. For the most part, I managed to do this successfully.

At times, I became overwhelmed and over-identified with their helplessness and rage. As I am by nature rather thin-skinned emotionally, I had a tendency to take some of my patients' intensely negative feelings personally, even when I understood them as manifestations of transference. Loud or angry voices were unsettling for me, whether or not I was the intended target. This was a real challenge, based on my early experiences of my father's harsh verbal and physical discipline. I used these experiences to further my own growth in therapy

Following my residency training, I worked at the Fort Logan Mental Health Center, a state hospital in a suburb south of Denver. One of my most difficult patients was a young woman who suffered from substance abuse and an impulse-ridden personality disorder. Following an altercation with the nursing staff, she had set fire to her bedding, forcing evacuation of the entire twenty-bed unit for a brief period as the local fire department came in to douse the flames.

In response to this incident I wrote orders for her to be searched for contraband, dressed in a hospital gown, and placed in a lockable seclusion room with personal safety checks every fifteen minutes. Following an animated staff meeting, I made the decision to place her on a ninety-day involuntary hold and arranged for her transfer to the Colorado State Hospital (CSH) in Pueblo which had more secure facilities and uniformed security staff. She was charged with arson through the local sheriff's office.

A few days later I received a call in the evening on my pager from a number I recognized as coming from Pueblo. I assumed it was clinical staff from CSH wanting to consult about my recent transfer.

I dialed the number, answering with, "Hello this is Dr. Graves, how may I help you?"

An ominous silence followed for several seconds....then I heard a muffled woman's voice: "You and your family are going to pay for this...I have friends in Denver who know where you live...You'll regret you ever laid eyes on me...." Click.

For a few moments I was stunned and speechless. My wife was cooking dinner and our young daughter was just a few feet away in the living room, watching TV. I explained to my wife what had just happened. I was certain it was my former Fort Logan patient. My wife and I were both shaken and scared. No one had ever threatened our lives before this.

By tracing the call, I determined it had come from a payphone on a hospital unit at CSH. I immediately called Dr. John MacDonald, professor of psychiatry at the medical school. I had worked on Dr. MacDonald's Forensic Unit during my residency years. Dr. MacDonald, a short, slender New Zealander given to grey suits, bowties, and a military bearing, was a national expert and had recently written a textbook on psychiatric evaluation of rapists, arsonists, and those who make homicidal threats and commit murder (1). Beginning with quotes from classic literature, MacDonald described in stark detail the dark, complex ruminations of the criminal mind.

Answering with his clipped accent, he queried: "You were in the class of '75 when Gaskill was chairman, right?" The professor was fond of addressing everyone by their last names. I described my experience with my patient at Fort Logan and my reasons for transferring her. Dr. MacDonald listened carefully without interrupting me, then said:

"First, don't pick up any more phone calls from that number. Don't speak with her if she calls from other phones. Notify the county sheriff's office immediately, describing her threats. I'll call Dr. Kort (then Medical Director of CSH) and the nursing unit she is on and request that staff notify you when she is discharged. Call the Denver Police requesting surveillance of your neighborhood for a while after her discharge....Please call me if you hear of any further threats and need advice on how to proceed."

Dr. MacDonald's no-nonsense, practical advice was both calming and reassuring. While I slept fitfully for the next few nights as I continued to work at Fort Logan, I never received any further threats. Two months later I was notified of my former patient's transfer to a hospital in the distant state where she was born. Following this, I never heard from or about her again.

My experience in the mid-1970s triggered painful memories of a previous frightening incident which occurred while I was completing my pre-medical studies at Columbia. Ten years earlier, I had worked several hours per week as a psychiatric aide at the Paine Whitney Clinic, the psychiatric division of Cornell University's New York Hospital. I was assigned to work with Jim, a young college student who had been admitted for treatment of his first paranoid psychotic break. Jim was a swarthy tackle on his football team who had been dismissed after arguing with his head coach for "putting the moves on me in front of everyone" during a difficult practice session. Jim had been given high doses of Thorazine and was beginning to show signs of recovering when I first met him.

In those days we were encouraged to play games with patients to develop an alliance. Since Jim indicated that he liked chess, I decided to engage him with a match in the day room. As we were setting up our pieces on the board, I noticed that his eyes began darting around the room, as if searching for intruders. In an instant, I felt chills running up and down my spine, but pushed my sensations aside as I concentrated on our opening moves. I soon realized that my chess partner had arranged his pieces in an impenetrable defense. He was avoiding all eye contact with me. I began to notice his right knee and ankle vibrating like a snare drummer's.

Suppressing my increasing discomfort, I advanced my king's knight forward, testing his vulnerability. Jim was beginning to stare right through me as the announcement came over the PA system: "Time for five o'clock meds...Patients please report to the nursing station." Relieved, I got up and said a hasty goodbye to Jim and signed out for the evening.

That night I slept poorly, awakening periodically with a vague feeling of dread. The steaming hot bath I was accustomed to taking in the evening to relax before bedtime had done nothing to settle me down. I decided not to speak with my wife about my apprehensions for fear of upsetting her. The following morning as I rode the crowded subway from our flat in Morningside Heights down to 72nd Street, I wondered how Jim had managed that evening.

In morning report I learned that he had continued to decompensate, engaging in a fight with evening staff which included breaking up a wooden chair and using a jagged chair leg to threaten them. He had been cuffed, taken to seclusion, and given several doses of intramuscular Thorazine. It was now my job to give him his breakfast while in seclusion. The head nurse indicated that there was backup ready to assist me just outside the nursing station if there were any problems.

Peering through the ten-by-ten-inch double plexi-glass window, I could see Jim crouched in the opposite corner, staring at the floor. As there were no video cameras facilitating staff-patient interactions, I opened the door a crack and said in my calmest tone:

"Jim, it's time for breakfast."

"GET THE FUCK OUT OF HERE!" he shouted.

I hesitated briefly, taken aback by his intensity. The next thing I knew, Jim had sprung to his feet, pushed the door into my face, knocked the tray out of my hands, hauled me into the room by my shirt collar, and was hitting me in the chest, just missing my face as I ducked and turned. I dropped to the floor, curled up in a ball on the floor protecting my head and face and yelled for help. My co-worker, a 250-pound West Indian aide came to my rescue, got Jim off me and "pretzeled" him. In a few minutes, he was given another high dose of intra-muscular Thorazine and was snoring it off on the floor.

I don't recall anything about my debriefing that morning except that I was sent to the nearby Cornell Hospital ER for medical evaluation and sent home with a few bruises, some Tylenol, and instructions to take the rest of the day off. I was deeply shaken by my experience and spoke about it at length with my wife at dinner following her return from teaching in White Plains. My physical bruises healed quickly and I soon returned to work. It never occurred to me to seek help to deal with my traumatic experience from the student counseling office at Columbia, or from any of the psychiatrists at Cornell. As with my father's beatings, I sucked it up, locked it away, and kept on working and studying.

If my experience had happened fifteen years later on a modern hospital unit, I would have been referred to an employee counseling service for evaluation and treatment and a clinical case conference would have been scheduled for all clinical staff on the unit to learn from this incident. I would have learned that I needed to trust my initial reactions as diagnostic: Jim's defensive chess moves, my spine-tingling chills, Jim's darting eyes, his vacant stare, his increasing physical agitation, my relief at leaving the game and my shift, my fitful sleep and vague feelings of dread and my hesitation to seek help. I would have been instructed to report everything that happened in writing to the head nurse and H.R. A clinical supervisor would have been assigned to help me deal more effectively with challenging cases going forward.

I now know that my choice of playing chess with a paranoid schizophrenic man was ill-advised. The very act of sitting close to him and engaging in a highly structured game of war must have been deeply threatening and over-stimulating for him. Jim communicated his agitation and fears entirely through his body language and his verbal shutdown. My tendency to deny and minimize my own reactions prevented me from recognizing a rapidly developing clinical emergency and also put the evening staff at risk. Not having had any therapy at that point, I did not know myself well enough to use my own physiologic reactions to stress to inform my clinical decision-making.

Jim was clearly having a psychotic reaction to what he experienced as my aggression. Within a matter of a few minutes, I had become the enemy, "putting the moves on him in front of everyone," just like his coach. His psychotic transference to me as the aggressor was diametrically opposed to how I viewed myself as his helper. It would take me a few years of therapy to learn how to use personal insight in the service of appropriate clinical interventions in an emergency such as this. When an agitated psychotic patient tells you to "get the fuck out of here," you need to close the door without hesitation. After this, with supportive colleagues in a safe space, you can discuss and learn from what just happened.

There were times, particularly when treating traumatized, depressed women like my mother or irascible, impulsive men like my father that I found myself dissociating for brief periods along with my patients. I was able to conceal these lapses from both myself and my patients with my soft voice and calm demeanor. These "spells" were so automatic that I didn't recognize them as such for several years until I engaged in treatment.

In my own treatment, I reviewed my family experiences and the experiences I had with Jim and the woman who threatened to kill me and came to recognize how changes in my patient's tone of voice and body language reflected triggering events. I discovered that my tendency to dissociate was a marker for my patients' growing connection with their own disorganized traumatic memories. Understanding these interpersonal phenomena and integrating them with my own musical experiences (see next chapter), I was better able to help my patients verbalize and gain control over their own traumatic affects, even as I managed to recognize and empathize with my own.

Several of my women patients were flirtatious and at times, sexually provocative (see chapter on Boundaries). While I was scrupulous about not becoming sexually involved with patients, I sometimes experienced an uptick in my flirtatious behavior with women in general. I was surprised when a hospital nurse I barely recognized once called my office phone requesting that we meet. I mistook her for a prospective patient and began to schedule an "appointment." She interrupted me and said: "But John, I just wanted to have coffee and talk about the possibility of our dating." Explaining that I was married, I wished her well in her dating adventures and ended the conversation. I came to understand this as an example of how I was displacing the increased sexual stimulation I encountered in my practice onto other women in my environment, often unconsciously.

Other aspects of my practice added to my stress level, including being reported to the state medical board. Despite rigorous continuing education and careful attention to maintaining high practice standards, few psychiatrists are immune from these occurrences. I dealt with three complaints to the medical board, one brief litigation process, and a handful of threats to sue. All three of the medical board complaints involved patients who were delusional at the time they filed and their complaints were ultimately dismissed. I was required to file detailed responses to the board and in each case waited several weeks before receiving notices of dismissal. During the waiting period my insomnia increased and I became anxious, hypervigilant, irritable at home, and more cautious in my practice.

During these periods, I declined new referrals and fantasized quitting my practice. My resentment was intense and I ruminated: *How dare they put me through all this stress... I've been trying to help them!* I learned from reading literature on doctors' responses to malpractice suits (2, 3) and speaking with colleagues and my practice consultant that my reactions were common and expectable. Simply normalizing my stress reactions helped relieve my intense anxiety and sense of isolation.

Threats of lawsuits were even more stressful. In one case the father of a teenage boy I had hospitalized after a serious suicide attempt threatened to sue me if I reported his physically abusive behavior to social services. He made several ominous phone calls to me and to the hospital administrator and screamed at me in my office about his right to use corporal punishment and threatened to "ruin my practice" if I reported him.

I informed him of my statutory duty to report, gave him and his wife information on what to expect from the agency involved, and made my report. During the course of the social services investigation he demanded that his son be transferred to another psychiatrist. I struggled with guilt feelings about abandoning my patient in what felt like a Solomon's choice situation. Ultimately I transferred him to a child psychiatrist. I later discovered that his mother had filed for a divorce and that her ex was mandated by the court to have supervised visitations. He never followed through with his threats to sue me. During this time I relived some of the more painful aspects of my father's overly strict discipline. This provided me with an opportunity to return to treatment to further resolve my own issues and to work towards forgiving him.

On the positive side, I have had many interactions over the years with my patients which have increased my self-awareness and provided an impetus for both personal and professional growth. Many of these growth experiences have arisen from observations of my behavior, feelings, or attitudes by patients (4).

One of the most useful observations came from a woman I saw many years ago for chronic depression and multiple somatic symptoms. After many consults and referrals to medical specialists to investigate her complaints, I found myself feeling increasingly depleted and helpless. I began to wonder if my sense of emptiness was related to how she felt growing up in a large family where she got very little attention from either of her parents. I arrived for our session one afternoon sneezing and coughing from a bad cold. After about ten minutes, she exclaimed, "Dr. Graves, you're sick. You ought to go home and take care of yourself." She was absolutely right.

We ended the session and I took a few days off to recover. She had reminded me of a basic axiom: "Physician, heal thyself." Her kind observation forced me to acknowledge that I had been overextended for months, ignoring my own physical and emotional needs and acting as if being a physician somehow exempted me from illness. In confronting my grandiosity and self-neglect, she gave me a valuable gift. I told her how much I appreciated this in our next session. We came to view her generous and assertive act as an important step in her own recovery and in mine as well.

In the 1980s and 1990s many women were referred for treatment who had experienced sexual assaults and/or domestic violence. There was considerable controversy regarding whether or not male therapists, including psychiatrists, should be treating these women at all. Feminist therapists frequently took the position in local and national conferences that therapy, even by well-meaning men, could be re-traumatizing for their women patients. Some psychodynamically oriented professionals advanced the opinion that cross-gender therapies where female patients expressed intense anger towards their male therapists could actually be *useful* in the hands of empathic therapists who were skilled at transference interpretations. Given this controversy, I accepted a few selected women patients and used consultation with senior female therapists to help insure that I was using helpful interventions.

Performing cross-gender therapies during this period coincided with a definite trend within health insurance companies to require more specific diagnoses and frequent utilization reviews to justify reimbursement for longer-term therapies. I treated a few women who, as a result of repetitive traumas, developed patterns of maladaptive behaviors or personality disorders.

In one memorable case, a woman who had a verbally abusive father and depressed mother asked me to provide her with a diagnosis. I made the mistake of saying she had a Borderline Personality Disorder. Sharing this felt like an insult to my patient who viewed my diagnosis as both pejorative and incorrect. I apologized for my error in the next session and we discussed the issue of how this kind of labeling was harmful for her in view of her history, especially coming from a male therapist. As it turned out, we later discovered that what initially appeared to be symptoms of a personality disorder were actually manifestations of a mixed bipolar disorder, where a depressed mood often coincides with intense affect and impulsive behavior.

I learned several lessons from this encounter: When dealing with someone with PTSD and current symptoms of depression, one should avoid making a personality disorder diagnosis, since PTSD and depression symptoms will generally subside with further treatment, often leaving few, if any, traces of a personality disorder. In situations with a male therapist and female patient, one needs to be cautious about any comments which may be perceived as blaming the victim. In cross-gender therapies where there is a history of rape, one should address on an ongoing basis how safe the female patient feels with seeing a male therapist. In this situation, the priority is creating a "safe space" both within the patient and in the treatment relationship (5).

Shortly after this experience, I joined a consultation group of men and women therapists focusing on gender issues in psychotherapy. Two of these women had experienced assaults and rape. All of them had endured varying degrees of sexual harassment. They shared many lessons from their painful dating and therapy experiences and what they had learned about how to foster a safe space for their clients. They also shared how male therapists could become better attuned to a whole range of sexual and gender issues by their use of more empathic language and careful timing of inquiries. These insights helped me both as a therapist and later on, in my personal relationships with women.

During my involvement with this group I treated a woman who had been the victim of incest with her father. She was currently in a physically and sexually abusive relationship with her husband and was experiencing difficulty extricating herself from her marriage. At the same time I was treating another woman who was also in the midst of a physically abusive marriage. After several months of working with these two women, I found myself becoming increasingly helpless and frustrated, feeling I was doing ninety percent of the work.

I sought consultation with Dr. John Kelly, who wondered whether I might be unconsciously engaged in attempting to rescue these women from their tormentors. As long as I participated in this dynamic, I was, in effect, depriving my patients of the opportunity to become more assertive. After two more meetings, Dr. Kelly asked if what we were talking about might be more in the realm of therapy than consultation. We agreed to begin treatment. In my treatment, Dr. Kelly helped me recognize that my "rescue operations" represented variations on the theme of my wish to protect my mother from my father's anger. This insight helped me let go of this old pattern and function more effectively in the treatment of these and other women who had experienced victimization.

During my forties, I experienced three depressive episodes, each coming on in autumn and lifting in the spring, followed by mood "switches" with periods of insomnia, racing thoughts, increased energy, irritability, hyperactivity, and hypersexuality. When my third depression came on in November 1991, there was no denying how serious it was. This episode took me by surprise since by that time I had remarried, bought a house, and was more active than ever with my practice, teaching, and professional leadership activities. I became suicidal (see Chapter 9 on depression) and was referred to a psychiatrist who immediately prescribed Prozac.

Despite my being a psychiatrist, it was difficult for me to admit that my depression was serious enough to require medication. I felt mortified and ashamed of my illness and feared that colleagues would somehow see through me and stop sending referrals. I thought I could beat my illness by the force of my own wits. Much of my excellent treatment focused on coming to terms with my diagnosis, dealing with self-imposed stigma, and resolving my resentment about being afflicted with this not uncommon familial disorder.

As I was beginning to resolve these issues and my depression lifted, new challenges arose. I needed less and less sleep and this time wrote reams of metaphysical essays until 3:00 a.m., including a lengthy epic poem, certain I would receive literary awards. When I wasn't writing furiously, I blasted out the beefy staccato chords of Rachmaninoff's G minor Prelude on the piano late into the night, keeping my family awake and annoyed. Many books arrived that I barely recalled ordering. On the ski slopes and highways I became reckless and narrowly escaped collisions. I set new records for speeding tickets and ignoring stop signs. My practice grew rapidly, and I took on more bipolar patients in my group. I was becoming quite unlike my former self, teetering on the brink of exhaustion.

My treating psychiatrist recommended a consultation with a faculty member who evaluated me and rendered his opinion. I had mild to moderate Bipolar II Disorder with mixed symptoms, most likely aggravated by my use of Prozac. I was embarrassed but also relieved to finally have an explanation for my irritability and agitation. In retrospect, I had struggled with symptoms of bipolar disorder for nearly fifteen years. Being a psychiatrist had provided neither immunity from my illness nor prevented me from engaging in extensive denial.

I was acutely aware of what lay ahead of me in terms of probable recurrence, higher suicide risk, and an aggravation of marital conflicts, which often leads to divorce. My mixed symptoms made me a higher suicide risk because my depressed mood coincided with increased energy and focus, potentially enabling me to act on self-destructive impulses. I was terrified and wondered if I would be able to survive another episode.

I was at a crossroads. I knew if I was going to support my family and continue my practice, I would have to prioritize my treatment above all else. My psychiatrist discontinued my Prozac and started me on Depakote, a mood stabilizer, along with a sleeping medication. I made every attempt to maintain consistent sleep and social and recreational activity schedules, and stopped drinking wine. I made a detailed list of my symptoms of depression and hypomania and used a bipolar mood scale to measure my mood changes on a daily basis, marking important events associated with them.

While I was getting adjusted to my treatment regimen, I continued to treat many bipolar patients individually and in groups and published an original article on my group work (6). Through my attempts to master my own illness, I became known as a local specialist, a complicated and fraught distinction. The extent to which I saw myself in others with bipolar illness amplified my empathy but also my vulnerability to relapse.

During the next few years I closely monitored my medication doses and eventually tried two other mood stabilizers, each with uncomfortable side effects. I elected not to take Lithium due to concerns about cognitive dulling and tremor, which I feared would interfere with my dexterity on the piano. I discovered I could function best on Carbamazepine, a mood stabilizer which I took twice daily. I worked diligently to keep my life organized and on an even keel. With a few "mental health days" off, I was able to maintain my practice schedule and avoid hospitalization.

In order to maintain my practice, I put numerous safeguards into effect. I informed my psychiatric consultant of my diagnosis and treatment plan. He agreed to help me monitor my practice stress, supervised difficult cases, and provided feedback if it became apparent that my mood swings could potentially affect my capacity to practice in a competent, ethical manner.

I discovered that with the onset of depression I was more empathic but also tended to be more passive and slower to make clinical interventions. When hypomanic, I was naturally more active, but sometimes listened less empathically and got ahead of where my patients were ready to go in therapy. My practice consultant helped me recognize these changes and decrease my practice to a more modest level during my acute episodes. Sometimes I just had to grit my teeth and do my best.

In the mid-1990s I formed a consultation group which met in my office for lunch on a monthly basis. This group of six men and women from different mental health disciplines provided a safe place to discuss difficult counter-transference and enactment issues (see Chapter 8 on boundaries) and to solicit feedback on the appropriateness of our treatment interventions. As group cohesiveness and trust increased, we became more comfortable sharing our vulnerabilities as they related to our clinical work. My experience in this group formed an excellent adjunct to my discussions with my practice consultant.

I struggled for several years with the question of whether or not to "come out" regarding my bipolar disorder with some of the bipolar patients I was treating individually and in groups. I was sorely tempted to do this at times, especially with bipolar patients who sensed that I was bipolar from the uncanny way in which I could empathize with their changing mood states. After much soul-searching I realized that my motivations for self-disclosure related more to *my* needs for empathy and connection, and less with theirs. In addition, I felt that such a disclosure would be unduly burdensome for my patients, given their own illnesses. So I remained circumspect.

After reading Kay Jamison's *An Unquiet Mind* (7), I decided to share my diagnosis with a few trusted friends and colleagues from my men's group. As I did this, my sense of shame and duplicity began to melt away and I felt more authentic. I ultimately chose not to disclose my illness to a larger community since, I believed that drawing attention to myself in this way would create additional stresses that I was not prepared to deal with. Personally, I believe I made the right decision. Now that I am retired and relieved of clinical responsibilities, I feel more comfortable sharing my experiences in writing in a way that I hope will be useful to other professionals who have mood disorders.

A combination of practice stresses, the symptoms of my bipolar disorder, and unresolved conflicts during my second marriage led to my divorce in May 2004. I was nearly sixty-one and wanted to work for at least another ten years. I understood that if I was to continue a successful practice, I would need to find a long-term relationship which could sustain me through the rigors of both my mood disorder and practice stresses. At this point I entered into an intense period of introspection, journaling, and therapy about my relationships with women.

I discovered that the combination of multiple erotic transferences and intense idealizations from men and women patients had combined to further augment my false self. As I became more attractive and more powerful in the eyes of my patients, I idealized myself. My grandiosity included an exaggerated view of what I deserved in marriage and consequently led to increased levels of frustration and irritability when I felt disappointed by the normal slings and arrows of married life. This was a unique occupational hazard, augmented by the tendency towards grandiosity and hypersexuality which accompanied my hypomanic episodes.

I came to realize that the practice of psychotherapy, as I had experienced it thus far, had periodically drawn me at times into a surreal world where I became increasingly isolated and distressed. In my attempts to adapt to this situation, I had ended up divorcing two women who had done their best to support me. If I was to continue my life and practice, I would need to find a different kind of intimate relationship with someone who could confront both my grandiosity and tendency to withdraw while at the same time providing the emotional and physical nurturance and support I needed outside my practice.

Around this time I discovered a book by James Guy, which addressed many of my concerns about intimate relationships and the stresses of my work:

"The importance of maintaining meaningful interpersonal relationships cannot be overstated. Psychotherapists need as much, if not more love, understanding, nurturance, support, confrontation, and guidance as any other person. Without these...the therapist may experience loneliness, depression, and ultimately, despair" (8).

From 2004 through 2014 I lived alone and pursued a number of dating relationships lasting from several months to four years. From these experiences I learned that I wanted and needed a long-term, exclusive, live-in relationship. In these relationships I openly discussed my mood disorder and what I needed from them to handle the stresses of my practice. In 2012 I found an energetic, bright, attractive woman with whom I am now living.

I have been a member of a men's group for nearly 25 years, many of whom are mental health professionals. Every month one of us cooks dinner for the group and we catch up on the unfolding dramas of our lives. We participate in annual retreats in a mountain cabin where we sing, drum, play guitar, hike, snowshoe, and share our life stories. Since I have lived far away from my brothers most of my adult life, these men have become like brothers to me. They have supported me through two divorces, two back surgeries, the loss of my parents and my brother Tom, conflicts within my family, the ups and downs of dating relationships, and the challenges and joys of my work. I have learned to be more openly affectionate with them in ways that have deepened my relationships with my own brothers. Together, we are finding ways to age with dignity.

My women friends have helped me grow and make up for not having sisters. From them I've learned how valuable non-sexual relationships with women can be. Some of them have helped me better understand my women patients, adding their valuable and varied perspectives. I have learned a lot from them about tact and timing when addressing touchy subjects such as obesity, traumatic sexual experiences, abusive relationships, employment, and gender discrimination.

My lifelong studies in classical piano have been stimulating and helpful in processing the stresses of my practice. Leaving my busy practice on Wednesday afternoons for 90 minutes with my teacher, Anne Pap, I entered a richly textured world of beauty, creativity, and hope for 23 years. I learned how to relax, breathe, and listen with increasing sensitivity. Playing a wide variety of compositions has allowed me to express powerful emotions while at the same time providing boundaries and structure for the internal disorganization I sometimes felt with traumatized or psychotic patients.

In the aftermath of the 2001 terrorist attacks, I felt an intense need to express my grief and find strength in community and with ritual. I began attending regular church services again and found solace and tears of joy in singing old familiar hymns and from the hushed rhythmic solidarity of saying prayers in unison. Being part of these services helped me rekindle my faith and prayer life, which I had neglected since leaving seminary. I discovered the power of forgiveness of self and others. As a result of these experiences, I began to encourage my patients to consider the wealth of benefits of incorporating forgiveness practices into their own lives (see Chapters 6 and 7).

My experiences with fly fishing, especially when alone, have been immensely restorative. Wading into the sparkling flux with the soothing melodies of water sculpting rock, I become one with the One and I am well-nourished. I focus my attention on the tiny fly dancing along the surface. My stress and tension are released to mingle and dissolve in the current. A hungry trout rises to my fly...I raise my rod tip and suddenly I am engaged in a brief struggle. I bring the fish quickly to my net so as not to exhaust it. As I release my brilliantly spotted friend and watch it return to its lie, I offer a prayer of thanks. I am at peace.

Psychiatric practice is not for the faint of heart. It makes great demands on the practitioner to tolerate long periods of ambiguity, the disorganization of psychosis, periodic dark tides of helplessness and despair, and the sharp fangs of hostility. Inhabiting these powerful force-fields on a daily basis has irrevocably altered my life experience, with my personal narratives often intermingling with those of my patients. At the same time, I've had the unique privilege of participating in exciting discoveries, transformations, and lasting personal growth in my patients and myself.

The fact that many of us enter this field to deal with our own wounds does not detract from the validity of our choice or our capacity to help others. In fact, it is precisely from the core of our own pain that we summon the courage to sit quietly with others and to lead them from despair to hope. The needs and goals of my patients are always in the forefront, but when their struggles have resembled my own, I am grateful to them for providing many opportunities for personal growth.

Few psychiatrists can succeed in this challenging work alone. More than any other medical specialty, we must rely on our family, our friends, our colleagues, and our own therapists for emotional support and understanding when things get tough. Since I have struggled with my own mood disorder, I have come to accept that periodic therapy provides a welcome safe harbor and a necessary anchor when I become weary from stormy seas. In reaching out for help, I am better able to help others.

With Anne Pap, piano teacher in Denver, Colorado, 1998.

Left: *With fishing buddies, Drs. Alan Levine (left), and Geoff Heron (right), 1999.*
Right: *With daughter, Jessica, atop Arapaho Basin, late July 1995!*

With Jack Bertman, M.D., sailing on San Francisco Bay, 2006.

With nice Rainbow on the White River near Meeker, Colorado, 2010.

With Janmarie Pilcher, San Miguel de Allende, Mexico, 2015.

CHAPTER 5

LISTENING AND EMPATHY

I was destined to be a listener. My early family interactions, a life-long interest in music, and an appreciation for the sounds of nature have all contributed to the development of my listening capacity. Empathic listening has been, and will remain, an essential foundation for performing successful psychotherapy of all types.

By *listening* I mean the act of focusing wholeheartedly on another person's communications, both verbal and nonverbal. *Hearing* is the complex process of making sense of these communications. *Empathy* involves understanding another person's mental processes and feelings and requires a sustained capacity for listening, hearing, and communicating this understanding in a way that makes the recipient feel validated. Listening, hearing, and empathy involve some interesting paradoxes and oscillations within the therapist which, in turn, can lead to occupational hazards such as compassion fatigue and vicarious traumatization.

At Wesleyan, "the singing college of New England," Professor Dick Winslow conducted the Glee Club. Winslow would start us on a piece and then abruptly step aside, a wry smile on his face, obliging us to continue, listening only to each other for clues as to how to proceed. It was assumed that we had mastered our parts. Initially we felt our guts tighten, fearing impending chaos. What transpired instead was surprising. Forty voices soon coalesced with vitality and an engaging sonority. Careful listening, like the sensory bands on the sides of brilliant tropical fish, enabled us to move together with grace and agility. Our glee club joined forces with several women's colleges, culminating in an exciting concert tour of Mexico in 1963 with the Smith College choir. These musical listening experiences proved to have far-reaching implications for my later work as a psychiatrist.

Fifteen years later, I began classical piano studies with Anne Pap in Denver. As I practiced difficult passages, I often heard the interpretations of Horowitz, Rubenstein, or Serkin in my head and inevitably became frustrated. Anne caught on to this, and said, "Forget Horowitz... listen to yourself...listen to the music...and *don't forget to breathe.*" As I matured as a pianist, I began to attend more sensitively to the nuanced sounds of my patients' stories and to the "music" of our interactions. Amazingly, I found myself breathing in sync with my patients and healing began to unfold.

In my studies with Anne, I became fascinated with the short keyboard pieces of Robert Schumann. Reading Kay Redfield Jamison's *Touched with Fire* (1), I learned that Schumann had most likely suffered from bipolar disorder and that there were compelling correlations between his shifting mood states, compositional frequency, and the tonal *quality* of what he composed. When playing his pieces, I could literally feel his mood states emanate from the scores. I spent a year studying his compositions in depth, listening for subtleties of intonation and mood.

In 1994 I gave a piano concert of Schumann's shorter works and described the composer's struggles with mood changes and how his compositions reflected these episodes. Later, I came to see Schumann's compositions not only as creative emanations of his mood states, but also as unique adaptations and attempts at self-cure. Through my piano studies I became more adept at listening to subtle shifts in mood and energy levels in my patients and in myself. I began, like the analyst Theodor Reik, to "listen with the third ear" (2).

In my early practice years, I treated a large number of bipolar patients in both individual and group therapy. While listening to them, I noted changes in pitch, rhythm, frequency of word production and pauses, and subtle dynamic alterations. The human voice, I learned, is an instrument *par excellence*, revealing mood, impulsivity, impending danger, and a wide range of other internal states. I was impressed with how well bipolar individuals listened to each other in my groups, picking up on subtle warning signs of potentially disruptive mood episodes.

As I listened, I was surprised to notice that my breathing patterns were changing along with those of my patients, in a kind of *somatic synchrony*. As certain patients became anxious and their breathing became more rapid and shallow, I found myself mimicking them and feeling tense. After learning about the importance of controlled breathing in meditation training, I wondered if I could have an impact on my patients by generating a more relaxed, deeper breathing rhythm in myself. I practiced dong this alone and with patients and was delighted to see some of my patients calming down without my uttering a word. Without knowing it, I was replicating earlier observations on the functioning of "mirror neurons" in primates and humans. I began to integrate my experiences in glee club, piano studies, and meditation with how I operated as a therapist.

Several years ago, I became engrossed in playing the piano works of Johannes Brahms, especially his *intermezzi*, which are complex, meditative gems. In these compositions, Brahms develops inner melodic voices of great subtlety. I find myself returning to the *Intermezzo in A Major*, Opus 118 No. 2 repeatedly, discovering intertwined inner voices, yearning to be set free from the score. Likewise, in listening to patients, I was delighted to discover and comment on their hidden inner voices emerging with increasing clarity and vitality. Together, we co-created a melody of healing.

As rests and spaces between notes, phrases, and movements are essential in musical composition, the capacity to enjoy silence and solitude are requisite for the practice of listening carefully. In his remarkable book *Silence*, the composer John Cage begins by pointing out that there is no such thing as absolute silence. After spending hours in an anechoic chamber, Cage discovered the sounds of his own heartbeat and nervous system. This experience led to his paying close attention to naturally occurring sounds and to their impact on the listener. Cage believed that once a sound is heard, the listener is forever changed (3). This is true for musicians and therapists alike. As my case studies illustrate, the lyrics and music of our patients can resonate within us for years, often for a lifetime.

I am reminded of an experience I had listening, for the first time, to Nathan Milstein's recording of Bach's *Sonatas and Partitas for Unaccompanied Violin*. I was transfixed by his performance. In the thundering silence that followed his final bowing, my whole being resonated with the music. In this transcendent and timeless experience, I realized that I was *both fully absent and fully present*.

The paradox of being fully absent and fully present has several implications for the life and practice of the psychotherapist. Regarding being "fully absent" (a paradox in itself), we try to listen without imposing our own values or preconceptions regarding our patient's mental processes or what might be best for them. Many therapists of my generation were steeped in the various "schools" of understanding mental functioning, e.g. Freudian, Jungian, interpersonal, and family systems. Being "fully absent" as a therapist entails emptying oneself not only of these theoretical constructs but also of one's own personal biases and beliefs. This, of course, is a goal never fully attained, but worth striving for if we are to optimize our healing capacities. It is only by emptying ourselves in this sense that we can be fully present for those we wish to help.

Another aspect of being fully absent is to be as free as possible from the exigencies of hunger, thirst, fatigue, physical pain, and sexual tension. This means that I must attend to these needs elsewhere and arrive at consultation sessions in a more or less relaxed state. When I become aware of these issues as potentially distracting, I address them promptly. In this context the injunction "physician, heal thyself" is *apropos*.

As with all therapists, I have good and bad days in terms of my empathic capacity. If I am tired from a late flight, hurried to make my first appointment, or have recently heard some disturbing news about friends or family, I recognize that I am not at my best. Patients often sense this, becoming more superficial, chatty about weather or news, or solicitous about my wellbeing. These are reminders that I am off center and out of tune. In these situations, I try to imagine a calming scene, take a few deep breaths, and carry on the best I can. As soon as possible, I make a point of walking outside, breathing deeply and grounding myself.

If I know that I will be stressed for a while, I make a practice of doing a brief walking meditation (4) on the way to my office entrance, asking for calm and equanimity as I face my practice. Before sessions, I give myself a few moments to imagine my patients' facial expressions and vocal tone qualities. Like some professional musicians who are able to "mentally rehearse" a performance, I try to "tune in" to the person I am about to see. Consistent with this, I try to take breaks between each session. This enables me to put aside my resonances from the previous session and to be as "fully present" as possible for my next patient. On occasion I have called a patient after a session and apologized for not being tuned in, or for misconstruing something important they have said. Patients are often surprised and grateful for this.

I pay close attention to my office environment and create one conducive to good listening, with a minimum of external distractions. My phone and fax are turned off. The lighting is soft but adequate. Chairs and couches are comfortable and allow for variations in interpersonal space and configurations. These items form the physical container for providing an adequate emotional "holding environment" for growth and maturation (5).

Several patients over the years have commented on how comfortable and "homey" my office is. This is gratifying, since I have tried my best to treat patients with all the warmth and solicitude I would offer a house guest. In the act of hospitality, I am conscious of withdrawing into my own comfortable space, or as Henri Nouwen has said:

"… by withdrawing into ourselves…we let others enter into the space created for them and allow them to dance their own dance, sing their own song and speak their own language without fear" (6).

Being both fully absent and fully present are, of course, unattainable ideals. But to the extent I am able to approximate them, I offer a gift my patients may never have received in their lifetimes.

At the same time, I am attending to my own internal processes. As I listen, there is an inner dialogue unfolding. My stream of consciousness is a comingling of my own and my patient's communications, but there may be significant issues of proportionality involved. How much is his or hers? How much is mine? What is most salient in the here and now interaction? Delineating this is no easy task. In any given session, I might be asking: are my fantasies about sailing double-reefed in a storm related to my patient's emotional turmoil, my own past or present stresses, or something as yet unidentified?

Is the affect I am experiencing something I can identify in myself prior to the session, or has it been primarily generated by my patient's verbal and non-verbal communications? If I begin to recall significant events in my own life, what prompted these recollections? If they are congruent with what my patient is getting at, how do I articulate what I am hearing in a way that will be useful for my patient?

James: Using my own dream to empathize with intense hostility

The following case illustrates what I mean by listening to internal processes. James, married and in his late forties, had a highly ambivalent relationship with his older brother Carl. A major theme in James' treatment was his conflict regarding assertiveness. While James and Carl were close as children, their relationship became increasingly strained followed their parents' divorce when they were in their teens.

Following their mother's death, Carl challenged the distribution of the family estate and James feared he would have to endure more of Carl's verbal abuse if he expressed his resentment about this. On the night before a scheduled session with James, I had an anxiety dream about training to be a bomber pilot. My dream took me by surprise, since I am a conscientious objector and had never had any experience in the armed forces or with pilot training. In the dream my anxiety increased as I learned to handle the levers which opened the bomb bays. I awakened with a shudder.

In James' session the next morning, I noticed how he was chatting away on superficial topics, avoiding talking about his brother. I wondered out loud if he might be experiencing some feelings that he wasn't addressing. He mentioned how relieved he had been during the past week about his brother's embarking on an ocean sailing cruise. In a monotonous tone, he added he thought Carl was deserting him at the very time their mother was on her deathbed.

Just then, I recalled my bomber pilot dream, which I now understood to be my empathic awareness of James' inhibited anger towards his brother. "Did you have any other feelings besides relief?" I asked.

James paused, looked chagrined, and blurted out, "I imagined blowing up his sailboat."

"You've been uncomfortable about your resentment of him for ages," I said. "Now that your mother is gone, you can own and express your hateful feelings and no longer be ashamed or afraid."

When I turned my understanding of my bomber pilot dream into a vehicle for interpreting James' suppressed rage at his brother, it was with what Heinz Kohut called "vicarious introspection" (7). First, I came to understand my dream as originating in my long-term work with James. The timing of the dream the night before my session tipped me off to its specific relevance for my work with James. A review

69

of my notes from the previous session reminded me that his resentment toward his brother was intensifying. In the portion of my dream regarding my anxiety in the flight simulator, I hypothesized that my unconscious was attuned to James' anxiety about expressing intense resentment, i.e., "bombing" Carl. My hypotheses turned out to be correct, as indicated by the fact that we *both* had an "aha! experience."

Ralph Greenson described empathy as an oscillation within the therapist from observer to participant and back to observer (8). In this pendulum swing, I find myself oscillating between detachment and emotional involvement with my patient. My capacity to engage and to be comfortable with these shifting functions requires a high level of personal insight and emotional maturity. I have to be "comfortable in my own skin" in order to temporarily empty myself and be truly empathic.

I learn to listen carefully by removing external obstacles and tuning in to my own internal processes. I articulate what I have understood of my patient's internal process in a provisional manner—aware of the subjectivity of my observing lens, biases, and values—and await confirmation. If I do not understand someone, I readily admit it, again following Reik's advice, and do my best to sit with and tolerate my own confusion, ambiguity, and ignorance, often a reflection of my patient's own existential reality (2).

I remind myself that wishes to be all-knowing, all-powerful, and all-caring are the three deadly sins of my profession. When I advance an empathic hunch, I am comfortable asking for confirmation with each closer approximation. Does what I just said make sense to you? Are we on the right track? If I am accurate, we both experience an "aha!" resonance. If I am off-base, I observe my patient's response carefully, admit my limitations, and try again. I know that my efforts to finally get it right will ultimately be rewarded by growth and maturation. I also remind myself that with every human encounter there remains an element of ineffable mystery.

While psychotherapy has often been described as "the talking cure," there are situations in many therapies where speech simply cannot do justice to the situation. Under these circumstances the most caring response to hearing a painful story may be an empathic and deeply connected silence. A Korean War veteran told me about finding a close companion left frozen to death after perishing in hand-to-hand combat. He, too, looked frozen as he teared up in silence. We both struggled for words and none came. There was a long silence as we gazed at one another, sharing the intensity of his profound pain. As we stood up to end the session, he gave me a hug, saying, "You've got a big ear and a broad shoulder."

There are some individuals who may initially lack the capacity to use our empathy or may be threatened by our attempts to employ it. In these cases it is best to keep our empathic understanding to ourselves until our patients are ready to hear what we have understood.

I learned this many years ago while treating a teenaged girl who had experienced an incestuous relationship with her step-father. She was the only adolescent I knew who had initiated her own admission to a hospital for a suicidal depression. Within the first few days of working with her, I could see that my attempts at empathy regarding her unfolding story were overwhelming her. At the same time, I began to feel hogtied, just as she had felt silenced by her step-father's threats to kill her if she revealed their "little secret." I gradually came to realize that she was getting me to experience her own terrifying internal reality. When I tried to make any observations about what she might be feeling inside (e.g., intense helplessness, betrayal, rage, and shame), she experienced it as a violation of her boundaries, often staring, then shouting at me with intense hostility. My attempts at empathy, at least for the time being, were abhorrent, and she had to spit them out and reject me in order to feel safe.

I concluded that very little, if anything, about my observations were interpretable or useful for her at this time. My job was to be quiet, to not be put off by her hateful rejections, and to somehow help her gain a sense of safety on the hospital unit and with me. During this time, I became better acquainted with the writings of Judith Herman (9) and learned how to monitor her sense of safety in real time, session by session.

I made it clear that she was in control of how much to disclose and we agreed that she could interrupt me at any time or end the session if my comments made her anxious. Gradually, she became more comfortable allowing me to make some "guesstimates" regarding how she might be feeling. During her hospitalization her mother and step-father were divorced with the court awarding custody to her mother with infrequent supervised visits with her step-father.

After a long period of intensive treatment, I discharged her from the hospital and we continued outpatient therapy for several months. A year later, she graduated from high school with decent grades and involvement in several extracurricular activities. Over the next 20 years she sent multiple messages updating me on major developments in her life, most recently the news of her enrollment in a doctoral program. There are no greater rewards than this.

The late Oliver Sacks, renowned neurologist and medical storyteller, was one of my professors in medical school. Dr. Sacks was a great listener who, with his warm bedside manner and a few pertinent questions, could elicit stories from patients who then virtually handed him their diagnoses. To watch him evaluate a patient was to witness a seamless comingling of compassion and science. Dr. Sacks was also a pianist who loved and played both classical and popular compositions. In his book *Musicophilia*, he shared his fascination with people who are "seized" with persistent melodies and lyrics, sometimes extending to whole movements of symphonies. His own similar experiences over many years led to his research into these phenomena and informed his sensitive, often humorous clinical vignettes (10).

After reading *Musicophilia* I began to ask patients more about their own musical experiences as they related to themes in our therapeutic work. I'd seen a number of widows who had very positive experiences involving singing with their spouses. Often they were surprised by the sudden appearance of lyrics of a song ringing in their ears for several days. When I asked them to repeat the words they would recite verses such as, "I'm going to lay down my burden…" "Down by the riverside…" "Bridge over troubled waters…" etc. Initially they were surprised and sometimes annoyed by these lyrical visitations. When I asked why this particular song appeared right now in their lives, they frequently described intense feelings of loss and loneliness.

I began to ask, "How would you feel about singing your song here so we can understand its meaning for you at this time?" As they began to sing, they frequently broke into tears, sometimes with intense sobbing, eventually experiencing relief. Combining their musical memories (temporal lobe) with singing words (frontal lobe) often helped them access complex feelings of guilt and remorse which helped them gain traction in their mourning. As I listened to their songs, I recalled my 97-year-old mother, who suffered from chronic back pain, having survived my father by sixteen years. While doing leg exercises from her kitchen rocker, she would sing "Amazing Grace" and reminisce about my father. It was her version of therapy, and it worked. For my patients, singing provided the best way of unlocking intense feelings of grief and longing, often frozen for years.

The following case illustrates how variations of intonation, timbre, and rhythm in my patient's voice provided an opening for empathic attunement.

Alice: Where I used vocal tone as an indicator of progress

Alice was a 50-year-old married woman whose early emotional abuse left her with a distorted body image and agoraphobia. Though quite attractive, she came to our sessions without makeup or jewelry, dressed in coveralls worn like body armor, which she later described as her way of remaining invisible to others when outside her home. In the waiting room she initially met me with a forced smile and saccharine greetings. Once in the office, she chose the closest seat to my chair, in marked contrast to the quality of her voice, which struck me as off-putting. I sometimes found myself pushing my chair backwards to distance myself from her harsh overtones.

The predominant message of her vocal tone was, "I'm in charge... stay away from me...I'm talking and I don't want or need a response." Her physical closeness to me transmitted another message altogether. Interspersed with her angry monologues I noticed occasional flickers of pleasant smiles of which she seemed unaware. Listening to her, I was reminded of Sue, an eighth grade girl in ski club I once had a crush on.

Over the next five years, Alice was able to let down her guard and share many of the uncomfortable and painful experiences she had had with men, beginning with her father. I chose not to comment on either her vocal tone or her attire during this period. As she gained more trust in me, I noticed significant changes in her appearance. Her hair styling was more attractive and she now wore tight-fitting clothing more flattering to her figure. Around this time she took the risk of revealing sexual fantasies regarding a tall, handsome man she had met at a conference. Her relationship with her husband improved and she began to describe enjoyable "dinner dates" away from his challenging teenage daughters. As a result, they were able to resume their sexual intimacy.

Accompanying these improvements, I noticed a steady transformation in her vocal sonorities. She now greeted me with authentic warmth in the waiting room. In our sessions, her voice was more relaxed, musical, dynamically varied, and inviting of response. Our conversations were marked by spontaneity, mutuality, and subtle humor.

These sonic cues allowed me to make observations about how much she had grown to enjoy her own femininity in more relaxed friendships, especially with her husband. From working with Alice I learned that it is possible to use observations regarding appearance and vocal tone as an indicator of therapeutic progress, even without explicitly commenting on them in sessions.

The experience of listening and empathizing with distressed individuals, year after year, can lead to developing a condition called "somatic empathy." Schwartz-Salant described marked transformations in his body and mood as he listened to severely narcissistic individuals. He noticed that often he felt short of breath and disembodied. With others who were experiencing dissociation, he felt physical pain and the onset of depression (11).

In my own practice, I've experienced similar changes particularly when listening to patients with severe traumas, physical illnesses, and those who have intense physiologic reactions to emotional distress. My version of "medical student disease" involved diarrhea and even a few episodes of projectile vomiting during my rotations on internal medicine and surgery. In psychiatric practice, my "somatic empathy" was more likely to involve nagging headaches, muscle tension in my neck and shoulders, and insomnia. I eventually learned to use my own bodily sensations to inform my interactions with patients. For example, I might say, "I find that I am tensing up as I listen to you describe how cruelly your sister treated you. Could it be that you are feeling tense as we speak? Can you put this feeling into words?"

During the past thirty years, primate and human research has begun to provide better explanations for both somatic and emotional empathy, which may be different facets of the same underlying phenomenon. The discovery of "mirror neurons," located in the frontal motor cortex of macaque monkeys and later in humans (12) has helped us understand how both sensory perceptions and motor behavior are mirrored between individuals. More recently, researchers have shown that mirror neurons respond also to auditory input and the visceral states of others, enabling us to share their emotions (13).

When I find myself breathing in sync with my patients and helping them breathe more slowly and deeply, while at the same time modulating my voice, I am utilizing the reciprocity of mirror neurons in my patents to bring about a therapeutic effect.

LISTENING AND EMPATHY

Listening, hearing, and empathy, formerly understood within the more abstract realm of metapsychology, have now emerged as significant capacities on the brain-mind interface (14). As it turns out, my "clinical intuitions" are more than mere whims. They have a basis in my own and my patients' brain circuitry. Freud, who started his career as a neurologist and later sought to connect his theories with neural connections, would be pleased.

It will be interesting to learn whether future research will enable neuro-rehabilitation or "neuro-enhancement" specialists to train people deficient in their empathic capacities, including therapists in training, to become more adept at this highly complex social and clinical skill. For now, the best we can do for therapists in training who lack empathy, is to refer them to an experienced, empathic therapist.

In addition to headaches, muscle tension, and insomnia, I also experienced hypertension, indigestion, depression, and anxiety for brief periods. Thankfully, many of these symptoms have subsided since my retirement. These conditions were accompanied by a poignant form of "compassion fatigue" which involved a loss of my listening and empathic capacities at home with family or friends, in which, sadly, I became temporarily emotionally deaf to those I loved the most.

Compassion fatigue is often associated with its more severe first cousin, "vicarious traumatization," which results from listening to large amounts of agonizingly painful, often tragic, stories, accompanied by hypervigilance, intrusive thoughts, a tendency to dissociate for brief periods, increased anxiety, and insomnia. These are significant occupational hazards for many mental health professionals and others in the helping professions. Coleman sums up the dilemma therapists and parents face in managing these conditions: "We need to be able to tune out the suffering of others to maintain our own sanity" (15).

When I become aware that my empathic capacities are supersaturated, I understand that I need more solitude. Contrary to what one might suppose, intimacy and solitude are not opposing experiences; rather, they form ends of a continuum encompassing our sense of self. I am able to enjoy solitude precisely because I have grown comfortable with being alone in the presence of a caring other (16).

When I find solitude I am not lonely or anxious. I'm actually processing many of the stories I have absorbed from others, just as I do in my sleep and dreams. I may do this at the keyboard of my piano, on a quiet walk in the evening, fly fishing on my favorite stretch of the

South Platte River, or simply by going into my backyard and tuning in to the soothing unison of summer crickets. These solitary retreats have been healing and essential in my life and work. When I reconnect with my family, friends, and patients, I can tune in once again.

A few years ago while in the Newark airport, I noticed a family of four standing a few yards away. Both parents were in animated conversations on their cellphones. Their teenage son was glued to his iPad watching a violent movie. His younger sister, perhaps six or seven, stood off to the side with a vacant, forlorn expression. She walked over to her dad and tapped on his free hand several times to get his attention but he was too preoccupied to respond. Meanwhile, as TV commentators hawked their opinions regarding the latest football upset, jet planes shrieked overhead, and shrill voices on the PA system announced gate changes and boarding instructions. This stunning family disconnect left a sad and lasting impression on me. I wondered, *What will become of this little girl? Who will listen to her? What will she hear? How will she learn to empathize with others?*

We humans are being increasingly inundated by unnatural sounds of our own making. During shore vacations, the soothing sounds of surf and seagulls are often interrupted by jet boats and the persistent beeps of our electronic devices. At home, video games, high volume TV ads, and cellphones set to every imaginable ringtone make uninterrupted conversation a rarity. Couples at "romantic" dinners often face one another, scanning social media to see if they are "liked," minimizing direct face-to-face conversation. What will become of them and their children? Will they too get disoriented and beached, like the whales washing up on our shores, impaired by submarine sonar? (17).

As parents, therapists, and citizens, we need to identify and remove those obstacles which erode our capacity to listen, hear, and empathize face to face in our families, communities, places of worship, and governing bodies. In a world of increasingly noisy distractions and political polarization, we need to find and maintain oases of tranquility where we can hold intimate conversations, tell our children stories, and listen to the wisdom of our elders.

These are social imperatives. If we lose these capacities, we will have lost much of what makes us human. Psychiatric training and practice can make a modest contribution in this area by expanding its focus on the art and science of listening and empathy.

CHAPTER 6

INTEGRATING SPIRITUALITY, RELIGIOUS FAITH, AND THERAPY

uman healers have been associated for thousands of years with supernatural powers or divine inspiration. The Hippocratic Oath (ca. 400 BCE) began with a prayer to Asklepios, the god of healing, and to his daughters, Hygeia and Panacea. For centuries physicians recited this oath, acknowledging that the ultimate healing power resided outside the methods honed by the best-trained practitioners. In 1964 a secular version of the oath was adopted, omitting all mention of Greek deities (1). In the twenty-first century, medical practitioners are once again acknowledging the benefits of spiritual practices and religious faith for human health and wellness in their patients (2).

When I entered Union Seminary's program in Psychiatry and Religion in 1965, I was unsure whether I wanted to pursue a calling in the ministry or in psychiatry. My coursework in this program included traditional courses in the Bible, Systematic Theology, and Christian Ethics,n along with extensive readings and discussions of the works of Freud, Jung, Adler, Horney, and Sullivan. Following my decision to pursue a career in medicine, my involvement in regular worship and prayer ceased almost entirely, overridden by the demands of mastering

77

the details of medical science, the skills of clinical practice, and specialty training in psychiatry.

In my residency program, discussions of the role of spirituality and religious faith in mental health were conspicuously absent, as if these topics were somehow taboo. This was puzzling to me, since American psychologist William James, in his detailed research on religious experience, had described widespread beliefs in a "larger power" which "provides an assurance of safety" (3).

By the time I had established a full-time psychiatric practice in 1980, I hadn't attended regular church services, except at Christmas and Easter, for nearly fifteen years. During the next two decades, I was drawn to participate as a consultant in a variety of Christian organizations. In 1975 I joined the medical staff of Bethesda Psychiatric Hospital, an institution "Dedicated to Christian Mercy." At Bethesda, patients had ongoing access to chaplains along with regular chapel services. From 1985 to 1996, I consulted with pastoral counselors at Bethesda and at the Samaritan Center for Pastoral Counseling regarding their clinical work. I served as the primary psychiatric consultant to the Denver Catholic Community Services from 1980 through 1999. For several years, I did psychiatric evaluations of candidates for ordination in the Episcopal priesthood.

While these consultation activities were gratifying and stimulating, I felt increasingly split off from my Christian roots. I felt like a sympathetic "fellow traveler," conversant with the theology of my consultees, but with only tenuous connections with my own spiritual center of gravity. When friends asked me about my own beliefs, I'd respond glibly that I was "theologically Reform Jewish and politically Quaker."

The terrorist attacks of September 2001 shook me to the core. On a personal level, I felt a deep sense of vulnerability and helplessness. As I was born nearly two years after Pearl Harbor, this sudden attack on our own shores challenged a basic sense of security which I had taken for granted. Like millions of Americans, I was perplexed as to why Islamic terrorists would want to attack innocent civilians in the Twin Towers and the seats of power in Washington, D.C.

Immersed in my patients' pervasive sense of shock and grief, I returned to church services for the first time in years, seeking a forum for collective mourning and a sense of grounding. Attending memorial services at a Lutheran church near my home, I was moved by the intimate unison of prayers and the solace of singing familiar hymns such as "A Mighty Fortress is our God." The organ and soaring choral music soothed me and reminded me of the inner peace I experienced as a baritone in my high school, church, and college choirs. I prayed for the souls of those who had perished and for their families. A patient who had lost several of her close colleagues in the South Tower of the World Trade Center wept inconsolably in my office. I listened quietly, struggling to help her find a shred of meaning within the immensity of her grief.

A priest I was treating gave me a copy of Hafiz's poems, many of which addressed God as "The Friend" and "The Beloved" (4). I was stunned by the irony of a Roman Catholic clergyman offering Islamic Sufi poems to console a lapsed Protestant psychiatrist. He must have sensed my grief and disillusionment. His gift was clearly an act of compassion. At a deeper level, I wondered: How could a loving God allow such a tragedy to happen?

Seeking clarity about my own faith, I began attending services at St. John's Episcopal Cathedral in Denver and entered spiritual counseling there with Reverend Elizabeth Randall, a wise and sensitive priest I had evaluated years before as a candidate for ordination. In our first meeting I described feeling spiritually empty and disillusioned. She suggested that we begin our sessions by lighting a candle and engaging in a period of silent meditation and prayer followed by a discussion of what I had just prayed about and its significance for me. I felt awkward doing this, fearing she would be critical of my doubts about the Holy Trinity, the virgin birth, and Christ's physical resurrection. Without missing a beat, she indicated that there were more important things for us to discuss, like reestablishing a regular prayer life, writing a spiritual autobiography, and discussing my need for forgiveness in several areas of my life. Intense periods of doubt and uncertainty were par for the course, she explained.

In my work with Elizabeth, I returned to a regular prayer life, found sustenance in attending Holy Communion services, and rediscovered the importance of my connection to what I can only describe as "Divine Energy." I augmented these activities with Buddhist loving-kindness and mindfulness meditation practices which I was already familiar with. In reading passages from the New Testament Gospels, the recently discovered Gospel of Thomas (5), and modern authors such as Marcus Borg (6), Elaine Pagels (7) and Henri Nouwen (8), I rediscovered the power of Jesus' ethical teachings in his parables which described the beneficial effects of developing tolerance, compassion, and a forgiving spirit.

After three years of attending these sessions and meditating on these and other readings, I felt more whole, enlivened, and grounded. As a result, I began to pay more attention to my patients' spiritual and religious issues. In describing my practice for the Colorado Psychiatric Society Directory, I indicated an interest in "spiritual and religious issues."

To understand how I began to address issues of spirituality, religious faith, and beliefs within the context of therapy, I'll define what I mean by these terms. *Spirituality* is an inner subjective awareness of a person's primary values and a sense of what gives life meaning and energy. *Religious faith* refers to an organized system of beliefs, manifest in worship, rituals, and symbols. Whereas spirituality is personally unique and private, religious faith is predominately mediated through communities of believers who meet on a regular basis. *Beliefs* include specific descriptions of higher powers espoused by members of a given religious faith. For example, in Christianity, most *believe* that Jesus was the son of God.

One can be spiritual without being a member of a specific religious faith or espousing a discrete set of beliefs. Likewise, one can identify with a specific religious faith and engage in a wide variety of spiritual practices unrelated to the traditions or rituals associated with that faith. Personally, I see no contradiction between my worship as an Episcopalian and my use of Buddhist meditation practices on a regular basis.

To be clear, I am in no way advocating a "spiritual" or "religious" approach for all patients, nor did I view myself as specializing in "Christian psychiatry." What has been helpful for me and a select group of patients, has emerged from the unique qualities of a trusting therapeutic relationship where I convey *an openness to discussing ultimate concerns initiated by the patient* which may have direct bearing on their mental and physical health. In so doing, I honor the fact that, as a healing professional, I stand on the shoulders of shamans, rabbis, and priests.

Worshiping a divine being, as I had learned from my studies of Paul Tillich, can encompass a wide spectrum of equally valid experiences of mystical union with the Ground of Our Being (God as Immanent) or a personal encounter with a Wholly Other Being (God as Transcendent) over whom one is powerless (9). Many individuals never report either type of encounter, while some experience mixtures of both types in different contexts. Reviewing Tillich's concepts of im-

80

manence and transcendence helped me better empathize with patients who were describing qualitatively different experiences.

During the next several years, I began to develop a more focused approach to integrating spiritual issues and religious faith into my work as a psychiatrist. Reading William R. Miller's book on this topic (10) helped me organize and refine my assessment of these issues in those who came for treatment. Miller stressed that a thorough understanding of spirituality and/or faith is not only relevant for all in the healing professions, but also a key ingredient in developing and maintaining psychological and physical health.

When new patients indicate they would like to discuss aspects of their religious faith and spiritual practices, I make it clear at the outset that I have no interest in advocating for my own beliefs or practices. Taking cues from how my patients introduce the issue, I begin with open-ended questions such as: What role does religious faith or spirituality play in your life? Do you attend services or engage in any type of meditation or prayer? Were you raised in a particular religious tradition? What was that like for you? Would you be comfortable describing your experiences within these practices or traditions?

Depending on individuals' responses, I often spread out the remaining inquiry over a number of sessions, as appropriate. I then ask: Have you ever considered using your specific practices of meditation, prayer, or worship to assist you with what brought you to me for treatment? Have you ever had any experiences which have challenged your religious beliefs or spiritual practices? Please describe these in detail and how you experienced your doubts. At this point the discussion may lead to recall of traumatic or disillusioning experiences.

Very often, at some point in my inquiry, patients begin to ask about my own faith or spiritual journey. I usually respond that I am Christian, worship in Episcopal services, and attended a non-denominational Protestant seminary for a year before attending a Jewish medical school. Some are surprised that I'm not Jewish, having seen my Yeshiva University Albert Einstein College of Medicine diploma. I find that clarifying my own background is helpful for most patients in providing a model for their own self-disclosure.

Occasionally someone will ask, "Have you accepted Jesus Christ as your personal Lord and Savior?" I generally respond by inquiring why this is important to them. Do they feel that we must have similar beliefs in order for me to be helpful? Very often this question represents a theological "litmus test" regarding whether I subscribe to a certain set of conservative Christian beliefs. In response, I explain that while I have not had a personal conversion experience similar to theirs, I do respect their beliefs and am open to supporting them any way I can. For some, this explanation is sufficient to remain engaged. For others who appear to be more wary or even offended, I may discuss referring elsewhere to pastoral counselors in a church setting whose specific beliefs and practices are more congruent with their own (see case of Ronald, below).

Sometimes the need to focus on putative differences represents a way of maintaining distance or generating conflict in our relationship, frequently mirroring their style in other relationships. When I am able to interpret this posture as part of a pattern, e.g., "Do you think your need to struggle with me regarding differences in beliefs might be similar to your conflicts in other relationships?" individuals can often put their struggles with me aside and refocus their work on themselves. Addressing this kind of potential impasse has an additional benefit of helping patients recognize that meaningful collaboration is possible between those of differing beliefs, an experience that some have never known before.

With some patients, especially Roman Catholics, I found that certain prayers could be very helpful in reducing tension and vengeful fantasies. One man who had been emotionally injured by a colleague he trusted and respected, developed vengeful thoughts towards his former friend. He was accustomed to using a short form of the Prayer to Saint Michael—"Satan, get behind me"—whenever he was tempted to act on angry impulses. I was familiar with dramatic and vivid Renaissance paintings of Saint Michael slaying the Dragon from recent visits to museums in Rome and Venice. I encouraged my patient to repeat this prayer every day at a designated time. These regular prayerful rituals eventually helped him diminish his angry impulses. I also recommended that he listen to Gregorian Chants (11) and Palestrina's *Missa Brevis,* which I had personally found soothing during periods of anxiety and agitation.

In working with him and several other patients, I learned that by tapping deeply into a person's religious rituals and prayer I could recruit powerful allies for therapeutic work and, in some cases, avert a crisis. These experiences repeatedly validated the usefulness of employing Jung's archetypes of the collective unconscious such as the Hero conquering Evil (12). The Prayer to Saint Michael slaying the Dragon enables one to externalize internal conflicts, thus gaining an additional means of controlling dangerous impulses. My patients invariably appreciated my attempts to speak the language of their religious faith and integrate my own experiences with art and music to join them in resolving the intense conflicts they faced within themselves.

Ronald: A Conservative Protestant I referred to a pastoral counselor

Ronald was one of the few people who persisted in asking whether I had "accepted Jesus Christ as my personal Lord and Savior." My interpretive approach which explored his need to provoke and judge me as he had in other relationships fell flat. After a while, I felt like he was trying to convert me to his version of the True Faith. I began to dread sessions and double-scheduled him twice. These were clear signals that I needed to seek consultation to prevent his treatment progress from unraveling. My consultant suggested that the best course of action was to refer him to another therapist. I told Ronald that I was having difficulties remaining helpful to him and suggested that he contact his pastor for a referral for ongoing treatment. We said our goodbyes, after which I learned from his wife that he had found a pastoral counselor and that his therapy was going well.

In reviewing his case, I discovered that my own defensive reactions were rooted in the uncomfortable experience I'd had as an eleven-year-old when two of Billy Graham's associates visited my parents' home after my mother's conversion experience. These well-meaning evangelists had pushed me into a corner when I was neither emotionally nor spiritually ready to respond to their message. I recognized that my resentment about this had gone underground, rendering me ineffective as Ronald's therapist. Making this referral was helpful for him and it provided me with an opportunity to expand on my personal insights and to integrate them with clinical experiences, one of the many intrinsic rewards of being a psychiatrist.

Elaine: Resolving conflicts in a Catholic-Muslim marriage

Elaine, a married Catholic woman, was referred originally for treatment of some problematic behavioral issues. After making significant gains, our focus shifted to addressing persistent conflicts with her husband Omar, who is a Muslim. Elaine had become increasingly resentful about Omar's refusal to allow her to engage their son Ibrahim in any form of Christian observance or holidays. His refusal to compromise led her to consider divorce, which she did not want to do, fearing that this would be harmful to Ibrahim and his sense of security. At the same time, her husband's unwillingness to compromise left her feeling frustrated, depressed, trapped, and guilty.

Meanwhile, she continued to attend Mass and practice her Catholic faith while Omar remained a devout Muslim. On occasion, Ibrahim attended social gatherings with his father at his mosque. While they exchanged gifts at Christmas, Omar prohibited them from decorating a tree, singing carols, or having any alcohol, which is *haram* (unlawful), in their home. When a close family member of Elaine's passed away, she assumed that they would all attend the funeral Mass together. However, Omar strenuously objected to Ibrahim's attending and being exposed to Catholic worship. Ibrahim, who by now was quite accustomed to his parents' regular religious skirmishes, exclaimed, "Dad, just because you go to a church service doesn't mean you have to be a Christian or believe in the faith."

Omar relented and they attended the funeral Mass together. I could scarcely hide my enthusiasm for Ibrahim's deft response and encouraged Elaine to offer loving support for her husband's willingness to accommodate her and their son's wishes.

Throughout the years they had attended various holiday meals, including Christmas with Elaine's extended family at her parents' home. As their marriage continued over the next ten years, Elaine explained that Omar had become even more observant of Islamic dietary law which forbids consumption of alcohol and allows only *halal* (lawful) meat. At this point I recalled my days at Einstein and what I had learned about kosher food and the dietary laws of the Torah. I did some research and discovered that the dietary restrictions were very similar in Islam.

Elaine had also told me that her husband enjoyed cooking. I wondered if she could discuss this with her parents, hoping that they could arrive at some arrangement that would allow Omar to attend an upcoming Christmas meal at her parents' home while observing his dietary restrictions. They agreed to have Omar bring the main entrée for the meal. In response, Omar agreed to bring an *halal* entrée that had been slaughtered and blessed in Allah's name. They all enjoyed their meal together on Christmas Eve. Afterwards, in recounting it, Elaine exclaimed, "This was the best Christmas since I married Omar!"

As I listened to Elaine describe the negotiations that preceded their Christmas meal, I thought of Niebuhr's Serenity Prayer. Over the years their marriage gradually evolved through small compromises by Elaine and Omar involving increased acceptance of their differences. Their relationship became less conflicted and more spontaneous. They were able to strike a creative balance between the courage to change and acceptance of the immutable. In my view, after all, they both worshipped the same God, only with different names.

Anita: A unique experience of Transcendence in a session

There have been rare moments in my practice when I sensed that something very powerful and unique was happening in the consultation room. These moments, in my experience, sometimes arise out of a period of silence during which a profound empathic awareness has developed. At other times, I had been struggling with my patient for what seemed like an eternity to unravel a knotty problem, when we were both close to calling it quits. Suddenly, a Powerful Presence enters the room, leaving me breathless. Words fail to describe it, but for me there is an electrifying sense of increased energy, illumination, and a feeling of being on sacred ground. I am aware that there are alternate explanations for what I am about to describe, but for me they are markers of Transcendence.

Such an experience occurred a few years ago when I saw Anita, a divorced black/Native American woman in her sixties who had experienced vicious racism from her supervisor at work. In working with her, I learned firsthand about the ravages of racism I couldn't have known in any other context. I was white and privileged like her supervisor.

I wondered aloud about how, under these circumstances, she could possibly trust me. She responded, "You may be white, but you are kind and you seem to care about me."

"I do," I said.

"You're not like my supervisor," she replied.

Over the next few years, I learned a lot from Anita about resilience, patience, hope, and forgiveness. I noticed that often in the waiting room she was reading quotes from a frayed stack of index cards held together by a rubber band. She explained that these were inspirational quotes from the Bible, various magazines, poems, and novels. She updated them and carried them in her purse for use at any time.

After reading the quotes she often prayed, asking the Lord's help in a variety of situations. Anita didn't have to describe her faith. It was readily apparent from her actions.

One night before our appointment, it snowed over eight inches in Denver. Many of my patients cancelled that day, but Anita had somehow managed to get a ride for our session. I scrambled up the stairs to my second floor office to discover her all alone in the common waiting room, looking serene as she read one of her cards. I was out of breath, ten minutes late, and had had a harrowing drive. As we settled into our chairs, we paused for a moment as whirls of snowflakes ticked against my office windows. I apologized for keeping her waiting and told her how much I appreciated her braving the elements to keep our appointment.

"You know, Dr. Graves, snowstorms are sometimes God's way of teaching us to slow down and be patient."

Her observation was stunningly accurate and I responded, "Thanks, Anita, I needed that." We were in one of Buber's "I-Thou moments" and we both sensed it. We were not alone on that snowy March afternoon. Her comment reminded me of the importance of faith in the healing process.

As I look back on my practice, I believe I made the right decision to become a psychiatrist. The peaceful, comfortable privacy of my office is always welcome. I can "tend my flock" without having to lead them all in the same direction from a pulpit. I can use compassion in my work without having to promote a particular religious agenda. I follow my own spiritual/religious journey without having to persuade others or be a moral exemplar. The religious diversity of my practice has been personally enriching and I have grown and benefited from observing how people of other religious faiths cope with many of the same struggles I face. When people ask me what I do, I simply respond, "I help people grow." I now know that, sometimes, when this happens in significant ways, God has been present.

CHAPTER 7

FORGIVENESS

Forgiveness is one of the most powerful behaviors available to heal the inevitable pain and suffering inherent in human relationships. Over the centuries, most of the world's major religions have embraced it as a preeminent value. The philosopher-political scientist Hanna Arendt, commenting on Jesus' role in discovering the power of forgiveness, stated: "The fact that he articulated it in religious language is no reason to take it any less seriously in a strictly secular sense" (1).

My earliest lessons regarding forgiveness came from my mother, who recited the Lord's Prayer with me every night at bedtime in which we said, "Forgive us our trespasses as we forgive those who trespass against us." My brother Charles, an ordained minister, worked most of his life as director of Interfaith International, a non-governmental organization affiliated with the United Nations Commission on Human Rights, promoting reconciliation and forgiveness in resolving disputes between religious leaders around the world. Charles exemplified a forgiving spirit and the need to seek healing interactions at all levels of family, society, and in international relations.

In my spiritual counseling sessions with Elizabeth Randall, I learned that I needed to forgive and receive forgiveness regarding several important events in my life that I had set aside for years, including writing some spiteful letters to my parents, intense arguments with my brother Tom during the period of our mother's decline, and angry words and behaviors during two marriages, both of which ended in divorce. In my three years of psychiatric training and two years of postgraduate training in psychodynamic therapy, the topic of forgiveness, which many now view as an essential ingredient in the healing process, was never discussed in seminars, readings, or clinical supervision.

During the 1970s when I was in psychoanalysis, I had written and said some hateful things to my parents in response to my father's abusive physical discipline and my mother's inability to protect me from this. As their health began to decline and I realized their time was limited, I experienced an increase in guilt and remorse for how I had treated them. With Rev. Randall's help I asked my mother to forgive me for what I had said and how I distanced from her and my father for several years. Muzz listened carefully, empathized with my resentment, and forgave me for my harsh words. She revealed that she had been feeling guilty about her passivity and inability to confront my father.

During his last visit to Denver three years before he died, I greeted Pop with a surprise hug at the airport and told him for the first time that I loved him. Startled by my gesture and words, he initially stiffened, then responded warmly. A man of few words when it came to feelings, I interpreted his warmth as a kind of forgiveness. During this visit, we played several rounds of miniature golf, went fishing, and reminisced about our time together fishing, hunting, and skiing. At age forty-seven, I felt the comfort and joy of being able to relax in his company.

Regarding my divorces, I felt ashamed that, despite all my psychiatric training and experience, I had not been able to resolve my marital conflicts more amiably. My bipolar disorder and the stresses of practice clearly played a role augmenting the intensity of my marital conflicts, but in no way absolved me from taking full responsibility and apologizing for my hurtful behaviors.

Rev. Randall suggested that we begin to address the issue of forgiveness by reviewing and reciting together the Reconciliation of a Penitent from the Episcopal *Book of Common Prayer* (2). Preparing for this, I made a list of all the things I had said and done in my marriages which I had regretted. I recited this list, requesting forgiveness for each instance from God, which was then mediated and given through a blessing by Rev. Randall.

This blessing was only the beginning of a process in which I learned that genuine forgiveness was truly reciprocal. Being forgiven by God in no way guaranteed forgiveness from my ex-wives. I needed to acknowledge my hurtful behaviors, acknowledge that I had caused them pain, and ask their forgiveness. I also needed to forgive them for ways in which they had hurt me. I needed to be willing to offer this freely, even in the absence of their forgiving me, and without expecting anything in return.

After completing the liturgy, I sent letters to my ex-wives asking their forgiveness for my hurtful behavior. I described what I valued in each of the marriages and thanked them for our time together.

Shortly after this, I got into some intense arguments with my older brother Tom regarding how to deal with our mother's decline in her late nineties. Tom, a former naval officer and I, a physician, were shouting at each other during one phone conversation until finally, in exasperation, Tom hung up on me. Reviewing this painful interchange, Rev. Randall suggested that I read the Parable of the Prodigal Son from Chapter 15 of the Gospel of Luke and the excellent essay on this by Henri Nouwen (3).

In reading the parable I identified with the prodigal son and Tom was clearly represented by the oldest son. Nouwen's essay focused in a compelling way on Rembrandt's oil painting depicting the son's homecoming with his father rushing out to envelop him with a tender embrace, in a powerful portrayal of God's steadfast, tender love and forgiveness. In the painting, the oldest son and two shadowy figures observe the scene with rapt attention and wonderment.

After meditating on this, I called Tom, asked his forgiveness for my angry words and said, "Tom, I love you and appreciate all that you have done to help Muzz. We need to work together as a team. Let's put our differences aside and do the best we can." Tom thanked me for reaching out to him. In each of our phone conversations after that, I made a point of telling him how much I valued his hard work on our mother's behalf. Our relationship became more spontaneous, warm, and loving and this greatly enhanced our collaboration during our mother's final years.

I finished my spiritual counseling sessions with Rev. Randall after three years in 2008. Following this, I dove into the sacred and secular literature on forgiveness. My research enabled me to tap into the significant power of forgiveness in my work as a psychiatrist with people of different religious beliefs and traditions. I include a few examples of what I learned in the summaries below.

FORGIVENESS IN MAJOR WORLD RELIGIONS

In Dallas Texas, ten days after the 2001 terrorist attacks, a Muslim from Bangladesh, Raisuddin Bhuiyan, was shot and critically injured by Mark Stroman, an American citizen who killed two other Muslims during a revenge spree. Bhuiyan, ten years later, motivated by his Islamic teachings on mercy, publically forgave Stroman and lobbied against his assailant's death sentence in Texas. This uplifting story by Anand Giridharadas, beginning with murderous acts of religious bigotry and hatred (4), inspired me to look more closely at Islamic beliefs regarding forgiveness.

I discovered from my readings of the Qur'an, that the name *Allah* is frequently translated from Arabic as "the Merciful One," "Compassionate One," and "One who is Most Forgiving," depending on the context. In fact, every surah in the Qur'an except one begins with *"Bismallah al Rahman, al Rahim,"* (Blessed be Allah who does mercy and who is Mercy). The Prophet Mohammed, like Jesus on the cross, on several occasions is pictured as forgiving his tormentors, even those who attempted to stone him to death.

From extended conversations with my friend, Rafaat Ludin, a Muslim engineer from Afghanistan, I learned how the concept of *jihad*, which was frequently translated in the U.S. media as an obligation to engage in "Holy War" with "infidels," had been distorted by Islamic fundamentalists to describe a duty to kill non-Muslims. According to Rafaat, *jihad* actually refers to an internal human struggle between vengeful, warlike impulses and Allah's commands to be loving, just, and merciful (5). These discussions helped me gain a broader perspective on the events of September 2001 as well as a deeper understanding of the preeminent role of forgiveness and compassion in Islam.

The Hindu epic poem, *Bhagavad Gita*, begins with an extended dialogue between the god Krishna and the reluctant warrior Arjuna wherein forgiveness, *ksama*, is described as a desirable quality of truly spiritual beings. In chapter sixteen, the anonymous poet describes laudable "Divine Traits" including "gentleness, compassion for all beings, patience and a benevolent, loving heart" (6).

In Hinduism the concept of forgiveness is best understood in the context of the doctrine of universal rebirth and *karma*. In this belief system humans sin regularly and, even if not caught and punished in this life, they will find punishment in future lives. Since one's enemy is also caught up in the inevitable cycle of birth and rebirth, he or she will eventually be punished for misdeeds. So why waste energy on exacting one's own private form of vengeance? To forgive one's enemy is to release oneself, if only a little bit, from the everlasting cycle of birth and rebirth.

Erik Erikson, in his 1969 biography of Gandhi, described the pacifist's lifelong meditations on the *Gita*, as crucial for his development of *ahimsa* (non-violence): "Ahimsa not only means not to hurt another; it means to respect the truth in him" (7). In respecting another's truth, we release them from judgment. Our empathic respectfulness becomes the foundation for forgiveness, the capacity for giving up our attachments to vengeful feelings and actions.

The writings of the Dalai Lama offered an entirely unique perspective from Buddhism. Up to this point, I had experienced forgiveness almost entirely within a Christian framework, where one sought God's forgiveness and forgave others because it was consistent with Jesus' example of practicing compassion *for others*. In contrast, the Dalai Lama teaches that one should pursue forgiveness as a matter of enlightened *self-interest*:

"Anger destroys your peace of mind. Your happy mood never comes, not while anger remains. That is the main reason why we should forgive. With calm mind comes more peaceful mind, more healthy body" (8).

Here was a clear, psychologically-minded rationale I could use to promote forgiveness with patients whose bodies and minds literally ached with resentment. As it turned out, two major secular research projects initiated by Drs. Robert Enright at the University of Wisconsin and Fred Luskin at Stanford had reached similar conclusions.

CLINICAL RESEARCH ON FORGIVENESS

In the 1990s Robert Enright and his colleagues established a forgiveness research center in Madison, Wisconsin which reviewed texts of all the world's major religious faiths and consulted with clergy, philosophers, and mental health practitioners. Enright's group concluded that religious faith, while important for many individuals, was not a necessary ingredient for forgiveness. In addition they discovered that their findings were equally applicable for individuals, families, ethnic groups, and nations (9). The remarkable thing about Enright's research from my perspective was that it provided scientific validation of many of the centuries-old precepts of the world's major religions regarding forgiveness. One commentator described the significance of Enright's work as follows:

"The research on forgiveness by Robert Enright and his colleagues may be as important to the treatment of emotional and mental disorders as the discovery of sulfa drugs and penicillin have been to the treatment of infectious diseases"(10).

In the Enright volume, Fitzgibbons defined interpersonal forgiveness as a twofold process involving giving up "resentment and thoughts of vengeance" and "fostering compassion" towards offenders (11).

Relinquishing resentment is no easy task. In psychotherapy, the dynamics and style of an individual's anger needs to be understood before the work of forgiveness can begin. For example, does one deal with anger by denial, minimization, passive aggressive behavior, or overt aggression with vengeful acts? Does the resentment derive from a current event or is it displaced from the past and projected onto readily available scapegoats such as one's spouse, children, co-workers, or friends? (12)

Enright's researchers agreed that forgiveness should not be confused or conflated with forgetting, accepting, tolerating, condoning, excusing, granting legal pardon, or pursuing reconciliation with the transgressor (13). I discovered that my patients often find this clarification useful in resolving internal obstacles to initiating forgiveness.

In my own professional work on forgiveness, Fred Luskin's writings have been most consistently useful. I have participated in his workshops and can attest to the helpfulness of his methods. Luskin takes a cognitive behavioral approach and includes detailed case studies in *Forgive for Good: A Proven Prescription for Health and Happiness* (14). His premise, like the Dalai Lama's, is that forgiveness has far-reaching beneficial effects on human health by reducing the stress chemicals which contribute to a significant number of physical and psychological ailments. I later learned from personal conversations with Luskin that he had immersed himself in Buddhist teachings while researching this topic.

One of Luskin's most helpful contributions is his concept of the "grievance story." These stories, via repetition, increase stress chemicals and further reinforce ill-health. In the grievance story we use the passive language of victimization and blame our perpetrators for our own feelings. Luskin's approach urges us to stop the "blame game," take responsibility for our own feelings, and transform our own narratives in ways that are empowering.

I found that Luskin's concept of "unenforceable rules" was also helpful for patients as well as myself. Examples include such illusions as: "I should not suffer," "people should love me," "my friends shouldn't lie to me," "my husband shouldn't have affairs," etc. Notice that the operative word is "should" followed by a series of illusory wishes. When we have a bad case of the "shoulds," our expectations, when frustrated, lead to feelings of disappointment, resentment, and sadness. When we discover and challenge our unenforceable rules and jettison the "shoulds,"we build a foundation for forgiveness by turning the focus from the offending other to relieving our inner distress by giving up resentment and changing the way we view ourselves.

MY APPROACH FOR INCORPORATING FORGIVENESS INTO THERAPY

When forgiveness appears as a viable process to use in therapy, I ask if my patients have ever considered using it and under what circumstances. If they appear motivated, I then inquire about whether or not they have a religious tradition within which they would like to focus their forgiveness work. I ask them to describe their beliefs regarding forgiveness and whether it has been useful to them in the past. I then make a concerted effort to support their connections, or make new ones, with their rabbi, priest, or minister and suggest that they meet with them and report back on their progress periodically. I reinforce this by describing how helpful my own experiences with spiritual counseling, worship, and forgiveness work have been. At the same time, I make it clear that I have no expectations that they follow the path I have taken within my own religious faith.

If they have not been raised in a religious tradition or have had disillusioning experiences within their religious institutions, I ask if they would be willing to pursue a secular path of forgiveness in light of recent clinical research findings such as Enright's and Luskin's. Patients are often surprised by my suggestion of a secular approach and by my willingness to work with them exploring this pathway. I then ask them to define what forgiveness means to them personally and what they hope to accomplish by seeking it or offering it to others. This often leads to a discussion about the differences between forgiveness, reconciliation, and condoning behaviors. If they are interested in pursuing the issue, I provide them with readings from several references depending on their unique experiences and interest levels.

In my work with patients, I have found they can get derailed from the path of forgiveness for a variety of reasons. They often rush into it, expecting quick results. For offenders, this often involves a need to be quickly exonerated before they become fully aware of just how hurtful their behaviors have been. This tends to short-circuit a period of true repentance and makes a mockery of their hasty apologies.

Among the injured, some seek to forgive before they truly understand how deeply they have been wronged and the complex, sometimes ambivalent, nature of their feelings towards their transgressor. An in-depth exploration of these issues, while it takes longer, generally brings more insight and lasting resolution.

Some people who are very bitter refuse to forgive altogether because they confuse forgiveness with condoning the offensive behaviors, agreeing to reconcile, or exonerating the offender from legal responsibility. It is interesting to note that some of the families who forgave Dylan Roof in the racially-motivated Charleston Church massacres of 2015 are now filing civil charges against him. These family members have been able to distinguish their Christian beliefs and practices from their legal rights and responsibilities as families of murder victims.

When obstacles to forgiveness arise in the context of psychotherapy, I have found the best approach is to slow down the process, ask individuals to think more carefully about what is unchanged or unacknowledged in their grievance story, and to take the risk of further examining painful details and feelings they may have missed.

Daniel: A Jewish man who used therapy to forgive his mother

Daniel, in his early forties, was referred for treatment of depression, conflicts with women, and low self-esteem. Daniel recalled his mother as being critical regarding his appearance, social awkwardness, and choice of girlfriends. When discussing these experiences, his face tensed up and his voice became barely audible. She would say to him, "Why don't you just marry a nice Jewish girl, have kids, and settle down near us, like your brother?" In his dreams he often felt helpless, devalued, and tongue-tied. He often dated women who treated their relationship as a low priority, leaving him feel frustrated, sad, and disappointed.

In treatment, he gradually became less inhibited with his anger. During visits home he noticed that his mother's mother treated her much as his mother treated him. Observing the palpable tension between them made Daniel very uncomfortable. For the first time, he began to empathize with his mother's situation. She was trapped by her resentment towards her own mother, just as he had felt with her. He avoided expressing his resentment, fearing she might explode or disintegrate.

Following his grandmother's death, Daniel returned home to sit Shiva. He said that he was able to speak more openly with his mother and felt some empathy for her complicated grief. He commented that she appeared more relaxed and spontaneous. When I asked him how he understood this, he replied, "I think she is finally free." He began to speak of how painful her life had been with such a controlling mother. I observed that this was the first time I had heard him express compassion and empathy for her.

The time was ripe for him to consider the possibility of forgiving his mother so as to release both himself and her from the unhealthy effects of his bitterness. I suggested that his mother, as part of her own mourning process, might be capable of changing her critical attitude towards him. If he could forgive her, I predicted it would help him reduce his chronic depression, insomnia, and widespread aches and pains.

Daniel was intrigued by my suggestion. He indicated that he would prefer to work on this process in therapy rather than doing it as part of Yom Kippur. Over the next several sessions, we discussed what he needed to forgive her for, how he would describe his feelings, and how he could begin a dialogue with modest expectations. I suggested that he work on writing a script to help him focus in his initial meeting. We collaborated on his script until he indicated he was ready to fly home and begin the process.

He returned from his visit and described how helpful his conversations with his mother had been. He could foresee, for the first time, the possibility of having a cordial, even loving relationship with her. Subsequent visits have validated his wishes. They are able to engage more spontaneously, reminisce, and even laugh a little. There are still times when his resentments resurface, but he understands that forgiveness is a process, not a single event. Meanwhile, his self-esteem has improved and he has been able to have more gratifying, emotionally intimate relationships with women.

When patients describe a positive connection with their religious upbringing, I often use an approach which involves reinforcing the tenets of their beliefs and practices regarding forgiveness. For example, I encouraged a number of observant Jews to use the Ten Days of Atonement and Yom Kippur services to ask for or offer forgiveness to friends and family members whom they had hurt or by whom they felt hurt. This was particularly useful when I was able to study the texts of their specific Yom Kippur services and discuss them for a few sessions prior to their attending services. I learned that the public nature of personal confession and forgiveness in Judaism is viewed as a communal act, binding the sins of one person to those of the community, in which the whole community shares responsibility, thus lessening the burden of guilt for the individual (15).

I was impressed with how the specificity and community context of this practice went considerably beyond the meaning of the more General Confession which I was accustomed to say as part of the weekly Episcopal Communion services.

There are some people, who despite their strong religious upbringing, are unable to use it to assist them in forgiving others. Many of these have had disillusioning experiences with clerics or with the church as an institution. A careful exploration of these issues is necessary before any meaningful forgiveness can take place. Even with regular attendance at religious services, distrust may persist and derail a faith-based forgiveness process. In these situations, a secular approach often works better.

Mary: A Roman Catholic woman who used a secular approach

Mary had suffered multiple experiences of trauma and loss, including an abusive father who left her mother when she was a child. Her mother responded to her loss by turning to alcohol and to many lovers for comfort, often leaving Mary and her siblings feeling abandoned. At the time of her referral, Mary had already been hospitalized for depression and was experiencing serious conflicts with her husband. Following her hospital stay, an outpatient therapist had made romantic overtures, which she rebuffed. She quickly left therapy feeling betrayed and resentful. Her husband had difficulties supporting her during her hospitalization and in the painful aftermath of her traumatic therapy experiences.

Early in therapy we dealt with the disillusionment she felt with her prior therapist and how this resonated with her sense of abandonment and betrayal following her parents' divorce. As Mary mourned these traumas and losses, she began to develop a more trusting relationship with me. In this context, two themes emerged: her need to be a perfect mother for her grown children and her increasing sense of isolation from her emotionally distant husband.

Mary began to idealize me in ways that made me uncomfortable, as if I were a hybrid of Father Confessor and God. It was not clear what she needed to confess or why I was supposed to be perfect. When I attempted to remind her that I was just a fallible human, she would have nothing of it. I eventually realized that she needed her idealizations to compensate for her own injured self-esteem.

Meanwhile, stories of Catholic priest abuse began to dominate the media. Mary was infuriated by the Church's avoidant and legalistic response and stopped attending Confession and Mass. "It's becoming harder and harder to be Catholic these days," she lamented. I empathized with this statement and then drew her attention to the importance of not conflating the human failings of priests with the eternally important messages found in Jesus' life and teachings.

I also described my own helpful experiences with spiritual counseling. This enabled her to initiate discussions with an empathic priest who validated her disillusionment. He recommended that she read and recite the centering prayers of Father Thomas Keating (16), which enabled her to soothe herself when she became tense or angry. I suggested that she listen to Gregorian Chants and the *Missa Brevis* of Palestrina. These readings and musical compositions based on the Latin Mass helped her regain trust in the process of worship and prayer.

While this was helpful, she remained resentful of her husband's lack of empathy regarding her depression and was unable to use her faith as a vehicle for forgiving him. I decided to try Luskin's secular approach and introduced her to his book, emphasizing that it was based on solid research and helped people of all faiths, even agnostics and atheists. I mentioned that reading it and attending his workshops had helped me in a variety of situations recently.

Mary was captivated by the idea that she had kept "unenforceable rules" and that her husband Richard should admit the error of his ways and be more loving towards her. Once she understood the futility of maintaining these "rules," we were able to explore some of the reasons Richard might have difficulty being more empathic and affectionate with her. His parents had been overwhelmed by raising their family on a subsistence income. She began to empathize with his difficult upbringing and how this had molded his character and his behavior towards her. He was, after all, a good provider, a faithful husband, and a devoted father to their children.

These insights about Richard helped her give up her resentment and develop a deeper appreciation for both the limitations and strengths of the man she married. She began to realize that she needed, first of all, to forgive herself for maintaining such a bitter stance towards a man who had experienced painful deprivation in his own family. She became less distant and more affectionate with him, joining him in his favorite hobbies. They began to have fun together with tennis and traveling. She became active in a new Catholic parish, assisting in serving at Mass and attending workshops there every year. Mary has come to accept that her forgiveness work will involve an ongoing process of asking forgiveness, forgiving self and forgiving others.

***

My father was in a hospital bed, paralyzed by a stroke the complications of which would claim his life a few months later. He spoke softly and haltingly as he drifted in and out of awareness. I sat quietly with him as increasing clouds in the November afternoon darkened the room. "I was hard on you three boys," he mumbled. His words astounded me, since I'd never heard him apologize before. I sensed that I might never see him again. There was a long, awkward silence. I thought of the many ways he had hurt me as a child with punishments in which he physically lost control and his disclosure on my wedding day about my accidental origins. I had hurt him by sending spiteful letters and distancing from him for several years.

Then I noticed the framed colored photo I had sent him many years before on his bedside stand. In the photo I was smiling and holding a large rainbow trout from the Bighorn River in Montana. He had taught me to fish and our times together fishing had been a precious part of his legacy to me. "Yes, Pop, I know you were hard on us…and I forgive you." A faint smile transformed his wizened face and his cheek moistened. I sat quietly for a few moments at his bedside, then hugged him and said goodbye.

Sharing a happy moment with my brother Tom in Dana Point, California.

CHAPTER 8

BOUNDARIES

I first became interested in boundary issues in the mid-1980s when articles and seminars on this topic began to appear with increasing frequency in the popular media and professional literature. It was during this period that numerous mental health professionals, physicians, and clergy were arrested and prosecuted for sexual and other boundary violations with their patients and parishioners. It was clear that these professionals were taking advantage of the power differential in their relationships to pursue their own selfish needs and thereby causing severe emotional damage in their patients, clients, and parishioners. In 1995 I organized a six-week multidisciplinary seminar on boundary issues for the professional staff at Bethesda Psychiatric Hospital in Denver.

After this seminar ended, the other participants and I formed an ongoing consultation group which met on a monthly basis for the next eight years. We discussed the rapidly emerging literature and treatment cases involving boundary crossings and dilemmas. My interest in this area intensified when I had to terminate a friendship with and report a clergyman who became sexually involved with one of his parishioners. Since this time I have treated both perpetrators and victims of sexual boundary violations and have done forensic evaluations of victims regarding psychological harm. Treating victims is especially challenging since reestablishing trust and safety in the new therapy must precede addressing the traumatic effects of boundary violations by therapists.

In 1990, Epstein and Simon conducted an extensive survey of boundary violations and found a 7-12% incidence of sexual behavior between therapist and patient, leading to a syndrome similar to that seen in child abuse and rape victims. They subsequently developed an "Exploitation Index" which evaluated behaviors in therapists most likely to be associated with boundary violations, including accepting expensive gifts, overtime sessions, excessive therapist disclosure, seductive behavior, revealing attire, etc. (1). Martinez surveyed the growing literature in 2000 and introduced the concepts of "dilemma" and "graded risks" to highlight the fact that boundary issues occur along a continuum with knowingly harmful violations by the therapist on one end and mutually unconscious enactments including therapist *and* patient on the other (2).

For the first several years of my practice I occupied a comfortable suite on the sixth floor of a modern office building in Denver. I had treated a number of challenging patients and felt reasonably competent in my work. Nothing could have prepared me for what transpired in the following session.

Debra: A dangerous enactment during an evaluation session

My pager went off at 7:00 a.m. I responded to the call and before I could introduce myself or inquire as to how I might help, Debra launched into strident demands to be seen immediately. She had been treated by several experienced colleagues over the years and "none of them had helped her." Her referring psychiatrist had told her I was "the best in town," and that she should call me right away. Her voice trembled as she described her husband's leaving her and fears of losing her job. Normally, under these circumstances, I would ask to speak to her most recent psychiatrist, but since she had communicated urgency, I agreed to see her later that day and sooner if I had any cancellations.

Debra was early for her appointment and knocked impatiently on my door. I explained that would see her in a few minutes. When she entered my office and insinuated herself onto the couch, she slowly removed her tight sweater. Her low-cut blouse revealed a more than ample décolletage. Facing me directly, she maneuvered her hips, hiking up her bright miniskirt, thus affording me an unobstructed view of her G-string. I blinked, struggling to avert my gaze.

101

Gripping the soft upholstered arms of my chair, I investigated her chief complaint, trying to maintain my composure, but feeling distracted and missing most of what she was saying. "I get involved with men quickly and then they always leave me," she complained. I surmised that she had struggled with abandonment issues, most likely early sexual trauma, with perhaps a borderline organization that impelled her to quit seeing other therapists before they could abandon her. *This is going to be tough,* I thought.

During the next several minutes I was inundated with her loud, hateful criticisms regarding men, feeling sucked into an intense emotional cyclone. I hesitated to interrupt her, fearing that she would see this as dismissive.

I finally asked her to pause for a moment and made a direct request. "Debra, what you are saying is very important, but I need to tell you that I'm feeling uncomfortable and distracted with the way you are seated on the couch. I would appreciate it if you would sit up, cross your legs, and pull down your skirt so we can stay focused on why you're here."

She looked agitated and upset with my request and burst into tears. As I was considering a response, she flew off the couch and bolted headlong towards my floor-to-ceiling window.

"STOP...STOP!" I shouted.

She pirouetted, gasping for breath, looking like a frightened child.

"Sit down and let's talk about what just happened," I uttered through clenched teeth.

Debra sat down on the edge of the couch, legs tightly crossed, looking down and away from me.

I knew this wasn't the time for therapeutic abstinence. I needed to say something that would help her reorganize. I also needed to compose myself. My mind raced. *How __dare__ you attempt suicide right in front of me...I'm here to __help__ you.*

I said, "Debra, it looks as though you just replayed something here that was very painful, so painful that you would rather die than remember..."

She sprang to her feet, glared at me, and bolted from the office, screaming, "You're just like all the rest of them!" as she slammed the door.

Catching my breath, I looked at my watch. It was 2:20 p.m. In a mere twenty minutes we had most likely enacted a piece of her life's drama. I felt bewildered, frustrated, and sad for her. Was she treatable, I wondered? Had I committed some grave error that drove her away?

I called the police and had them do a welfare check. They informed me that she had been taken to an emergency room where she had been admitted on an involuntary seventy-two-hour hold to a hospital where I had no medical staff privileges. I attempted to obtain a follow-up from her hospital psychiatrist and was told that Debra had refused to sign a release for him to speak with me.

Understanding this case and those that follow requires some definitions. A *boundary violation* describes a situation where the therapist knowingly takes advantage of the power differential inherent in the treatment relationship and acts in a way which is harmful to his or her patient. An *enactment* describes a complex, often unconscious, interaction between therapist and patient where some aspect of the patient's (and often the therapist's) previous problematic life experiences are dramatically played out in the treatment situation. As one of my colleagues said: "Before you know it, you're a leading actor in your patient's impromptu script."

In some cases there is a gradual evolution of a *folie á deux*; in others, as with Debra, the drama erupts with awesome speed. Enactment experiences are unavoidable for any therapist with a busy practice. The therapist's challenge is how to recognize, discuss, and use them to therapeutic advantage.

Debra's capacity to rapidly overstimulate and disorganize me was an important sign of a traumatized internal state. Rather than speaking about her treatment needs, she communicated behaviorally via "action languages" which provided a brief glimpse of her internal disorganization and unbearable psychic pain (3). It was my job as her therapist to evaluate these behaviors, much as I would palpate and consider the implications of a fast, irregular pulse in a patient with cardiac arrhythmias.

Transference describes those feelings, fantasies, and wishes which a patient experienced in the past regarding a parent or other significant caretaker which get *projected* onto the therapist. In classical psychoanalytic treatment, the analyst uses transference interpretations to understand and resolve neurotic conflicts and to decrease unhealthy behaviors in more current relationships.

I speculated that Debra, with my request that she sit up and pull down her skirt, had instantly associated me with a critical or seductive male figure from her past. Her transference was most likely *psychotic*, in that she experienced it as a violation and reacted to me as a perpetrator, with minimal reality-testing involved.

Part of her reaction most likely involved a form of *projective identification*—a process where a person denies his or her own uncomfortable feelings, projects them onto the therapist, and then proceeds to struggle with the therapist as if (s)he is endowed with the feelings projected. These phenomena are not unique to therapy. They can arise in many types of human encounters.

Debra needed to test whether or not I could handle her overtly sexual adaptations to what was most likely boundary crossings and violations at multiple levels. Her behavior with me during the first twenty minutes raised several questions simultaneously: Could she trust me to maintain my own boundaries and not exploit her? Did I have the requisite knowledge and skills to understand and help her make sense of her chaotic, traumatized state? Could I provide a safe and nurturing environment to allow her to heal, mourn, and grow? Would I judge, reject, and abandon her like so many other men in her life?

Succumbing to her need to flatter me as "the best in town" I had agreed to see her immediately, rather than asking her permission on the phone to speak with her most recent psychiatrist regarding the circumstances of her ending therapy. This would have given me important data regarding whether I had the time and energy and skills to take her on as a patient.

My brief interaction with Debra also provides an entrée to discuss the difference between *erotic* and *erotized transference*. *Erotic transference* is generally <u>ego-dystonic</u>, i.e. the patient is aware of sexual longings towards the therapist and may feel some anxiety regarding them. He or she generally has the capacity to talk about these thoughts and feelings in the treatment (see case of Amanda, below). With *erotized transference*, there is little awareness or anxiety <u>(ego-syntonic)</u> accompanying the sexual behavior, which may also involve coercive and aggressive components (4).

Debra's expression of erotized transference with me most likely had little to do with conscious sexual wishes or fantasies. She managed to set up a situation where I instantly became an intrusive and critical *voyeur*. Her inappropriate self-exposure was more aggressive than sexual. It was as if she were saying, "I'm going to force you to help me whether you want to or not and, by the way, don't you dare get aroused, or I'll destroy myself and your practice." Patients who display this degree of aggression and self-hatred invariably drive away multiple therapists. They are best treated in long-term residential facilities where staff, while providing a safe holding environment, can understand their fragmented internal experiences of self and others and help them begin the process of integration and healing (5).

Amanda: Hot pants, and erotic counter-transference

Amanda was an attractive woman in her forties who came for help following the break-up of an intimate relationship. During the course of therapy her older brother, with whom she was very close, died from a rapidly metastatic tumor. In the process of mourning, Amanda commented on how much I resembled her brother. As she was speaking, I began to fantasize how she might have been the sister I never had but longed for. With a sister I could have learned a lot about how women think, feel, and operate in the world of relationships. The last phase of my work with her came on the heels of my finalizing a divorce.

Back in the 1980s I smoked a pipe, a habit I had indulged since I was a teenager. In one session Amanda became quite animated as I was puffing away. I became aware of a fragrance quite unlike my favorite Latakia wafting up from the region of my groin, accompanied by a warm sensation. I looked down to find my pants smoldering near the bottom of my zipper. There was no way I was going to risk pressing my yellow notepad onto my genitals to smother the conflagration, so I stood up suddenly, did a 180 and brushed the glowing embers out. I was aghast to find two holes burned clean through my slacks. I screwed up the courage to face Amanda again and we both burst out laughing. "So much for Joe Cool," she smirked. "Yup," I replied.

My boundary dilemma with Amanda came a few weeks later in our penultimate session when she asked me out for coffee. I would have accepted her invitation outright but something about it made me uneasy, so I said I'd think about it and let her know in our final session. It was only then that I became aware of fantasies about dating her, imagining in considerable detail where we could go hiking and how our relationship would progress from there. What I had initially experienced as a brother/sister transference had transformed into an erotic counter-transference involving fantasies about dating her.

The intensity of my feelings startled me and I realized I was in a very precarious position. Acting out my fantasies would not only undo our treatment progress but also put my practice and reputation in harm's way. I sought consultation from Peter Mayerson, a senior analyst and teacher whom I respected. Peter immediately picked up on my post-divorce vulnerability and we discussed how I might decline Amanda's coffee invitation in our final therapy session.

In our last session I told Amanda how much I appreciated her invitation and that, under different circumstances, I would have really enjoyed having coffee with her and getting to know her as a friend. We talked about the deep respect and caring we had for each other as a result of our therapeutic work and how useful it had been. She indicated that she had become increasingly anxious over the past week and was relieved that I chose not to honor her invitation. We joked about the "hot pants" incident and I told her that as a result I had decided to give up smoking in the office.

As we both stood up to say goodbye, she asked for a hug. Without hesitation, and for the first time, we hugged briefly and said our goodbyes. Since then I've received a postcard or two from her from her international travels. For a long time I hung a print which she gave me (a boundary crossing which we had discussed) on the wall of my home study.

In many ways the depth and intensity of therapeutic relationships, with their sustained periods of non-judgmental empathic communication, can match or even exceed that found in many intimate love relationships. Looking back on my work with Amanda, it is clear that we experienced a unique form of love for each other in which some professional boundaries were crossed and others were maintained.

Amanda's father had never been able to acknowledge her warmth, sense of humor, and professional accomplishments. To have refused Amanda's gift would have felt like a slap in the face. That I allowed her to give me the print was based on the fact that we had established a new kind of real relationship enabling her to fill in some developmental needs which had never been met (6). The fact that I kept the print on my wall for several years was indicative of my enduring affection for her.

Dr. T: A physician who was sexually involved with his patient

The experience of treating a physician who has been involved in sexual boundary violations can be a profound test of a therapist's empathic capacities, self-knowledge, and technical skills. I was asked to treat an internist, Dr. T, when he experienced a depressive episode twenty years after becoming sexually involved with a female patient. Dr. T's patient, Lucille, was an attractive woman with chronic pain, hypochondriasis, and borderline personality disorder who had begun to request late afternoon appointments, then back rubs and hugs. Their sexual petting soon evolved with full intercourse on Dr. T's examining table.

Dr. T's recent depressive episode occurred in the aftermath of his wife's discovering letters from Lucille which he had kept hidden away years after terminating their relationship, which had resulted in a civil lawsuit. The litigation ended with Dr. T being placed on probation by his medical board, required to see all female patients with a female nurse present, and an out-of-court financial settlement. His wife's more recent confrontation about the cache of letters reawakened guilt feelings and traumatic memories regarding the chaotic aftermath of his ending his sexual relations with Lucille, in which she became suicidal and required hospitalization.

In treating Dr. T, I faced a number of challenges, not the least of which involved my own disillusionment and resentment. My liability insurance rates had quadrupled in the past decade, largely due to similar boundary violations. Female patients who had learned I was on the hospital board of a local psychiatric facility were asking why we didn't just "fire the bastards." The medical profession, once highly esteemed, was under attack, besmirched by the selfish behavior of a few bad actors. How, I wondered, was I going to muster the equanimity to treat my medical colleague?

While hearing Dr. T recall his transgressions with Lucille, I recalled my feelings about Amanda. Eric Clapton's lyrics, "Before you accuse me take a good look at yourself," flashed through my head and I recognized that Dr. T and I were close cousins in our temptations. Dr. T had had an affair with his patient and I had entertained the idea with mine. Armed with this awareness, I was able to understand and empathize with Dr. T and move forward with his treatment. In working with Dr. T, I frequently referred to Glen Gabbard's helpful article on transference and counter-transference issues involved in treating perpetrators of boundary violations, where the treating therapist's own vulnerabilities may take the form of critical judgments (7).

What unfolded with Dr. T was a tragic tale of deprivation, loss, and misguided attempts at restitution. Dr. T's father, a solo family practitioner, had practiced in a small town. He was overwhelmed with patient care responsibilities and physically and emotionally absent from Dr. T and his family during his childhood. Dr. T's sparse memories of his father involved going to his office on Saturday afternoons to help him sterilize instruments and clean his examination rooms.

When he was twelve, he discovered his father's dead body on the floor of his waiting room. An autopsy revealed he had died from an overdose of pain medications. His mother, in her bitterness, was poorly equipped to help Dr. T or his sister mourn their loss. Dr. T had hardwired the horrific scene of his father's lifeless body and banished his grief, disillusionment, and revulsion to an impenetrable lockbox in his mind.

Dr. T's adolescence was a barren, lonely desert. He related to his mother by becoming her caretaker and protector. Frozen in her grief, she rarely showed affection for him. He avoided dating in high school and college, fearing his mother's disapproval and not wanting to abandon her. During his medical training, he moved away from his hometown and found a warm, affectionate woman whom he eventually married.

Lucille's background bore a striking resemblance to his own, with multiple early losses and deprivation. Dr. T had deeply empathized with her and felt he could, by his own affection and care, make up for her deficits. In the early weeks of their treatment relationship, the lines between his own needs and Lucille's had become increasingly blurred.

She was warmer, more responsive, and more affectionate than his mother and always grateful for his attention. He was quite aware of his ethical responsibilities but this relationship somehow felt *different*. He was certain he could cure her chronic pain and depression with love.

In his therapy we needed to deal with his guilt regarding his transgression with Lucille, as well as how his emotional deficits and unresolved mourning regarding the loss of his father had become interwoven with rescue fantasies, built on the patterns developed during his teens with his mother. We came to understand that his sexual acting out primarily represented maladaptive coping with his traumatic deprivation rather than a simple response to sexual frustration.

I began to notice Dr. T's subtle capacity to "disconnect" from me as we touched on painful issues regarding Lucille. I addressed these disconnects in the here and now by pointing them out when they happened. I shared my hypothesis that he needed to cut himself off from intense longings to be close with me and to hear words of affection and encouragement, while at the same time fearing I would harshly judge and disown him as a sexual predator and a traitor to the highest ideals of medical practice. His growing awareness of these longings towards me was a precursor in the process of mourning his father for the first time.

I was able to allay his fears by confirming that I would not abandon him as a predator and that I saw him as having been tragically caught up in a complex nexus of enactments involving his own and Lucille's deprivation histories. Yes, his behavior was wrong and caused significant harm to Lucille. But it was also understandable and with continued therapy, unlikely to be repeated. As we worked together to consolidate his insights regarding these issues, his depression lifted and his relationship with his wife improved.

Currently, many therapists who commit sexual boundary violations with their patients are divorced as a result of their behavior, convicted of felonies, and forced to retire from their practices. Dr. T's case was different in that with careful practice monitoring, supervision, and therapy, he was able to return to independent practice and to continue his marriage. His wife's supportive role in all of these developments was extraordinary. She was, despite all of her resentment, able to use her own treatment, the support of friends, and her undying love for her husband to stay the course. Dr. T was truly blessed to have such a kind and empathic spouse.

Cecilia: Managing erotized transference and my brief disability

There are some treatments where the management of boundary issues becomes the primary fulcrum around which the gains of treatment are leveraged.

Such was the case with Cecilia, who was referred by a colleague for treatment of depression in the context of a marriage devoid of sexual intimacy. The early weeks of treatment involved a traditional medication and cognitive behavioral approach for her depression which proved to be helpful. I referred her to couples therapy with a colleague and took a history of prior relationships.

Cecilia had divorced her first husband due to his abusive behavior. A counselor she had gone to following her divorce became seductive with her and she fled therapy, disgusted and disillusioned. "Do I have a knack for bonding with predators?" she wondered. I suggested that we keep this question in mind for future exploration.

As I began to empathize with her regarding these losses, traumas, and disappointments, I realized that our work was likely to take longer than we had originally estimated. Accordingly, we reset our goals to address her inability to enjoy trusting relationships with men, including her husband. As her comfort level increased, we discussed the importance of creating a trusting environment in our work together and increased our session frequency from once to twice per week. I suggested readings on trauma recovery (8) and mindfulness meditation (9) to deal with her resentment and anxiety. Using guided visualizations of tranquil scenes, I helped her create an internal "safe space" that she could enter whenever she felt stressed and panicky.

In her second year of treatment, she began to pepper me with questions about my personal life in a way that felt like a cross-examination by a trial lawyer. I was initially stunned by her intensity and persistence and responded with silence. I began to inquire about what *she* was experiencing during these interrogations, to which she responded with a testy defensiveness. This process continued for a few sessions until she announced suddenly that she felt like quitting therapy.

My first thought was *fine, go right ahead.* Reflecting further, I realized that we were probably enacting something closely related to why she had come for help.

I told her that I thought quitting would be a mistake and that what was happening with us was undoubtedly a variation on the theme of her distrust and resentment of men. She reluctantly agreed to continue with me on a trial basis. We began to discuss how pushing me into a corner interfered with her getting what she needed from me in her therapy. I wondered if this had also happened in her prior relationships with men. This had been a problem for years, she concurred.

At this point her resentment softened and her demeanor shifted. She began to bring in cartoons playfully poking fun at analysts, along with a book regarding the spiritual aspects of sexual intimacy. I quickly learned that the book constituted a probe regarding how comfortable I was with discussing the details of sexual intimacy. Within a few weeks Cecelia began disclosing explicit fantasies about ending treatment and beginning a sexual relationship with me outside the office.

She wanted to know what I thought about this and whether or not I thought she was "my type." I answered the first question directly, saying that my professional ethics forbade this. I then described how a sexual involvement would negate any gains we had made in therapy and

110

ultimately prove to be harmful for both her and me. I wondered out loud if she thought propositioning me might be an example of behavior which would result in her, once again, feeling hurt and rejected. We were at the end of our session, so I asked her to think about this issue during a vacation break.

Upon my return from vacation I found a long letter she had written during my absence. Her letter began with a warm welcome, quickly moving to her resentment about what she saw as my aloof, judgmental stance in the last session. I was probably aloof, she ventured, because she had pushed me into a corner, where I had no choice but to become defensive. She apologized for her behavior with me and, in further discussions, came to see this as part of a familiar pattern: pushing away those she most needed and loved.

I was impressed by Cecilia's accurate perceptions of my aloofness, which I'm sure felt judgmental. I told her how much I appreciated her disclosing her thoughts and feelings and suggested that we spend the next several sessions discussing what she had written. We were able to put this letter into the context of her marital therapy, where she had decided to leave her husband, who had longstanding difficulties showing approval and affection. She then began to mourn never being truly known by her inattentive father.

During her treatment I had taken four weeks off from my practice to have back surgery. I decided to share only the date of my surgery and information about coverage during my absence, and arranged for a post-op message from one of my colleagues that my recovery was going well. I had been taking significant doses of pain medications prior to and following my surgery. Several patients, including Cecelia, noticed that I appeared preoccupied and less active during sessions.

Cecelia became concerned and solicitous during this period and I validated her perceptions that I was functioning less than optimally. During this time I felt physically and mentally very shaky and wondered how attuned I would be in doing psychotherapy following my recovery. I did not share these concerns but I am certain that she picked up on my sense of vulnerability in a way which must have increased her concerns about her own aggression.

Towards the end of therapy, she thanked me in a letter for continuing to see her in spite of her attempts to push me away. She had resolved to "stop scaring the crap out of me" and other men. We discussed the possibility that her request that I become her sexual partner was her way of gaining power and getting me to feel the helplessness and resentment that she felt towards her husbands and her previous therapist. She was grateful that I had been able to hold the line with her when she attempted to seduce me.

In our final sessions she informed me that she had moved into a comfortable condo and was excited by the challenges of furnishing it entirely on her own. She had gotten a promotion at work and felt optimistic about pursuing new and healthier relationships.

My work with Cecilia in the aftermath of my back surgery taught me how to better manage patients during a period of temporary impairment. Cecilia had experienced my reduced activity level and absence as an abandonment, which led to her pursuing me more aggressively. For some, my temporary disability evoked caretaking responses; for others, it stimulated unresolved mourning of family members who had died in the aftermath of surgery. I also learned that I needed to pay closer attention to how my use of pain medications was affecting those I was treating.

With some patients, this required a degree of self-disclosure I had not previously been comfortable with. Others needed to discuss how they experienced my diminished activity levels and how this resonated with issues regarding deprivation, neglect, or abandonment. Some simply needed to know that I had a good prognosis and was recovering well. In a few cases of patients with chronic back pain and multiple surgeries, I disclosed what I had learned about the value of non-prescription pain management, physical therapy, meditation, and acupuncture.

I found that judicious amounts of self-disclosure in this context were welcome and useful. While making these disclosures, I continually monitored my efforts. Was I about to disclose this for the patient, or for myself? If I sensed the latter, I kept quiet.

Therapists who practice long-term dynamic psychotherapy are often vulnerable to powerful pressures from their patients to become involved sexually or in other ways which can ultimately harm their patients and their practices. An understanding of the power differential in the therapist-patient relationship as well as the psychodynamics of boundary violations forms a necessary bulwark against destructive acting out by the therapist.

The mental and physical health of the therapist are often key factors affecting the capacity to manage boundary issues. When a therapist becomes vulnerable, as I did following my divorces and back surgery, boundary issues can intensify in a way that requires a careful balancing of transparency, clinical acumen, and ethical decision-making.

While boundary violations, such as sexual involvement are never acceptable, boundary crossings and enactments are common in many therapies and can be used collaboratively by astute therapists and their patients to facilitate significant insights and personal growth.

CHAPTER 9

DEPRESSION, SUICIDE, AND
THE DIALECTICS OF HOPE

I begin this chapter with a mixture of urgency and sadness regarding the growing epidemic of suicides in the U.S. Any suicide involving a close relationship ultimately confronts us with two complex issues: first, the limits of how well we can actually know and care for another human being; and second, how we can maintain hope in the face of profound despair. Psychology, which began as a branch of philosophy, has described the disorders and risk factors associated with taking one's own life. However, mental health practitioners have only recently begun to use a more systematic approach to treat those who are suicidal and to prevent fatal outcomes.

An understanding of the dialectics of hope is essential if one wishes to help suicidal patients. Hope may be defined as the capacity to imagine and create a more positive future, based on internalized experiences with nurturing caretakers. In a suicidal crisis, there is an increasing tug of war between hopes and fears, hope and despair, and between realistic and false hopes. Make no mistake, feelings of hopelessness and despair can be contagious. Therapists who are dedicated to working in this field need to carefully monitor their own levels of hope and despair and to seek consultation when despair gains ground.

DEPRESSION, SUICIDE, AND THE DIALECTICS OF HOPE

Four of my patients died by suicide during their treatment with me. Two of my colleagues suicided within two years during their residency training, coinciding with my own training. One of my surgery mentors at Einstein suicided several years after I graduated. My first high school sweetheart died by hanging herself, an event I learned about many years later. Two of my close friends and two members of my extended family have also had suicidal episodes from which they survived. Two other friends lost their sons to suicide.

I know that my own losses are by no means unique. These ten losses and a brief suicidal episode of my own have had profound impacts on how I view myself and my work as a psychiatrist with those who seek to end their own lives. As a psychiatrist, I have learned to monitor my own emotional reserves, engaging the dialectics of hope within myself and my patients in order to help them wrest hope from the clutches of despair.

Following the suicides of my two psychiatric colleagues in the mid-1970s I sought out Dr. Joan Fleming, a senior analyst at the University of Colorado Health Sciences Center who had written extensively on mourning. Dr. Fleming suggested that I view my own experiences as an opportunity to do research and publish my findings, much as Freud used his own dream analysis to further understand the operations of the unconscious. Adopting a research attitude allowed me to distance from my painful feelings of loss while developing an appreciation for the complexities of my own lived experience.

Over a three-year period, I wrote multiple drafts and published an article on how I helped two teenaged boys deal with their mourning as I struggled to manage my bereavement regarding the loss of their psychiatrist. Research and writing anchored me, facilitated my own mourning, and allowed me to further model mourning for my patients (1). Mining and sharing my own experiences, I became a more attuned, active therapist. Emotional authenticity became the mantra for my interventions.

In recent years, there has been a transformation in how helping professions and researchers view and respond to individuals who are seriously considering suicide. In the past, psychiatrists have viewed suicidal thoughts and behaviors as a symptom of severe depression, anxiety, or other psychiatric disorders. In the medical model, risk factors are aggregated and treatment regimens with varying levels of care are initiated accordingly.

More recently, several researchers have come to view suicidal episodes as distinct clinical entities engendered by specific triggers which involve a marked loss of cognitive capacities, rendering the individual incapable of managing intense feelings of worthlessness, hopelessness, and being trapped without a path for escape (2). It is the job of the mental health professional to understand, empathize with, and educate patients about their cognitively regressed states, assuring safety while gently assisting them to discover unrecognized pathways of hope (3).

In medical practice, hopelessness and despair are often the results of an incapacitating or possibly terminal illness. *In psychiatry, hopelessness and suicidal despair may represent the illness itself.* In both situations, a careful exploration of the dialectics of hope and co-creating a positive vision of the future self are crucial. The research of Baumeister (3) and Schneidman (4) has begun to shift the focus from the medical model of suicide as a symptom of depression to an understanding of a suicidal crisis as a complex set of processes involving cognitive, affective, and behavioral changes triggered by stresses unique for the individual, each with its own developmental history and personal flavor. A central concept in Baumeister's and Schneidman's approach involves the therapist's maintaining a consistently empathic stance regarding suicidal thoughts and impulses. The role of the therapist is not to prevent suicide; rather, it is to fully understand the suicidal state and to maintain a conversation seeking alternatives. The clinician explores the specific triggers to the "psychache" of suicidality; identifies the features of cognitive regression, educates patients about their regressed state, and formulates a detailed safety plan with the patient and his or her family and support system.

A few years ago, a bold new treatment paradigm called Zero Suicide was developed by the Henry Ford Health System in Detroit. Zero Suicide literature states unambiguously that suicide deaths for people in treatment are preventable. This powerful declaration throws down the gauntlet and challenges all caregivers, family members, and advocacy groups to rethink their previous assumptions and to do a better job. Since the program's origins in Detroit, health plan members have experienced an 80 percent reduction in their suicide rate. The key to this program lies in its focus on developing a suicide prevention alliance (SPA) with the patient and his or her family. The success of Zero Suicide lies in its high standards, multidisciplinary focus, emphasis on closing loopholes in a fragmented care system, rigorous training programs, and insistence on long-term follow-up (5).

Joan Heron, a psychoanalyst and suicide specialist, refined this approach in her own practice and helped me reformulate the four cases of completed suicide which I discuss below. In speaking with her I came to recognize the shortcomings of the medical model I had been using. She has proposed that clinicians eliminate the expression "committing suicide" (as if it were a criminal act) and instead, speak of "death by suicide," helping me and my colleagues to view the act less judgmentally (6).

In medical school, internship, and residency training, when we lost a patient from a medical illness, we had the benefit of clinical pathological correlation (CPC) conferences, where fatalities could be reviewed in detail with senior faculty, after which there were discussions regarding how the treatment might have been pursued in a more helpful manner. In private practice, unless a suicide occurs within a hospital, these formal structures and supportive learning communities are often absent. This places the burden for initiating a case review on the treating professional, the very person who is often struggling with intense feelings of shock, guilt, and grief. In addition, there may be conflicts between the human impulse to reach out to support grieving family members and a need to protect oneself from possible litigation.

I have generally followed the path of offering support to family members and have never experienced litigation regarding a patient who died by suicide under my care. I have had the benefit of monthly meetings with my practice consultant and my consultation group to assist me in managing my responses to losing patients by suicide.

Of the four individuals who were in treatment with me when they suicided, one was in a hospital, the second was seen primarily for medication maintenance and supportive therapy, the third, whom I saw for a single consultation, was the son of a long-standing patient, and the last was in an intensive outpatient program for a period of less than two weeks. All these suicides involved men, three of whom used violent means to end their lives (two by hanging and one by gunshot to the head). The last one took an overdose of prescription medications.

Arthur: A schizoid, depressed young man in a hospital

Arthur was a single high school dropout who was admitted for treatment of depression. His parents were divorced when he was a child and he was raised by an aunt with whom he still lived. He was a loner who had never dated and had no friends outside his family. Video games were his main hobby. At intake he described vague suicidal ideation and denied any past attempts and personal or family history of psychosis. His admission to the unit coincided with those of two acutely agitated schizophrenics.

During the second week of his hospital treatment, Arthur began to describe thoughts of self-harm to a male mental health worker on evening shift. He stated that, prior to admission, he occasionally had a strong impulse to inhale carbon monoxide, which he never acted upon. The main deterrent to acting on these impulses was that, "My aunt would be angry at me." Day staff, in follow-up, found that he minimized these suicidal thoughts and became irritable when pressed for details.

I placed him on suicide precautions with medication mouth checks, confiscation of "sharps," restriction to the unit with staff checks every fifteen minutes, and added Lithium to his antidepressant regimen. These precautions were in place for five days when a strong opinion developed among the evening shift that he no longer needed them, while the Head Nurse and many day shift staff favored keeping them.

During my reevaluation of Arthur, he denied active suicidal ideation or plans; however, I noted that he was guarded in his interactions with staff and with me. I ultimately signed an order to lift his suicide precautions. Three days later, he was found in his room by evening staff, hanging from bed sheets which he had secured by placing a knot in the doorjamb. Resuscitation attempts were unsuccessful.

I felt awful, lashing out at myself with self-criticism. The staff split regarding suicide precautions intensified, including some scapegoating of the evening mental health worker for his "nonchalance" regarding Arthur's risk. Staff interactions were becoming toxic at the very time we needed to offer each other maximal support for dealing with our guilt and grief.

To address these issues, I invited an outside psychiatric consultant to conduct a case review with our entire clinical staff. Our consultant empathized with our collective pain and helped normalize our feelings of guilt and regret. He reminded us that we were dealing with the most challenging and dangerous patients with limited resources.

He suggested we view risk factors involving three interacting variables: those intrinsic to the patient, the patient's family, and the state of the treatment milieu. Given Arthur's depression, plus his avoidant and schizoid behavior, he was less likely to approach staff consistently regarding any worsening of his condition. He was a loner who carried deep wounds from his parents' divorce and repeated job losses.

The presence of agitated patients on the unit had diverted us from fully appreciating Arthur's suicidal crisis, resulting in my taking him off precautions, possibly making him feel abandoned. The staff splitting may have repeated his experience of parental conflicts. Amid the noise and chaos of the unit, feeling isolated and abandoned by staff, his fragile balance tilted toward oblivion and death. No one seemed to notice that neither his aunt nor his parents had visited him. As he knotted his bed sheets and carefully soaked them in water to ensure the knots would hold, he must have felt totally alone.

Several lessons emerged from our conference. Psychological testing would have been helpful to rule out an occult psychosis, which often increases suicide risk. Self-harm precautions need to be maintained even in the face of denial and minimization following any escalation of reported symptoms. Shame, especially in men, needs to be addressed thoroughly as it often interferes with full disclosure (7). Staff splitting is often symptomatic of the patient's ambivalence about continuing to live. I should have identified this at the outset and emphasized that it be dealt with more proactively in clinical staff meetings.

Arthur should have been placed in a safe, lockable seclusion room while deemed a safety risk. If none were available on this unit, he should have been transferred to another unit or hospital where adequate staff for implementing safety precautions was available.

The distinctions between active, passive, or vague suicidal ideation are ultimately of little use and may preclude further, more detailed investigation of an acute, rapidly shifting, suicidal state. If someone is "thinking they would be better off dead," then an active ongoing pursuit of similar thoughts, fantasies, mental rehearsals, writings, and communications with others needs to be undertaken, followed by a key question: *"Is there anything else you haven't shared regarding suicidal thoughts or actions in the last few minutes, hours, days, or months?"* In terms of modern psychiatric hospital practice and assessment procedures, this was a preventable suicide.

Ethan: does suicide necessarily mean a failure of treatment?

A sense of inevitability hovered over my treatment of Ethan, which involved supportive therapy and medication management.

119

Ethan had engaged in mild suicide gestures at an early age and experienced multiple suicidal episodes, one of which required hospitalization. His final attempt, by gunshot to the head, was therefore not altogether surprising.

In reviewing his treatment, I became aware of my increasing use of minimization and denial as the years progressed. I knew that guns are invariably the most lethal means of suicide and I had confiscated his gun on two previous occasions. His past history placed him at high risk, while his recurrent episodes implicitly challenged my role as a helping professional. With each successive episode, I developed more emotional calluses to protect myself, which ultimately decreased my vigilance and clouded my clinical judgment.

Ethan's death raises a number of questions of whether a treatment ending in suicide is, by definition, a failure. I had helped him choose life over death for many years, during which he had loving connections with his family and a productive life at work. This provided a modicum of reassurance that my efforts had not been entirely in vain. Nevertheless, the sting of his death lingered for a long time and I experienced painful flashbacks from my experiences with Arthur.

In some psychotherapies profound inner transformations may occur, where the old self must be grieved in order to make room for the new. The new self is often very vulnerable, like a young chick tentatively emerging from its eggshell. These developments can be both exhilarating and terrifying for patients, who may become suicidal at a time of maximal growth. It takes a seasoned clinician in close collaboration with his or her patient to distinguish between the development of suicidal "growing pains" and the onset of a truly lethal episode.

Dexter: A young married man with an anxious depression

In many ways this is the most painful case for me to summarize. Dexter was referred to me by his father, who had seen me in psychotherapy for chronic depression. Dexter's older brother had suicided several years previously. I had witnessed the intensity of his father's grief and helped him deal with this loss in therapy sessions over many years. I agreed to see Dexter for a single ninety-minute evaluation session, after which I planned to refer him for ongoing treatment to another psychiatrist. Dexter's father described him as having increased signs of depression and anxiety over the past few weeks, including vague suicidal thoughts. Both of his parents, in reviewing this summary, commented on Dexter's apparent weight loss and noted that he had been avoiding contacts with them during several weeks prior to his seeing me.

I saw Dexter within a few days of his father's referring him to me. He was a handsome, well-dressed young man who was soft-spoken and somewhat guarded when sharing details about himself. He described having a stable marriage, an absence of past suicide attempts, steady employment, absence of drug or alcohol abuse, love for his two young children, and long-lasting friendships. Risk factors included work stresses, a family history of depression, his brother's suicide, and a significant anxiety component in his depression. On a standard checklist for depressive symptoms, he had vague suicidal thoughts but denied any specific method or plans. He denied that any specific event could push him over the edge to take his own life. He also denied ever wishing to join his brother in death.

When I inquired about his brother's suicide, he said that he had sought grief counseling through his employer's EAP for five or six sessions. He denied becoming clinically depressed following the loss of his brother and denied experiencing any anniversary reactions during the month his brother died by an overdose. When I asked what he had learned from his EAP counseling, he said, "I learned how much I valued being alive." He admitted that he often wished he could have done something to prevent this brother's death.

Due to his high level of anxiety and some obsessional traits, I discussed the option of his enrolling in an intensive outpatient treatment program involving cognitive behavioral therapy (CBT) and dialectical behavioral therapy (DBT). I prescribed small amounts of an SSRI antidepressant and a sleeping medication. He promised not to overdose with these prescriptions.

At this point he informed me that he was scheduled to leave in two days for a one-week vacation with his wife and two young children. He was looking forward to this but was concerned about whether his work responsibilities would be adequately covered during his absence. We discussed the option of scheduling phone sessions during his vacation. He declined my offer but said he would call me if needed. We set an appointment for follow-up immediately upon his return and I promised to help him find referrals for his ongoing treatment. He signed a release of information allowing me to discuss my evaluation with his father and his wife.

A week later, Dexter was found dead by his wife, having hung himself by his belt in their hotel room while she and their children were outside. He had been somewhat reclusive during their vacation, but had played golf on the morning of his death. According to his wife, a few days before his death, he had sent text messages to a friend about being a failure and had spoken to his family about "spoiling their vacation."

I responded to this news by seeing Dexter's wife, his father, and speaking to his mother by phone to offer my condolences. I facilitated referrals for his wife and children and referred his mother for grief counseling. I also consulted with a local expert on communicating with families victimized by a member's suicide.

In my first session with Dexter's father, I revealed my own shock and grief, adding that even though I had seen his son just once I had felt a sense of connection from his descriptions of him in past sessions. I couldn't imagine the depths of his pain and I hoped that my own feelings would not interfere with our ongoing work in therapy. He told me that he appreciated my honesty. We sat silently for a while. He was in tears. I fought to suppress mine.

I inquired about anything I might have missed in my evaluation. Had Dexter mentioned that he was also very agitated, pacing, and muttering self-criticisms for the past two weeks prior to his vacation, his father queried? No, I hadn't known about these behaviors. In our session Dexter had appeared to be rather controlled and shut down.

During the next few sessions we continued to process his father's devastating losses. He was now actively mourning both of his sons simultaneously. I struggled to stay attuned, due to the intensity of his losses and his tendency to distance himself emotionally. I met with my practice consultant and monthly consultation group and received support and validation regarding my work. Other members shared about their experiences of suicides, which helped diminish my sense of isolation and guilt. I informed the group that I also had two actively suicidal physicians in my practice, stretching my emotional reserves to the max.

Over a number of monthly sessions, the group helped me mourn Dexter's suicide and supported my decision to refer both of my physician-patients to other practitioners. I no longer felt jinxed by suicidal patients. At his parents' request, I attended Dexter's memorial service and found this helpful in dealing with my own feelings. His family was grateful for my presence and support.

In my discussions with Joan Heron and my consultation group, I learned several lessons. I did not inquire about Dexter's high levels of agitation and anxiety, which pointed to an acute suicidal cognitive regression triggered by the changes at work, particularly involving his reactions to a new critical, distant supervisor. I should have evaluated his reactions to his new supervisor in greater detail, focusing on how this affected his self-esteem, sense of competence, and capacity to problem-solve regarding his sense of helplessness and suicidal thoughts.

Dexter's vacation plans suggested hope regarding his future; on the other hand, they distracted me from engaging in a more extensive evaluation process, which would have also included seeing his wife and parents. With these additional perspectives, I would have learned about his agitation and guilty ruminations and been in a better position to assess his family's ongoing capacity to offer support and encouragement regarding his treatment. This is of crucial importance, since the signs and symptoms of depression can cause emotional withdrawal and sometimes resentment in the family, which may tilt the scales towards suicide.

The combined effects of physical agitation, guilty ruminations, and insomnia are a volatile mix for a depressed man with suicidal ideation. Furthermore, the sudden emergence of a plan can override a large array of protective factors. Depressions with agitation may indicate mixed manic states where the combination of depressive affect and increased energy levels and impulsivity increase lethal risk (8).

Routine inquiries regarding psychotic symptoms such as delusions and hallucinations may miss subtle but significant impairments of reality-testing. For example, my observations regarding his excessive sense of work-related responsibility, his obsessions about his perceived inadequacy, and fear of being trapped in his work may have represented markers for a cognitive regression bordering on psychosis. Psychological testing would have been helpful to rule out an underlying psychotic or manic process.

I felt tense when Dexter revealed his vacation plans. My anxiety response constituted crucial data indicating the seriousness of his suicidal crisis. In retrospect I might have said, "Dexter, as you began to describe your upcoming vacation, I found myself tensing up. Is it possible that you yourself might be anxious about your commitment to travel at this time with your family, given the seriousness of your depression? If so, can you share why this might be?"

Questions remain as to whether I should have agreed to see Dexter in the first place. While I had discussed the pros and cons with his father, I did not explore the issue with Dexter. His father had communicated a sense of urgency in making the referral. In light of this and his other son's suicide, I didn't want to delay the process of Dexter being seen. On the other hand, I was already feeling burdened and depleted in my work with other chronically depressed and suicidal patients.

Had I reached my limit? I rationalized that this would be a single consultation leading to a referral, thus avoiding any significant ethical or boundary issues. But things in practice are rarely this simple. I did not consider the possibility that Dexter might feel inhibited in making more open disclosures to his father's psychiatrist regarding suicidal intent, which he most likely knew I would be obligated to communicate to both his parents and his wife.

Dexter must have embarked on his consultation with me with considerable caution, considering his likely fear of activating additional anxiety and mourning in his father. In retrospect, I should have begun our session with: "How do you feel about consulting with me?"

A large Swedish study found that in the two decades following the death of a family member by suicide, men were 2.44 times more likely to commit suicide than men who lost a family member from other causes (9). Dexter's brother had suicided several years prior to Dexter's death. I should have given this issue more weight in my assessment.

Dexter was in a suicidal crisis. Had I conceptualized this more accurately, I would have recommended he postpone his vacation, gathered more information from him and his family, performed psychological testing, and admitted him to a twenty-four-hour hospital program, where his treatment could be initiated in a safe environment.

An important lesson from this and other cases is that an exclusive focus on identifying "risk factors" for suicide is often inadequate in predicting any individual attempt. Risk factors are based on statistical findings in large population studies, not in individuals (10). While risk factors (trait indicators) need to be carefully considered, the clinician must seek to better understand the fluctuations in cognition, affect, and behavior (state indicators) which reflect a suicidal crisis.

Edward: A married man with increased marital conflicts

Edward was referred by his therapist to an intensive outpatient program for depression and suicidal ideation in the context of increased marital conflicts. He described periodic suicidal thoughts of taking an overdose of prescription medications used for a medical condition which was currently stable. He denied any stockpiling of these medications, owning guns, or other lethal means. He also denied any past history of suicide attempts or of suicides in his extended family. The only thing that would push him over the edge to suicide was if his wife had an affair or said she intended to divorce him.

During the first week of treatment his Beck Depression Inventory (BDI) Scores decreased and he denied suicidal intent both on the BDI and upon daily questioning by clinical staff members. He attended various educational and therapy groups, but was noted to be superficial in his contacts. I prescribed a one-week supply of antidepressant medications and met with him three times for ongoing assessment of suicidal intent and response to medications. In each of our sessions he denied suicidal intent or stockpiling of medications. Clinical staff made multiple attempts to contact his wife to include her in the treatment process, but she never returned their calls.

This striking lack of involvement, while not surprising to Edward, generated considerable anxiety within the staff and me. We began to feel we were handicapped by a lack of critical information. In his third appointment, I scheduled an appointment time for him and his wife in three days and asked him to confirm it as soon as possible. A message was left for Edward's outpatient therapist requesting that he also attend the meeting. Over the weekend neither the patient nor his outpatient therapist responded.

Edward failed to report for treatment on Monday morning. Calls were made to the patient and his wife. His wife finally responded and informed staff that Edward had left home over the weekend. He had taken all of his prescription bottles and a small knapsack with him. She had told him prior to our third and final treatment session that she had rented an apartment for herself and was filing for a divorce.

Edward had left no suicide note nor had he voiced any specific suicidal intent to her. He had failed to disclose any of this information in his final sessions with me or other staff. The sheriff's department in the town he told his wife he was traveling to was notified and activated search procedures. Two days later, Edward's lifeless body was found in his car, the victim of an apparent overdose.

Edward's suicide best exemplifies the importance of forging a suicide prevention alliance. His treatment was notable for its superficiality, lack of transparency, and ultimately, his inability (or refusal) to form an alliance. His improved scores on the Beck Depression Inventory diverted our attention from the fact that we were unable to mount an effective suicide care management plan involving him, his family, and clinical staff. All of these factors hindered a full investigation into his acute lethality.

A tragic combination of high levels of marital conflict and an unwillingness to disclose crucial information by both the patient and his wife handicapped the treatment team from developing a suicide prevention alliance. These confounding factors are by no means unique to this case. The increasing anxiety in myself and other clinicians no doubt paralleled the intensification of a developing marital-suicidal crisis. Staff countertransference, especially anxiety (similar to mine with Dexter), needs to be carefully understood, communicated, and monitored in the course of assessing patient risk and the intensification of a suicidal crisis.

In the current treatment climate, it can be difficult to hospitalize a patient who denies having an immanent suicide plan. Due to local psychiatric hospital bed shortages, I have had patients whom I placed on a seventy-two-hour involuntary hold denied admission to a hospital where I was on staff. The rationale given was that "the patient is no longer suicidal." Because of this and similar situations, many mental health professionals are now advocating modifying involuntary admission criteria from "imminent danger to self or others" to "substantial risk of harming self or others." This is especially important since there are a significant number of cases where the impulse to harm oneself can fluctuate rapidly and in which the fatal impulse develops less than an hour prior to the terminal act (11).

In cases such as Edward's, where there are high levels of marital conflict and a limited capacity for a therapeutic alliance, transfer to twenty-four-hour care within the first few days would have been more appropriate. Hospitalization can buffer the effects of covert or even overt hostile spousal messages escalating suicidal risk.

Edward's suicide occurred just two months following Dexter's. I initially found myself very frustrated with Edward and his family for their lack of openness and how this handicapped me and the treatment team. I realized later that my feelings were part of a *cumulative bereavement process* involving not only Arthur, Ethan, Dexter, and Edward, but also the previous losses of my friends and colleagues. The close proximity of these more recent losses helped me clarify how stressful my practice had been for many years and that this could have an impact on my effectiveness as a therapist going forward. Shortly after these suicides, I decided to forgo treating any new patients with a history of suicidal behavior or current suicidal thoughts.

While my personal and clinical experiences have been painful and challenging, I believe that I learned in many ways to be more sensitive to the needs of my suicidal patients and their families. With the helpful support of colleagues, I was able to regain confidence and reaffirmed that I am treating complex, deeply troubled persons who struggle with illnesses no less fatal than aggressive cancers, strokes, or cardiac diseases.

It is clear from recent demographic studies that there is an epidemic of suicides in the United States, a significant portion of which are carried out with handguns. Suicides and gun violence have emerged as defining issues for our time. Mental health professionals thus have a clear mandate to educate themselves, fellow citizens, and leaders at all levels of government regarding risk factors, the nature of the suicidal crisis, assessment methods, and prevention strategies, including reduction of access to lethal means, particularly guns. The institution of Extreme Risk Protection Orders in several states, enabling family members and law enforcement officers to confiscate guns from those who are dangerous, is clearly a move in the right direction. Nevertheless, gun rights advocates, including some local sheriffs, have mounted highly vocal opposition to these orders. To remain silent on this issue is to countenance more carnage.

The sad fact that several of my medical colleagues have a significant vulnerability to depression and higher than average risk of suicide (approximately 400 per year die by suicide) suggests that there is an urgent need to de-stigmatize mental health screening and increase depression awareness and burnout recognition in our medical training programs (12). Psychiatrists have a special responsibility in this regard to provide resources and expertise to their local practice and training programs and to offer individual consultation and therapy support groups for physicians who suffer from depression and other mental illnesses, which can be exacerbated by the ongoing stresses of practice.

During my own suicidal episode, I had developed a fantasy of using a handgun to kill myself in late November. I disclosed this to my second wife and she helped me arrange for an emergency consultation. My psychiatrist immediately placed me on an anti-depressant and I began twice per week therapy. In my treatment I discovered that, among other things, I had identified with a patient, treated by another psychiatrist, who had suicided just a year previously in his bedroom on a hospital unit where I consulted. In my fantasy, I imagined going to the same store where the hospital patient had purchased his lethal weapon.

I had helped the clinical staff on the unit process their own shock, grief, and guilt associated with this event but somehow minimized my own feelings. One of my roles as a consultant involved training clinical staff to be alert for subtle warning signs of suicidal episodes. I had managed to convict myself of negligence in my training methods. If I had done a better job, I imagined that clinical staff would have been more vigilant and that this would never have happened. My fantasy was patently absurd, yet it exerted a powerful influence by further shaking up my vulnerable self-esteem. In addition, I was re-experiencing some of my earlier painful experiences of losing Arthur ten years previously.

In addressing my own depression and suicidal episode in treatment, I learned that healing from depression and suicidal impulses involves much more than eliminating symptoms. The experience of severe suicidal depression involves a traumatic assault on one's self-esteem and competence which can become walled off and encased in shame. I was able to identify and dispel my own shame and to forgive myself for a sin based on irrational grandiosity.

I also learned that as much as I as a physician sought to prevent suicidal behavior, I ultimately had very little control over it. My therapy enabled me to carry these insights over into my treatment of others by focusing on their unique and irrational senses of shame and guilt and by giving them a new language for their depressive experiences while on the path to hope.

Psychiatrists face life and death issues every day, often in environments significantly different from other practitioners. A surgeon faced with a life-threatening injury, lesion, or tumor can often save lives by performing a single, skillful procedure. In psychiatry, we see large numbers of patients who are silently suffering chronic depression with recurring suicidal episodes, often treatment-resistant, disrupting work and relationships and requiring lifelong interventions with varying degrees of success.

In my own practice, I lost four patients to suicide but many others have thanked me for not only saving their lives but also for helping them build foundations for significant growth and resilience. For this reason I have kept a file of positive patient comments and thank-you notes as a bulwark against the inevitable periods of burnout and decreased confidence (see Appendix Two). I recommend this habit to anyone practicing in the mental health field.

In order to continue functioning at the highest level, I learned to address my cumulative bereavement burden more proactively. This has involved periodically decreasing my practice load of severely depressed patients, reentering personal therapy, describing my experiences with trusted colleagues, seeking consultation, and speaking with my monthly consultation group. These combined supports enabled me to continue practicing effectively for forty-four years.

The most important lesson from these cases, in addition to making a detailed assessment of risk factors and the suicidal crisis, is the creation and maintenance of a Suicide Prevention Alliance (SPA), as recommended by Zero Suicide. The main ingredient of this is a clear understanding with the patient that he or she has a potentially fatal but treatable condition and that our main goal is to continually address together how to discover options for acquiring hope and preserving life. It is also important to recognize those conditions in which the capacity for an SPA may be compromised, such as in latent psychosis, bipolar disorder, and severe personality disorders, particularly borderline, paranoid, or schizoid.

Factors in the patient's environment compromising his or her ability to form an SPA include intense family conflicts, family history of suicide, absent or deficient family support systems, and current issues such as empty nest phenomena, worsening medical illness, and impending retirement. Critical factors in the therapist affecting the SPAs include clinician burnout, illness, cumulative bereavement, and disillusionment, all of which can compromise both the treatment alliance and clinical judgment. When any of these factors are present, more conservative treatment approaches, including consultation and referral for hospitalization, must be considered, even in the absence of expressed imminent suicidal intent.

The tendency to hide specific plans regarding suicidal intent is an obstacle that needs to be studied further to allow for more effective assessments. Recently, Shea has developed a detailed, highly-structured, sequenced interview technique for use in adults where lack of full disclosure is suspected (13). Further research and implementation of these techniques will likely result in better treatment outcomes.

The internal world of the suicidal patient takes up residence, sometimes for years, in the antechamber of Dante's *Inferno*, with its dreadful warning: "Abandon all hope ye who enter here." Any therapist who treats suicidal patients must be comfortable living on the threshold of Hell in allowing him or herself to vicariously experience the terror and agony, much as Virgil did as Dante's guide. This is no job for the weak-hearted. As mentioned, despair can be contagious in therapists, especially for those who have known it themselves. It is also true that therapists who are fortunate enough to have conquered their own hopelessness and despair may have a distinct advantage in treating these individuals.

Grasping the dialectics of hope involves an understanding of profound paradoxes (14). On the one hand, therapists naturally wish to assist suicidal patients in finding hope. On the other, simplistic exhortations to be hopeful when the patient has lost it or never had it are often experienced as naive and insensitive, especially when coming from a therapist whose interventions are based on their own insecurities. In this situation, the patient often shuts down or worse, flees treatment, leaving the therapist to struggle with frustration, guilt, and despair. To empathize with hopeless suicidal despair, the therapist must be grounded enough to place one foot in Dante's vestibule with the patient and the other in his or her own carefully nurtured haven of safety.

This involves a capacity to empathize with impulses that are often seen as taboo, terrifying, or malevolent. To paraphrase Paul Tillich, it requires that we find "the courage to accept the unacceptable." Facing the option of suicide together requires that the therapist has accepted the inevitability of his or her own death and is not threatened by the possibility that patients may well be the agents of their own.

While treating chronically depressed, suicidal patients can be very challenging, it has also been a privilege for me to be a guide in the healing process. One of my patients, whom I had seen for a number of years in individual therapy, put it this way: "In working with you I got my life back."

130

CHAPTER 10

GROUP THERAPY AND CONSULTATIONS

When I entered private practice, I had no idea how much I would come to enjoy doing group therapy. As with many other developments in my practice, my clinical activities were based on a combination of chance patient referrals and what I viewed as interesting professional challenges. During my residency, I participated in three types of group training: an experiential group of seven residency classmates led by Dr. Carl Zimet, short-term inpatient groups, and an extended outpatient group where I teamed up with a fellow resident as a co-therapist.

In the experiential group, I found that I was reenacting some of my own family dynamics, especially concerning competition with my brothers who were a half generation older. In our family, competition with my brothers tended to preempt playfulness, spontaneity, humor, and emotional intimacy. I idealized Tom and Charles, while at the same time striving to be as smart and accomplished as they were. In the residents group I became quite competitive with my classmates, often trying to impress our leader with "brilliant" interpretations of group process and individual dynamics.

My arrogance kept my classmates at a distance until one day one of them confronted me. "Why don't you just get off your high horse and tell us how you're feeling today." I was immediately chagrined but ended up thanking him as the group ended. His blunt observation was not only accurate but way more helpful than a multitude of analytic sessions. Over the next few weeks I took the risk of describing how anxious I felt in my role as a second year resident on the inpatient service. Expecting to be bruised and shunned for my comments, I discovered that admitting my vulnerability actually brought others closer to me. A few of these men became lifelong friends.

I learned firsthand that there was a special kind of intimacy and excitement in working groups that is hard to duplicate elsewhere. Immediate interpersonal feedback coming from peers is often much more effective in bringing about lasting change than the best-timed and accurate interpretations made by a professional. In being more open and honest with my peers, my sense of isolation and uncertainty as a young psychiatrist began to melt away.

My group experiences in the early 1970s happened to coincide with the emergence of rapidly growing developments of group therapy techniques and practices in the United States and the U.K. These techniques were summarized in Irvin Yalom's books on outpatient (1) and inpatient (2) group therapy which literally became bibles in the field. With vivid examples, Yalom described the power of interpersonal feedback, catharsis, insight, cohesiveness, universality, developing hope, and learning in the present via family reenactment. Participating in Carl Zimet's group validated many of these concepts directly and launched me on the path of being more comfortable and affectionate with other men.

In my psychodynamic outpatient clinic group, I collaborated with the only woman resident in our class. She was bright but also somewhat scattered with her interventions. In working with her as a co-therapist I developed rescue fantasies not unlike those I experienced with my mother and some female patients I was treating individually. In the beginning, these preoccupations made it difficult for me to maintain a focus on group process and patient interactions. I described my dilemma in supervision and my supervisor helped me move out of my neurotic interactions with my co-therapist. Operating with these insights, our group members began to do more productive work. From this, I learned that the quality of my relationship with my co-therapist was a crucial element in determining the effectiveness of group treatment.

MONTHLY OUTPATIENT GROUP FOR BIPOLAR PATIENTS

In the early 1990s I became frustrated with the fact that four of my manic depressive patients were cycling in and out of hospitals, despite my careful medication management and supportive psychotherapy efforts. In my work at Arapahoe Mental Health Center I had conducted outpatient groups for chronic schizophrenics who used the groups productively as their primary social network. Many of these men and women had been able to avoid hospitalizations for several years. It occurred to me that individuals with bipolar disorder, who generally functioned at a significantly higher level, could also use groups to decrease their stigma and isolation, discuss concerns about medications, and possibly reduce their rates of relapse and hospitalization.

I was aware that I was walking into a minefield, given the large number of publications, including Yalom's, which offered dire warnings against frequent exacerbations, negative transferences, regressions, denial, and problematic interpersonal styles in this population (3). This professional skepticism had not deterred a large number of volunteer support groups, such as the National Depressive and Manic Depressive Association, and National Alliance for the Mentally Ill, from offering valuable services to these individuals. In addition, a growing number of memoirs by bipolar patients was emerging with powerful testimonials regarding the value of support group experiences. For example, Patty Duke, in her 1992 *New York Times* bestseller, wrote:

"Many people with depression and manic depressive illness say that their most effective therapy—the kind that helps them move past their illness and on with their lives—comes from attending a support group" (4).

Armed with this and other testimonials and the knowledge of a growing network of voluntary support groups throughout the U.S., I met together for the first time with my four patients. We five formed a kind of "steering committee" that developed the mission and designed the structure of the groups that evolved over a nine-year period. I was very frank with the members that I had not done this type of group before and that I needed them to be consultants regarding how the group should best operate.

We agreed that members should have clear diagnostic evidence for the disorder, be in individual therapy, comply with their medication regimens, and be free from alcohol or drug abuse. We met for ninety minutes on a monthly basis in the late afternoon to accommodate work schedules. New members were asked to commit to three consecutive trial sessions. Our main goals were psycho-education, offering mutual support, and decreasing hospitalizations for serious episodes (5).

Over the nine years that we met, a total of 14 patients actively participated for an average of nearly three years each. Group members averaged 0.97 hospitalized episodes per year prior to group attendance. During the years of their group participation, they averaged 0.18 hospitalized episodes per year for depression or mania. Many of the group members felt that what they learned in group was responsible for helping them preempt hospitalization both during and after their group involvement.

In the early phase of our group, individuals spoke openly of their fear of losing control in episodes, increased conflicts and arguments with family members and friends, enjoyment of their "highs" during manic episodes, social ostracism, and stigma when their behavior became bizarre or inappropriate. They all spoke of difficulties with medication compliance and described how this led to relapses.

As the group proceeded, I became more intrigued with understanding the meaning of manic delusional experiences. The prevailing attitude towards delusions in bipolar illness was to divide them generically into paranoid or grandiose types, often viewed as unrelated to the individual's actual lived experiences. What I discovered was quite the opposite. There were a number of patients who described paranoid delusions which, when carefully investigated in the group, related to actual traumatic experiences in their families of origin or from negative experiences with prior hospitalizations and physicians. In other words, their delusions were not simply arising *de novo*. As with neurotic symptom-formation, they appeared to represent efforts to recover from extraordinarily painful life events.

I found that grandiose delusions, often seen in mania, were likewise found to have clear personal origins, often related to significant but short-lived successes. For example, one man, who had recently been fired from his position as law clerk in the office of a federal judge, told me in the midst of a manic episode that he was likely to be appointed to the Supreme Court. This young attorney's grandiosity was obviously serving as a means of coping with his embarrassment about being fired.

A woman who had been promiscuous during her manic episodes revealed that she had an emotionally incestuous relationship with her father and a mother who ridiculed her as a whore. She had often attended church with her father while her mother stayed home to tend to her younger siblings. These experiences coalesced into a manic delusion that she was "married to God and was having his baby." Group members used this revelation to empathize with her experiences in childhood and to help her understand the risks of her current hypersexuality. In her individual sessions with me, we explored her reactions to her father's poor boundaries and her mother's traumatizing criticism. As she began to resolve these issues further, her episodes decreased in frequency. This woman's openness in group clearly enhanced her progress in areas that individual therapy alone would have taken much longer to access. It also demonstrated that a combination of group and individual therapy formed a robust addition to the medication component of treatment.

This group provided an excellent opportunity to explore a wide-ranging repertoire of coping mechanisms associated with managing intense mood episodes. Older members who had experienced repeated severe episodes tended to use what I came to call "camouflage of affect." This variation of denial and minimization dealt with fears of unleashing embarrassing aggressive and sexual impulses. An example of this involved a man who had hidden his affairs from his wife of ten years and other manic symptoms from me. His wife finally discovered him with a paramour, confronted him, and asked for a divorce. I met the couple in my office and changed his diagnosis from unipolar depression to bipolar disorder and asked him to join the group after he stabilized on meds. With gentle confrontations in the group, he was able to discard his camouflage efforts and describe details regarding multiple episodes of sexual indiscretions.

As he talked about these behaviors, other group members began to speak about their difficulties trusting good feelings or even spells of mild exuberance as inevitable precursors of mania. Similarly, they often experienced periods of normal sadness as dangerous pre-

135

cursors of depression. Describing these experiences enabled them to put their fears in perspective, normalize their concerns, and decrease their sense of isolation. Reporting on self-charting and group discussions involving details of their bipolar mood scales formed a helpful tool for discriminating between normal exuberance and significant hypomania.

In some patients, a kind of defensive non-manic grandiosity developed to ward off sadness and mourning. A group member who was no longer on speaking terms with his son following a divorce, boasted, "I think I've licked this bipolar thing...I've been hunting for Suzie (his current girlfriend) all my life...now I feel whole." Three months later Suzie left him during his next manic episode and he quickly sank into a deep depression.

I was impressed by how cohesive this group had become over the years. This ran counter to previous reports in the professional literature and was due, I believe, to several factors: careful selection and preparation of new group members, the fact that I was seeing many of them concurrently for individual therapy, my adopting a learning and consultative role, the use of role-playing to deal with conflicts at work and in relationships, careful setting of boundaries regarding extra-group contacts, and using group feedback and individual sessions to diffuse intensifying transference issues. In addition, the emergence of my own bipolar symptoms and treatment around this time gave me a unique advantage in being able to empathize with their struggles with medication side effects, their embarrassing painful indiscretions, and their fears of being stigmatized.

The evidence for cohesiveness in this group included patients calling each other to detect early warning signs of episodes and the use of the group as a surrogate family and buffer against social and familial ostracism. When members did require hospitalization, they were often visited by their compatriots from group for support and encouragement. One woman developed terminal cancer and several members, including myself, visited her in hospice. All of us joined together in attending her funeral and offering our condolences to her family. Our group grieved together and ultimately grew closer from this experience. This experience was especially useful, since many bipolar patients have difficulties managing the affects of grief and mourning.

The functioning of this outpatient group over a prolonged period period demonstrated that group therapy was not only possible for patients with bipolar disorder, but that active participation in it could significantly improve the course of their illnesses. Members demonstrated increased medication compliance, decreased camouflage and denial, increased awareness of stress factors leading to episodes, and decreased frequency of hospitalizations during participation in the group. Following the publication of my article on this group several local mental health centers and other outpatient treatment facilities began to include bipolar support groups in their therapy offerings. Several of my patients, having stabilized the course of their illnesses, developed a sense of altruism and became involved in Colorado Alliance for Mental Illness (CAMI) support groups.

While this group work was very gratifying for me, I ultimately decided to allow the group to taper off and dissolve when patients terminated or moved away. I found that maintaining this group as a solo therapist was increasingly demanding and time-consuming, especially as my own mood changes intensified. In a way, my work with this group and writing about it helped me begin to recognize and come to terms with the emerging mixed symptoms of my own unique variation of bipolar disorder. My next group, I vowed, would involve working with an experienced co-therapist who could provide both support and creative stimulation.

WEEKLY MEN'S PSYCHOTHERAPY GROUP:

In the 1990s I had three valuable experiences with groups that stimulated my interest and led to my creating a men's psychotherapy group with a co-therapist. These included a consultation group for therapists treating abusive men, a group of men and women therapists dealing with gender issues in therapy, and my own involvement in a leaderless men's group composed mainly of mental health professionals.

I consulted on a monthly basis with the AMEND (Abusive Men Exploring New Directions) Program with six therapists who treated men who were either voluntary or court-ordered into treatment. Listening to their case presentations, I learned that verbal and physical abuse often represented a last ditch attempt to compensate for intense fears of being devalued or abandoned, leaving them feeling inept, weak, and vulnerable (6). Cycles of violence were often triggered within seconds of a man's feeling devalued by his spouse. Rather than experience this and verbalize it, these men attempted to manipulate and control the women they loved and needed the most. Their impulsive anger was a final common pathway for expressing a wide variety of feelings these men neither understood nor had words for (7).

The therapists in my consultation group and I, vicariously, often felt overstimulated and overwhelmed by feelings of helplessness and despair. This made it difficult for them to remain empathic and objective when hearing their patients speak openly about impulses to control, maim, rape, or kill partners who triggered feelings of vulnerability. Maintaining an empathic stance while at the same time training these men to increase their self-control was a Herculean task. Listening to the therapists' struggles became increasingly challenging for me, as it often stimulated memories of my father's overly aggressive discipline. After eight years, I decided to resign from my consulting position. I left with great admiration for the therapists who had the courage and fortitude to continue in this difficult and necessary work. In the last few months of my consultations, I began to wonder if treating healthier men in group therapy might serve as a preventative intervention for men at risk for violent behavior.

Shortly after I ended my consultation role with AMEND, I joined a peer consultation group with seven men and women therapists. This group was founded by a husband and wife team, Drs. George Hartlaub and Joan Shapiro, to explore cross-gender interactions in conducting psychotherapy. Joan had recently published a book entitled *Men: A Translation for Women* which described how men's ways of coping with their vulnerabilities, such as denial, obsessive rituals, and work addictions, often interfered with intimate marriage relationships (8).

Most of the women in our group were ardent feminists who had experienced a wide range of gender discrimination, physical or sexual assaults, and/or prior emotional abuse in their families of origin or past relationships. Listening to them describe their deep-seated resentments and humiliations and how they managed to heal with other women in treatment was, for me, a very touching experience. It helped me not only find new ways of empathizing with my women patients, but also forced me to look inward to better manage some of my own controlling behaviors. Listening to the long-standing traumatic effects of the Patriarchy on these women was, to say the least, a chastening experience.

At the same time I was involved in this group, I invited Dr. Judith Herman to address the Bethesda Hospital Speakers' Forum regarding her brilliant essay on the effects of physical and emotional abuse on development and subsequent relationships (9). The combined insights from my consultation group and learning about Dr. Herman's research deepened my capacity for empathy with both traumatized women and men who struggled daily with their aggressive impulses.

One of the members of my consultation group, Paul Walker, Licensed Clinical Social Worker, invited me to join a leaderless men's group in which he had participated for several years. I was excited by his invitation and joined, eager to learn how to be more affectionate and less competitive with men. Paul and I had shared many activities together in fly fishing, hiking, and snowshoeing and had become close friends. Both of us had dealt with aggressive fathers and had attended seminaries prior to our clinical graduate training. Paul's association with the Colorado Men's Leadership Alliance gave him additional expertise in understanding men's developmental issues and the unique ways in which men manage conflict. As we participated in the men's group, we discovered a common interest in how some of the newer writings on men's issues had responded to the feminist critique of Patriarchy (see references 10-18). These authors described, in varying ways, how a number of feminist authors had misunderstood some essential features of men's experience. These views, espoused by some of our female colleagues in the men's and women's issues group, held that men were inherently violent, controlling, and sexist. While galvanizing the women's movement, these stereotypes failed to acknowledge the pervasive issues of men's emotional disconnectedness from self and family, their unique vulnerabilities related to work and identity, their longing for intimacy *with both men and women*, their shame-based behavior, and feelings of entrapment in traditional gender roles.

After several months of discussion, Paul and I decided to form a men's psychotherapy group to explore these issues. By defining our group as a "men's issues group," we hoped to emphasize men's common struggles and downplay any focus on pathology. We fostered a safe environment by operating on a first name basis, using selective self-disclosure, and encouraging transparency. We emphasized that members, as much as possible, use "I statements" about how they are feeling about others, as opposed to "you statements," which often generate hostile defensiveness. We intervened quickly if anyone became aggressive or devaluing of others in the group and promised to intervene quickly to avoid harm. We invited men to give direct and honest feedback on how their communications felt for the guy on the receiving end. Advice, which is a tactic men often use to avoid their own issues, was not to be given unless asked for.

Initially, we formed the group with men from our own practices; later on, we solicited referrals from other clinicians. We included men, ages thirty-five to sixty-five, who had ongoing problems with work or personal relationships, difficulties with anger, and those who felt isolated from their feelings and from other men. We carefully screened out those with current drug or alcohol abuse, recent psychiatric hospitalization, impulsive personality features, or a history of psychotic episodes. We asked newcomers to commit to three consecutive weekly group meetings on a trial basis, after which they and other group members would discuss whether there was a good match.

Paul and I frequently described our understanding of typical men's issues and recommended readings in order to normalize their struggles. At the time we formed our group, there was only one other similar group in the entire Denver metropolitan area. Our group met weekly in the late afternoon for 90 to 105 minutes. We extended the duration on rare occasions by consensus if a man needed more time to focus on urgent or painful issues. Our general format followed Yalom's model for insight-oriented outpatient groups (1) with minor modifications.

A brief sampling of four men's group interactions demonstrates how this group helped them grow.

George, a 50-year-old married professional, came to me for treatment of anxiety and panic symptoms which seriously hampered his functioning at work. He described his marriage as a stalemate of smoldering resentment with little intimacy and frequent anger outbursts on his part. Prior to referring him to group, I used cognitive behavioral techniques and medication to treat his anxiety and panic. He was highly motivated for change and improved within a few months. As we began to work on some family of origin issues, it became clear that he was repeating childhood traumatic experiences in his relationship with his wife and with other men. Despite his persistent hesitation, I strongly urged him to consider attending our group as an adjunct to his individual therapy, explaining that there was a good chance it could help him with his anger outbursts and increase his capacity for intimacy at home.

George entered the group with intense fears of being seen as vulnerable, even fraudulent. His fears were based on his traumatic experiences with a borderline psychotic mother and a father who was withdrawn and unable to protect him from her outbursts. In his work setting he maintained a cool professional façade which allowed him to isolate from intense feelings. He maintained a similar façade for months in the group until Frank, the son of an abusive construction worker, told him to "cut the crap and get real." George recoiled from this confrontation, looking chagrined. Frank persisted, saying, "I know you've got some feelings stuck in there…just let them out…it's not like we're going to beat you up."

I was concerned that Frank's heavy-handedness might push George further into a corner, so I asked him to describe how he felt about Frank's comments. George paused for a moment and then responded, looking at me for guidance. "He's right, I'm scared of my own feelings…I let resentment build up until I blow." Another man chimed in and observed that George had been looking at the floor during Frank's confrontation and suggested that he look Frank in the eyes and address him personally. George looked up at Frank and thanked him for helping him be more direct about his fears of being judged as weak and vulnerable.

Over the next two years George found his voice and became increasingly assertive with other group members about his own needs and their behaviors. Ultimately he was able to discuss his feelings of frustration, without erupting in anger, with his wife about their lack of sexual intimacy. In his individual therapy we worked on his fears of his mother's psychotic outbursts and helped him differentiate his wife, who was very well organized, from his mother. Eventually, their sexual relationship improved. He was able, by identifying with more assertive group members, including Paul and me, to outgrow his identification with his emotionally constricted and passive father. When he graduated from the group, George summarized his progress: "Now I can speak up for myself. I'm a better father and husband."

Milton was referred to me for treatment of depression, low self-esteem, and underachievement in his profession. His older brother, with whom he was initially quite close, was verbally abusive to him following their parents' divorce. His relationship with his brother was now strained to the point of his wanting to cut off all ties. In his work environment he described difficulties with sabotaging himself and being assertive with his boss.

After a few weeks, Paul and I noticed that Milton was generally last to claim "air time" for working on his own agendas. Frequently the group would end before he got to speak up. We brought this to the group's attention and discussed how men needed to be more assertive about bringing up their own issues. Some men indicated that this was the very reason they had joined the group. We agreed that we would support Milton in taking more responsibility for his needs but that we wouldn't do it for him. The focus shifted to why he felt so inhibited in the group. He realized that he was afraid that Frank, like his abusive older brother, would "walk all over him." The group agreed, with Frank's permission, to confront him if they saw this develop. This discussion also helped Frank connect with how frightening he had become at times in his two marriages. Frank's involvement in this group helped him decrease his own tendencies to be abusive.

In the next several meetings, Milton began to claim more time, which he used productively to discuss how he tended to sabotage himself during faculty meetings at the school where he was teaching. In addition, while he had worked in this district for years, he had been hesitant to ask for a raise. Group members role-played with him to prepare for a meeting with his department chairman in which he intended to propose a raise. He engaged his "chairman" in an increasingly active and persuasive manner. Two weeks later, he could hardly contain his excitement when he announced that he was actually getting a raise. The group spontaneously broke into applause. In the next two years Milton was able to confront his brother directly about his abusiveness and made the decision to apply for advanced graduate training in his specialty.

Eli entered our group after being referred by another therapist who described his individual treatment as stuck regarding his wish to develop more intimate relationships with women. Eli was in his mid-forties, lived alone, and worked in his family's business. He had had only one brief dating relationship which ended when the woman accused him of stalking her. In his description of their relationship he was strikingly unaware of how his eccentric behavior might have led to these allegations. What he had assumed was a close relationship appeared to be a distant infatuation characterized by his awkward intrusions and inability to read the woman's body language indicating her lack of interest. In addition, he was unable to describe any friendships with men. Paul and I accepted him into the group on a trial basis indicating that we would need to evaluate with him whether it would be a good match.

Eli's initial interactions with other men were inconsistent and off-putting. While he was always early for meetings, he rarely exchanged greetings in the waiting room, choosing instead to bury himself in magazines or books. Once the group started, he checked in by reciting overly detailed, rambling descriptions of his past week's activities, rarely making eye contact with other group members, often glancing at me as if he were a little boy needing approval. After a few sessions it was clear that he had a limited capacity to formulate an agenda for himself. During other member's check-ins, he often appeared disengaged, often looking out the window, anxiously twisting his long hair.

Paul and I both agreed that Eli most likely had mild Asperger's, now called autism spectrum disorder. We informed his therapist of this and indicated our skepticism as to whether our group could help him. His therapist replied that Eli had told him the group was the "high point of his week." He added that our group most likely provided the only opportunity for Eli to have regular social interactions. I was uncertain whether this constituted a good rationale for his continued group involvement, but agreed to shift the focus from psychodynamic work to a social skills-training effort. We would have to weigh the potential gains for Eli remaining in the group against the possibility that his continued presence might lead to others fleeing from the group.

During the following session we asked other men to describe their reactions to Eli. While he was initially defensive about their observations, he gradually acknowledged that his frequent interruptions and lack of direct eye contact when addressing others caused frustration, resentment, and decreased trust. It was, in addition, inhibiting others from being more openly disclosing with their own issues. We agreed as a group to call these behaviors to his attention whenever they occurred and to offer him support when he was able to suppress them. As Eli began to interact more appropriately, other members were able to more confidently address their own issues.

In time, Eli became more adept at talking about himself and his painful family history, which included Holocaust survivors. He was even able to empathize on a limited basis with other group members. He graduated from the group several months later, indicating how grateful he was for his involvement and how he would miss several group members. At follow-up, his therapist said he was listening better, interrupting others less at work, and feeling more spontaneous with others. He continued to avoid dating or initiating friendships. While his progress was more modest than we had hoped, it was, for him, significant.

Irwin was a warm, sociable man with extensive past group experience. He sought help for dealing with a devastating divorce from a woman with whom he'd had a sadomasochistic relationship. In the first few weeks he looked like an ideal newcomer, reaching out consistently to empathize with others. We soon realized that this behavior diverted him and the rest of the group from focusing on his own issues. His check-ins were boring "data dumps" of dry details, further disguising his personal agendas and feelings. The other men were more than willing to allow these monologues to continue, since it served their own avoidance as well.

Paul and I responded by making a simple request in the following session:

"Irwin, we are having trouble understanding what you need from the group. From now on we ask that you come prepared to say what you are feeling and what you need from the group."

With frequent reminders he began to do this and other men followed suit by being more assertive regarding their own needs and agendas. Irwin's increasing assertiveness in the group carried over into outside relationships and helped him mourn his marriage.

One of the most delightful and unanticipated results of our co-therapy experiences was a deepening of our personal friendship and mutual growth. Paul and I met for up to forty-five minutes following each group in my office. These meetings became cherished encounters for reacting to what the men stimulated in us and how we collaborated as co-therapists. Paul's style was warm, spontaneous, and often sprinkled with gentle sarcasm. I tended to be more thorough, meticulous, and analytical. After a while I became much more comfortable with sharing my own experiences of Paul and openly disagreeing with him in the group. I came to see Paul as a true brother, with whom I could be more open and vulnerable than I had been with my own brothers. This helped me become closer to Tom and Charles in our later years. As the group came to a close, I was more able to laugh at myself and to accept the challenges and the absurdities of being a mature male in our society. I will be forever grateful for this experience.

CHAPTER 11

TREATING PHYSICIANS

When I treat physicians, I feel a heightened sense of responsibility for them, their families, and their patients. We physicians share tight kinship bonds from our similar experiences with prolonged training and facing the ravages of disease, disability, and death. Likewise, we appreciate the joys and triumphs of practice when our persistent efforts lead to survival and healing. Society rewards our profession by conferring high levels of status, power, and respect upon us. When a doctor becomes a patient and the power differential is reversed, things get complicated due to a number of factors on both sides of the therapeutic relationship.

Physicians who come for psychiatric treatment are often in the midst of severe personal stress such as divorce, physical illness, acute psychiatric disorders, or addictions. They frequently are struggling to shoulder the cumulative stresses of unexpected patient deaths, malpractice litigation, or critical reviews from colleagues. These developments involve simultaneous threats to their self-esteem and professional identity which are invariably interwoven. Under these circumstances, as Myers and Gabbard point out: "The last thing physicians want to be is a patient. They prefer to deny their vulnerability to illness and to concentrate on the diseases of their patients" (1).

In addition, physicians in all specialties frequently share the biases of laypersons regarding mental illness and psychiatric practitioners. These biases continue to be propagated in medical schools and residency programs, where rotations in psychiatry are often shorter than in other specialties and focused on severely disabled hospital populations. A leg cast from a skiing accident may prompt a lively conversation about a daring adventure whereas seeing a "shrink" for a bout of depression becomes a closely-guarded secret often encased in shame.

Three issues can complicate treating fellow physicians: identification, idealization, and the psychiatrist's own transference reactions. These issues are often comingled, making this population particularly challenging to treat. Understanding and managing these complex dynamics is essential for assuring positive outcomes.

The first order of business in treating physicians is to focus on their feelings of vulnerability in becoming a patient. The very idea of engaging in a role reversal often triggers intense feelings of shame and embarrassment, challenging longstanding grandiosity. The psychiatrist's capacity to recognize and empathize with these issues at the outset of treatment is paramount if the physician is to feel validated and to gain maximal benefit from therapy.

When a psychiatrist treats a fellow physician, various forms of collegial identification may obscure important issues, leading to blind spots and therapeutic passivity. For example, a psychiatrist who had a very stressful call schedule during residency may identify with the exhaustion and irritability of a colleague who speaks of similar experiences and thus fail to vigorously explore the reality of how these issues have eroded marital intimacy and triggered alcohol abuse.

Idealization of the physician-patient may interfere with doing a comprehensive evaluation and making an accurate diagnosis. Dr. Miller, a prominent surgeon, was referred for treatment of depression. In his initial session he focused mainly on his wife's complaints regarding his irritability and then proceeded to brag about innovative surgical procedures he had developed recently. I was captivated by his descriptions and initially distracted from my primary task of evaluation. Regaining a more active clinical role, I soon discovered that he had a long history of emotional and physical abuse in childhood. With tears streaming down his cheeks, he blurted out, "Men don't cry in my family...I became a surgeon hoping for love and approval...Now I'm

alone and ashamed to cry…I guess that's what I have to do to get help."
Dr. Miller was on his way to becoming a patient, needing to gain my
approval before he let down his guard.

The idealization process may involve situations where *psychiatrists develop transference reactions to their physician-patients* based on
their own past positive experiences. Transference reactions are usually
defined as feelings, fantasies, and wishes projected *by the patient* onto
the therapist, but in the case of treating physicians, transferences can
easily become bi-directional.

An idealizing transference to my physician-patient can interfere with the development of a good therapeutic alliance and recognition of more severe pathology. A *therapeutic alliance* involves a generally positive relationship in which patient and therapist agree to work as
a team on well-defined treatment goals. The degree to which I may
idealize my physician-patient carries a risk for our developing a *pseudo-alliance* in which therapy sessions become imbued with mutual admiration and thus diverted from therapeutic tasks. Sessions involving
pseudo-alliances are characterized by their superficiality and lack of
affective depth and intensity. When this is recognized, the treater
needs to shift to a more traditional hierarchical, as opposed to collegial
role, much to the patient's relief (2).

Since I am the first and only physician in my extended family, I
had few models for how a doctor lives and works other than those who
treated me over the years and those I knew from medical and psychiatric training. For this reason, I read widely in an increasingly rich repertoire of medical memoirs to further understand the specific challenges and stresses inherent in various medical and surgical specialties. I include a brief summary of these works in the notes for this
chapter.

What I remember most about our family doctor, Harold Brown,
was his spontaneous warmth and no-nonsense approach. He met me
and my mother with his sleeves rolled up, round headband mirror, and
with a hearty, "What's up, Johnny?" His home office was unpretentious
and easily accessible, less than a mile from our house. His jovial demeanor quickly calmed my fears about shots or uncomfortable diagnostic procedures. My parents often told me how much they liked and
respected him.

I have returned to treatment on several occasions when life circumstances or the stresses of practice aggravated my mood disorder.

Apart from a difficult analysis in the 1970s, I have had positive experiences with several psychiatrists with each experience augmenting the previous one, depending on what I viewed as the best fit for issues at various times in my life. With each of these treatments I experienced a different style of empathic understanding and communication, which has enriched my capacity as a therapist.

In the three case vignettes below, I describe how I managed issues of identification, idealization, and transference with physicians in treatment.

Dr. A: Brief therapy for sexual harassment and depression

Dr. A sought my help, complaining of chronic low-grade depression and widespread aches and pains. She was near the end of her second year of residency training and was fearful that she might not be advanced to her final year.

An attractive married woman in her late thirties, she had obtained her nursing degree and had worked for several years in a variety of clinics before applying to medical school. Dr. A complained of being exhausted from her long hours on call. In the previous year she had to take medical leaves for brief illnesses.

Her male attending physicians had been insensitive about her need for these leaves, treated her condescendingly, and took liberties touching her during rounds. One of them had hinted at liaisons in the evening on-call rooms. Outraged, she told him that she would report him to her department chair if this continued.

"'Go right ahead,' he replied…'he's a good friend of mine and we're not sure you have what it takes to be advanced to your final training year.'"

This interaction pushed her over the edge. She felt angry, humiliated, and hesitant to speak with her husband for support. She disclosed her situation to a nursing colleague, who had referred her to me.

In our first session Dr. A explained that her insurance plan only covered six sessions and that she couldn't afford to extend treatment beyond that limit. In addition, she was considering a move out of town. I was impressed that she had considerable warmth, despite her somewhat guarded presentation.

I asked how it felt as a woman to be seeing a male psychiatrist, given what she had just described. She quickly dismissed my inquiry by saying that I came highly recommended. I then asked if this was her first treatment and how it felt for her, a physician, to be seeking help from me. She had never seen a psychiatrist before, but had a good experience with a priest who counseled her during nursing school to deal with some guilt feelings regarding an affair she had prior to getting married.

Near the end of the first session, I summarized by saying how painful and degrading it must have been for her to endure these indignities from her male attending faculty. It was understandable that she was depressed and having physical pain. I suggested that she arrange for a complete physical exam and lab work to rule out any concurrent medical issues that might aggravate depression. I stressed that we needed to pay close attention to how she was feeling with me in our sessions and that, if at any time, she felt uncomfortable, she should let me know. She agreed to do this.

I explained that I viewed therapy as a collaborative process, very different from surgery. We would need to agree on our agendas and stay focused, given our time limitations. This approach appealed to her. She agreed to write out a list of topics she would like to cover over the next five sessions and bring it to our next meeting.

Dr. A looked markedly less guarded and anxious as she arrived for our second session. Without hesitation, she presented me with a list of topics for us to discuss in the remaining time. Together, we consolidated her goals as follows:

1. Treating her depression.
2. Dealing with sexual harassment at work.
3. Decreasing her isolation.
4. Supporting her progression to her final training year.

I told her how impressed I was with her diligence in defining our treatment goals.

I prescribed a dual-action antidepressant, which addressed her pain symptoms, and a limited prescription of a sleeping medication, requesting that she keep me informed regarding any side effects having an impact on her on-call responsibilities. We discussed the importance of making prescription decisions together and she agreed to not make any changes without consulting with me. She was clearly relieved that I cared enough to take charge. At the end of the session I said that her therapy would address depression as a symptom of her experience of gender discrimination, sexism, and burnout, and that she might need more therapy at some point to address these issues more fully. I found myself wishing I could be the one to do more extensive work with her.

Our next four sessions were very productive. We discussed the details of her sexual harassment at work, including her prior history of trauma (she had been date raped in nursing school) and behavioral factors she thought might be contributory, such as her soft-spoken presentation and lack of assertiveness in relationships. I supported her for her openness and honesty and we discussed whether she might see a female therapist in the future to deal with these issues.

I also recommended that she check out support groups for women to deal with her isolation. She made a commitment to call some of her women colleagues for breakfast and bike rides on a regular basis. We discussed how harassment can affect intimate relations within marriage and I called her husband for a phone session to discuss this with him. I referred her to a female attorney I knew who dealt with workplace harassment issues and recommended she take advantage of a free initial consultation.

I asked her if she knew any senior female faculty whom she liked and trusted. She did not, but there was a general practitioner in another town who had supported her in her decision to enter medical school. I suggested that she contact her colleague and discuss whether they might develop a regular mentorship via Skype to brainstorm her progression in her residency. We considered the pros and cons of her transferring to another residency program which might be more sensitive to gender issues. She diligently researched several programs and at the time of our ending treatment had narrowed her program options to two.

In our last session she brought me a thank-you note, enclosing a picture of her and her husband. The card, signed by both, said simply, "Thank you for believing in me." Two years later, I received a note from her indicating that she had completed her residency in another town and had recently joined a group practice. She was pleased to report that she had found a new psychiatrist to work on issues we had discussed. I responded with a brief note congratulating her and wishing her well.

This case demonstrates the value of a dynamically-informed brief psychotherapy for a traumatized woman physician-in-training.

The architect, Mies van der Rohe, famously said: "Less is more." This comment is especially relevant for the treatment of physicians whose work or life situations are currently too stressful to accommodate a lengthier exploratory therapy. The supportive, structured approach I took in this case immediately addressed the issues of therapeutic alliance (agreement on the goals for the remaining five sessions), the issue of role reversal (her positive prior experience with the priest), transference (my addressing the gender issue in the here and now of our sessions) and my use of brief forays into past history to enable me to more directly empathize with her current experiences of sexual harassment.

The use of organized written goals for each session had the effect of galvanizing Dr. A's adaptive compulsive traits which served as the daily currency of her life as a doctor. She was able to use this carefully designed short-term treatment as a dress rehearsal for a more leisurely exploratory approach as her life became less stressful.

Dr. B: The benefits of combining individual and group therapy

I recommended that Dr. B. join my men's group in order to increase his self-confidence as a physician and improve his romantic relationships, which followed a pattern of choosing unavailable partners. In his medical practice his overly meticulous style and indecisiveness led to unnecessary delays for patients and waiting room backups, and generated frustration in his practice group. He also complained of periodic depressive episodes, during which he would withdraw socially during his time off, struggling to gain enough energy to face patients again.

His psychosocial history included parents who each followed busy schedules and who displayed little affect or physical intimacy. An older brother, whom he envied, was married with kids and overshadowed him with regard to earnings and social standing. He described his father as a passive, intellectual man and his mother as very critical and demeaning. He felt he could never live up to his mother's expectations or match his brother's stellar accomplishments. Most of his high school friends were smart, motivated, sociable teens who shared his interests in the visual arts.

He was the first and only doctor in his family and did very well in medical school. In residency training, he had struggled with adapting to a demanding schedule and critical superiors. By contrast, he became very animated when describing an externship in infectious disease in Central America. In this setting, he felt useful, autonomous, and appreciated by the local indigent population. Prior to moving to the Denver area, he described a helpful experience in a coed therapy group, explaining that feedback from others had made him more aware of some of his self-defeating behaviors in relationships.

During his first group meeting, he greeted everyone spontaneously and was articulate in explaining his goals. However, in later sessions, when the group began to focus on his self-confidence, he became anxious and tongue-tied, often searching for the perfect word before he spoke.

Over the next year he developed complex transferences in the group. He viewed the older members, including a physician colleague, as more secure and accomplished and was hesitant to claim his rightful "air time" when he was speaking. On the other hand, when I was relatively quiet in the group relative to my co-therapist, Paul Walker, he became aware of feeling resentful. In our individual sessions we were able to identify his resentment as deriving from his feelings about his father's passivity when his demanding mother would criticize him. We agreed in individual sessions that he would actively ask for feedback from me about his group behavior whenever he felt a need for it.

In the following group session, he mustered the courage to do so and I complimented him and asked the other group members to give him additional feedback. Several members, including the other physician, Dr. W, added their supportive comments. During the next few sessions he began to interact more with Dr. W. Dr. W's marriage was in crisis and he struggled to deal with two teenagers who were acting out. Dr. B was able to make useful observations about Dr. W's difficulties with parenting. This generated support from other group members and myself regarding his excellent listening skills and how helpfully he communicated his insights.

Meanwhile, during our individual sessions, we explored his wishes to have an older mentor for both personal and professional development. He shared how gratifying and meaningful his experience with Dr. W had been in the group and began to indicate his admiration for me and my successful practice.

At first I was tempted to interpret his idealization and temper it with comments regarding my own foibles. I decided to forgo this, with the understanding that he probably needed this for a while, given his emotionally deprived upbringing. Instead, I opened the door for him to say more about what he admired and how he saw me as a physician.

He surprised me with his response. "You seem to really enjoy your work...and from what I can see, you really have been able to balance your work and personal life."

I confirmed his observations, describing my involvement in this group as one of the highlights of my practice. I got along really well with my co-therapist Paul and considered him my mentor in group work. Dr. B was thus experiencing an *in-vivo* mentorship in the group. As our co-therapy relationship matured, Paul and I became much more comfortable openly discussing our disagreements in the group, thus offering further modeling for Dr. B and other group members. In individual sessions, I described helpful aspects of participation in my own men's group, a reading group, piano studies, a consultation group, my own psychiatric mentorship, and recreational activities.

I actively encouraged Dr. B to develop a trusting mentorship outside the group with a senior practitioner in his specialty. He pursued this and learned ways of streamlining his evaluations and decision-making. For a brief period he did daily self-charting focused on eliminating self-critical thoughts and setting goals to improve his medical practice. Dr. B brought these written goals to the group and read them during the initial agenda-setting phase. Other group members began to employ this tactic for their own benefit.

I saw Dr. B individually for several years, punctuated by his accepting a medical position overseas in his specialty. During this time, we communicated via emails enabling him to relay his latest medical and dating adventures to me and the group. When I retired, he called to say goodbye and described his engagement to a woman he had met during his practice overseas. He added that he had recently been appointed as medical director of a new clinic. I told him how impressed I had been with his persistent hard work and growth over the years.

In my view, several factors led to a positive outcome in Dr. B's treatment. He had had prior group experience; thus, the usual beginning group issues of developing trust and negotiating feelings of vulnerability were less pronounced.

He was able to use his connections with an older physician in the group to increase his self-confidence and decrease his anxiety. His confidence grew when he realized his insights about this colleague's parenting were helpful.

The combination of group and individual therapy provided an opportunity for Dr. B to further explore the transference implications of his reactions to others beyond myself and Paul, and also facilitated important insights regarding his needs for a mentoring relationship in his practice.

My own use of self-disclosure in both group and individual treatment settings helped him deal with some of the disappointments he had experienced with his own father. As a result, he gained confidence in approaching his father more directly regarding his needs. I allowed him to idealize me, leavened with periodic doses of self-disclosure focused on balancing professional involvement with social and recreational pursuits.

Dr. C: Where my idealization resulted in missing a personality disorder

As soon as Dr. C walked in the door requesting help for depression, I was reminded of my childhood physician, Dr. Brown, by his slightly disheveled appearance, warm voice, and relaxed countenance. I felt drawn in by his penetrating gaze. He whispered while recounting how a hypomanic episode a few months earlier had brought his marriage to the brink of dissolution and threatened longstanding relationships with his radiology group. During his episode, he had impulsively invested large sums of money in a risky venture and was currently emailing an old flame from residency years. As he was speaking, I noticed the incongruity between his soft delivery and the turmoil he described.

Since he had never been diagnosed with bipolar disorder, we spent considerable time in the first few weeks establishing his diagnosis, discontinuing his anti-depressant and starting him on mood stabilizers. While he did not feel initially that his mood episodes interfered with his capacity to perform invasive procedures, I made it clear at the outset that we would need to monitor this carefully as treatment progressed.

In describing how he had decided to become a doctor, he said that his father had "almost made the decision for me." His father had wanted to be a surgeon, but there wasn't enough money for him to attend medical school.

As a child, Dr. C had been drawn to playing the violin and his dream had been to perform or teach. When he practiced at home, his father would make fun of him for mistakes. He feared sharing his own vision with his father, concerned that he would be subject to another dose of derision. As he talked about playing the violin, I recalled that Dr. Brown had played first chair violin in our local orchestra.

As I listened to him describe his feelings of deprivation and loneliness, I began to have fantasies of adopting him and promoting his musical talents. One day he disclosed that he was playing fiddle in a bluegrass group and asked how I would feel if he brought his violin in and played for me. I hesitated for a moment and then agreed to his proposal. He arrived for his late afternoon appointment, excited as a puppy, and proceeded to spellbind me for fifteen minutes with his virtuosity.

As I clapped enthusiastically, I was filled with a bittersweet mixture of joy and sadness. "I'll bet you never got to do that for your dad at home as a kid," I said. Suddenly he started sobbing. In the following sessions, he began to mourn the mirroring and empathy he never had as a child from either of his parents. He brought in CDs of his own recordings and asked if I would listen to them. I realized that while I had idealized him, he was also idealizing me on the way to developing a more secure sense of self.

At around this time, he disclosed that he had unilaterally decreased his mood stabilizers, saying that he was feeling much better and that his mood swings had decreased. I accepted these statements at face value without pursuing the ramifications.

In the next few months, his wife announced that she was filing for divorce. Soon thereafter, one of his patients died shortly after he injected contrast material during a scan. The hospital quality control committee initiated an investigation of the case and advised him to speak with his liability insurance carrier. The concurrence of these two events was devastating. Within weeks he became depressed and actively suicidal, and shared that he had been stockpiling lethal drugs at home. The only way he could tolerate these blows to his self-esteem was to maintain a suicide plan.

I immediately advised him to notify his practice partners and the hospital that he was taking a leave of absence and asked his wife to help confiscate his contraband analgesics. I hospitalized him at a local psychiatric facility where he was treated for a week with the addition of an atypical antipsychotic medication and discharged to an intensive outpatient program. In the this program, clinicians noted that he had remained superficial and demonstrated very little motivation to work on his assignments or to practice new skills such as charting irrational thoughts and using mindfulness to promote affect regulation. The staff, like myself, felt that they were doing the bulk of the therapeutic work.

At this time I strongly recommended that he enroll in the Colorado Physician Health Program to monitor his treatment and any future practice involvement. During this period he revealed that he was experiencing an almost constant state of empty panic regarding losing his wife. He could no longer soothe himself by playing violin and had stopped jamming with his group. In addition, he was terrified of losing his medical license. He said that he had been unable to open up in the outpatient groups which involved blue-collar workers who "were not like me." We discussed how difficult it was for him, a doctor with years of higher education, to see himself as a patient in this program. He anticipated being stripped of his marriage, his career, and of every last ounce of self-respect. He and I both feared for his life.

As we spoke further about the events leading up to his patient's death, he revealed that for the past few years, he had taken a cavalier approach to his work, frequently not following accepted practice standards, providing less than fully informed consents, and becoming careless in performing invasive procedures. When I asked him to describe how he understood these developments, he said that he almost wanted to be caught, sued, and ordered to quit his practice. "I never wanted to be a doctor. I did it for my dad. Now I'm going to be punished for killing someone...I'm such a failure and a fraud."

I responded by telling him that while I appreciated his honesty, it was of the utmost importance that we focus now on how he could suspend his practice and use further therapy to recover from his losses and to develop a more authentic self.

Dr. C's depression and suicidal thoughts continued, despite multiple medication changes, crisis phone calls, and extra sessions. I ultimately transferred him to a two-month inpatient program in another city designed for professionals. During his treatment, psychological testing revealed a Mixed Personality Disorder. There were no major changes made in his medication regimen; however, he was able to decrease both his intense self-criticism and suicidal thoughts. Following his discharge, I decided to transfer him to a younger psychiatrist who did psychodynamic therapy and whose practice was better suited to respond to brief regressions and provide hospital care when needed.

In our last session, I asked him for feedback on this therapy experience. "You saved my life," he said. His new psychiatrist told me several months later that his mood swings had decreased in intensity and that he was no longer suicidal.

Viewing him initially through the transference lens of my own family doctor, we had formed a kind of mutual admiration society with a pseudo-alliance. Dr. C's minimization and attempts to reassure me regarding his improved mood states distracted me from addressing the medication adherence issue earlier and left him vulnerable to increased mood swings. His deepening depression and suicidality appeared to represent a cumulative reaction to an impending divorce, mood destabilization, and the emergence of his personality disorder.

Had I confronted his lack of medication compliance directly as symptoms of denial and minimization, his next depressive episode might have been less severe. My own fantasies of adopting him should have tipped me off to the profound nature of his early emotional deprivation and the possibilities of a severe regression as his wife moved towards divorce. My own sense of depletion in shouldering the bulk of the therapeutic burden reflected the emergence of his dependent traits.

Transferring Dr. C was painful for me since I felt a close affinity with him regarding his mood disorder and his impending divorce. At the same time, I did not feel I had the emotional reserves to go the distance with him. Part of my depletion related to two patient suicides in my practice which coincided with Dr. C's becoming actively suicidal. In struggling with my decision to transfer him, I recognized for the first time that I was at the limits of my energy reserves. It is possible that Dr. C picked up on my depletion and that this also contributed to his regression. Under these circumstances, I felt that transferring him was justified on both clinical and ethical grounds.

Treating physicians in psychotherapy is a heartfelt privilege as well as a challenge. The sense of kinship that we share forms the foundation for complex therapy relationships. When we see a physician for therapy we may idealize them as often as they idealize us. Physicians, in spite of their training, often experience the same kinds of stigma associated with psychiatric treatment as found in the general population.

They frequently enter treatment in situations where their professional identities have been challenged in significant ways.

In addition, the process of becoming a patient involves a role reversal which can be daunting. Psychiatrists, if they wish to be effective in treating their medical colleagues, need to consider all of these issues carefully and address them actively in the treatment situation.

Mutual idealization in the treatment dyad is a double-edged sword. On the one hand, it can facilitate positive change; on the other, it can sometimes blind us from recognizing more severe impairments such as personality disorders. Psychiatrists can form positive or negative transferences with physician-patients, and these can exert powerful influences on the therapeutic alliance and treatment outcome. Recognizing and addressing shifts in the therapeutic alliance and understanding pseudo-alliances are important ingredients in successful therapies. The coexistence of affective disorders and personality disorders in physicians is not uncommon and can complicate treatment progress.

Personality disorders can be partially masked by the demands and structure of a busy practice and may only emerge with full intensity when their practices are compromised or when they face divorce or retirement. A flexible treatment approach is essential to allow doctors to function at the highest possible level in their practices. Often, this requires the therapist to move quickly from exploratory to more structured supportive modes, or in some cases to use a brief, solution-oriented approach. The combination of dynamically-oriented group and individual therapy is often the best form of treatment for physicians seeking lasting change. This is best done when the group is composed of high functioning individuals, at least two of whom are physicians.

Many of us begin our psychiatric work as wounded healers. In treating our physician colleagues we are often challenged to recognize and heal our own wounds.

In this process we become better guides on the road to hope and healing. The rewards of our efforts extend well beyond our patients to their families, their patients, and to the profession as a whole. Treating other doctors is a gratifying and honorable task and one in which we often reap the benefits of our own growth as well.

CHAPTER 12

HERMAPHRODITES, GAYS, AND BISEXUALS

W hen I started practice in the 1970s, homosexual behavior was still viewed as a disease by most American psychiatrists. The *Diagnostic and Statistical Manual* (DSM-II) of 1968 (1) included it in the category of "Sexual Deviations." The prevailing psychoanalytic view was that male homosexual behavior developed as a result of being raised by seductive, overbearing mothers and absent or ineffectual fathers (2). There were few clinical studies at this time describing the origins of lesbian orientations. None of my residency clinical conferences included cases focused on gay or lesbian issues. Thus, I began my practice largely unaware of the complex issues facing this population.

Beginning in 1970, gays and lesbians held demonstrations in San Francisco and other cities during the American Psychiatric Association's (APA) annual meetings, challenging its leadership to abandon this biased and unscientific labeling. It took ten years of protests, assisted by the research findings of the Association of Gay and Lesbian Psychiatrists within the APA, before the "deviance" label was omitted from the DSM-III (3). This was the first instance in which a "disease" had been totally eradicated by growing social and political protests. Dr.

Philip Hickey summarized the process: "The homosexual community… managed to liberate themselves from psychiatric oppression" (4).

Similar protests have forced the APA to end its discrimination against transsexuals and transgendered individuals within a rigid binary system. In the DSM-III and DSM-IV (5) these individuals were described as having "Gender Identity Disorders." It was not until the publication of the DSM-V in 2013 that "Dysphoria" replaced "Disorder." In Gender Dysphoria, there is a "marked incongruence between one's experienced/expressed gender and assigned gender, of at least 6 months duration" (6). It is now clear that dysphoria is not, and never was, a disease.

Recent studies in the U.S. indicate that transgender individuals face more bullying in school environments (7), lower percentage of coverage by health insurers (8), high unemployment rates, and higher rates of depression, anxiety, paranoia, and suicidality than in the general population (9). In 32 states there are virtually no statutes outlawing discrimination against transgender people (8).

In Colorado, where I practiced, Gay Pride parades are now held with widespread support and in 2018 Colorado elected the first gay governor in the U.S. While the U.S. Supreme Court upheld the constitutional right to enter into same sex marriages in *Obergefell v. Hodges* (2015), many LGBTQ individuals continue to live their lives in painful isolation. Recently, a bisexual man I treated, despite his helpful therapy, declined to have a carefully disguised case study included in this memoir, fearing negative repercussions involving his extended family.

During my practice years, LGBTQ individuals often got referred to therapists who were themselves out. For this reason, my own experience treating them and their partners has been somewhat limited. In this chapter I describe a successful treatment with an hermaphrodite, during which I gained important insights regarding my own homophobia and sexuality. I also briefly summarize some of my experiences treating gays and bisexuals and discuss how ongoing stigmas involving this population are likely to present challenges for psychiatrists.

Given my profession's shameful history with this population, I have found that disclosing my own heterosexual orientation at the outset of therapy is useful.

During initial consultations, I invite prospective patients to give me feedback if they feel I am being insensitive or biased. I also describe my view that sexual orientation and behavior takes place along a continuum involving heterosexual, homosexual, and bisexual elements, determined by a complex array of biological and environmental factors. I make it clear that I have no interest in either "converting" them or advocating for them in political movements. My job as their therapist is to assist them in understanding and validating their authentic selves.

My upbringing and previous encounters with gays undoubtedly influenced my responses to these patients, especially when they became sexually attracted to me during their treatments. I was raised in a conservative community in upstate New York where homosexuality was both taboo and profoundly misunderstood. Some of my swim team members sneered when talking about "fags," "queers," and "pansies," no doubt reassuring themselves and others of their solid heterosexual attributes. My father was a typical homophobe who combined repulsion with fear and bristled around gays. My mother was more tolerant and spoke of gays as "nice, considerate fellows."

I knew two men in college who didn't come out as gay until decades after graduation. One recalled, at Wesleyan's 50th reunion, how depressed and isolated he felt when rejected by a fraternity as a freshman and later experienced the sadistic teasing of our classmates.

I had one brief homosexual experience involving a minister who fondled me at age nineteen. I had no inkling that he was interested in me sexually. It was very hot that summer in the ghetto where I had volunteered in a vacation church day program. He invited me to sleep in his air-conditioned bedroom to escape the sweltering heat. I awakened at 2:00 a.m. to discover he was fondling me. I was not aroused by his overtures and simply turned over without uttering a word and slept fitfully for the rest of the night. Following the incident, we never discussed it. While I was initially surprised and upset, I felt more confused than traumatized. I later discovered that two of the other male volunteers had been involved with him.

Shortly after this experience, he offered to pay for weekly piano lessons given by a friend of his who had a studio adjacent to Carnegie Recital Hall. I accepted his offer and began lessons with Richard, a brilliant, soft-spoken man in his fifties who taught me to appreciate the melodic nuances of Chopin's *Preludes*. During our final lesson he put his hand on my shoulder and propositioned me. I remember feeling squeamish and politely declining his offer.

161

I have no regrets for having spent time with him. Through him I caught a glimpse of the diverse lifestyles of the gay musical and dance community in Manhattan in the early '60s. My experience with him piqued my curiosity about a world of experiences drastically different from what I had known as a teenager.

What was upsetting about my experience with the minister was his subterfuge and hush money offer, which I didn't fully appreciate at the time. Had this happened a few years later, I am certain I would have confronted him about his subtle predation and refused payment for my lessons. For a brief period after this, I wondered if my decision to sleep in his bed meant I was gay. In my psychoanalysis I uncovered no fantasies about sex with men or boys. What I discovered was my own homophobia, no doubt originating with my father and the prevailing Calvinist views of my early social environment. These biases had little or no basis in my experience and, in fact, were quite contrary to my positive relationship with my piano teacher. Decades later, I resigned from an Episcopal Search Committee which was engaged in heated discussions regarding whether or not to interview gay priests for placement in a suburban parish.

One of my paternal cousins came out in his forties and remained in a loving relationship with his wife until her death. As a couple, they were very active locally and nationally with Quaker committees supporting LGBTQ causes. A talented baritone, he gave me a fine CD he had recorded with songs of the gay experience (10). He and I discussed my work with gay men on several occasions. He described a frustrating experience with a male therapist in the late 1960s, who viewed homosexual behavior as a symptom of arrested development. Hearing about his disappointment regarding this experience increased my sensitivity with patients who were understandably skeptical about entering treatment with a straight psychiatrist.

Andy: A chromosomally male hermaphrodite with anxiety

(I presented this case in a different format at the June 2007 American Psychoanalytic Association Meeting in Denver, Colorado.)

Andy was in his mid-forties when referred by a colleague for treatment of anxiety and guilt feelings which accompanied an intensification of homosexual fantasies which arose during business trips.

While in the grip of these fantasies he described being increasingly confused regarding his sexual orientation and gender identity.

Andy was born with ambiguous external genitalia, a uterus and undescended testicles. His father acquiesced to his mother's wishes to name him Mary Jane and to dress him as a girl until age five. While Andy had no memories of long hair or being dressed as a girl, he did recall as a four-year-old that he could urinate while standing. This must have been quite a feat, given the fact that his "penis" was actually an enlarged clitoris, separated from his urethra. Andy's parents divorced when he was five and during the following year his mother had a number of relationships with men, one of whom fondled him. His mother married his stepfather when Andy was six. During the early weeks of therapy, Andy showed me a prized picture of himself at age six with short hair, dressed in overalls. He was quite certain that his stepfather was responsible for insisting that he be identified as a boy and that his name be changed to Andy, for which he was grateful.

Andy had limited memories of his biological father, with whom he spent long summer vacations on a mountain ranch riding horseback and fishing. He recalled his father telling him that he had worked in a uranium mine and speculated that his radiation exposure might have been responsible for genetic changes leading to Andy's genital ambiguity. His father was never evaluated medically and thus Andy was left in a quandary regarding the causes of his hermaphrodite origins. Andy's summer vacations with his father were cherished times during which he never felt his father questioned his identification as a male. He sensed that he was favored by his father over his two older sisters.

When Andy was fourteen his father died suddenly from a fall related to his work on their ranch. Although he was not present when his dad died, he struggled with guilt feelings that he had not been there to revive and rescue him. Since neither his mother nor his stepfather were able to help him with his mourning, much of our work together focused in this area. Andy's father remained a distant, revered, and idealized figure and a model for his early transference relationship with me, whom he always addressed, with noticeable deference, as "Dr. Graves."

Andy's few positive memories of his mother were intertwined with intense feelings of devaluation, despair, and confusion. She frequently labeled and treated him like a freak, lamented that she had not aborted him and repeated bizarre stories about how people used to

163

mutilate little boys and eat their penises, leaving him feeling that she wanted to destroy what little masculinity he possessed. On the other hand, he recalled her speaking openly with her friends about the special powers of hermaphrodites as deities in ancient mythology. In these situations, he felt like an exotic display piece existing entirely for his mother's aggrandizement. He hated her profound lack of acceptance and empathy for his ambiguity.

From ages eight through twelve Andy engaged in rough and tumble play typical of boys. As a teenager he fantasized about and engaged in heavy petting with girls his age but made no attempts at intercourse due to feelings of embarrassment regarding his genitals. He imagined that his mother had contributed to his genital ambiguity by drinking heavily and using a "toxic douche" during her pregnancy in an attempt to abort him. He denied that his mother's sadistic treatment of him had in any way complicated his marriage relationships.

A few months after his father's death, Andy awakened one night to discover his stepfather lying behind him, naked and erect, spooning him. He smelled alcohol on his breath and knew he was intoxicated. He was surprised by his own sexual arousal and "instant orgasm," after which he eventually fell back asleep. There was no forced activity or penetration and the two of them never spoke of this incident afterwards. Hearing this material reminded me of my own experience with the minister and I empathized with how surprised and frightened he must have been. "Surprised yes; frightened no," he responded. He believed his stepfather was a kind and nurturing man who would *never* want to hurt him.

At age seventeen, with his stepfather's encouragement, Andy underwent a series of several genitourinary surgeries to form a functional penis and external urethra. These procedures also included a hysterectomy and closing of his vaginal opening. Surgery was complicated by abscess formation in his new penis, which evolved into a nearly fatal septicemia and forty-pound weight loss, for which he received last rites. During his recovery from this terrifying odyssey, he recalled handling his anxiety by flirting with and fondling a young nurse. His mother and stepfather rarely visited him during his two-month hospitalization, leaving him with intense feelings of abandonment. Fortunately, an aunt and uncle visited him a few times during his recovery and offered consistent emotional support.

Andy was so exhausted and terrified by his multiple surgeries and complications that he refused to have a surgical repair of his hypospadias, a condition in which the urethra opens on the underside of the penis. As a result, he was obligated to remain seated while urinating, thus reinforcing ongoing doubts about his masculinity. Despite these complications, he was able to achieve and maintain an erection, experience penile pulsations (he was unable to ejaculate) and to have intercourse with women in several different positions. His two wives insisted that they enjoyed intercourse with him, though he frequently doubted their assertions.

Andy was a good student, finished college with honors, and pursued a career which involved considerable travel. He married his first wife in his mid-twenties and was able to have pleasurable intercourse but was unable to conceive children. In his late twenties he had surgery to remove undescended testicles, one of which was cancerous. Not long after this procedure, his wife left him for another man. Andy was devastated by this loss, convinced, despite his wife's denial, that her reason for leaving him was related to his defective sexual apparatus and functioning.

Andy had one helpful psychotherapy experience fifteen years earlier related to his cancer surgery and divorce. His previous therapist was able to review his early surgical procedures, some of which he had repressed. With his therapist's help he was able to discover, to his immense relief, that he was chromosomally male.

An increase in work and travel responsibilities drastically reduced his time at home with his wife and he found himself once again questioning both his sexual orientation and gender identity. Prior to entering treatment with me, his wife had begun to encourage him to pursue surgery to correct his hypospadias. This was a frightening prospect, given his past near-fatal surgical complications.

During the first two years of weekly therapy sessions, Andy related to me in a very ambivalent fashion. We observed a pattern in which he would be quite warm and affable in a session and then show up late for the next one. He began to cancel sessions to accommodate his travel schedule, over which he had considerable control. I began to interpret this ambivalence as manifestations of a complicated father/stepfather transference. If he got close to me, I would desert him, die, or take advantage of him. While he acknowledged these offerings superficially, his responses lacked emotional voltage. I found myself becoming irritated when he retreated to a more deferential mode or canceled a session. I realized that my irritation paralleled my growing affection for him and immersion in our work.

Late in our second year of treatment, I suggested that we meet twice per week to develop more continuity and to better access his ambivalent feelings. I explained that understanding the ebbs and flows in our relationship could be helpful in understanding other relationships and especially his persistent gender identity and sexual orientation issues. Coincidentally, we began to cross paths in the parking lot, the hallways in my building, and in the men's room which, until more recently, he had been avoiding.

I noted that he would sometimes blush during these encounters and asked if perhaps he felt overstimulated or anxious. He initially denied this, but soon thereafter began to admit to intense longings to join me outside the office. Stimulated by my Trout Unlimited wall calendars, he shared vivid fantasies about our fly fishing together and became curious about my favorite streams and best catches. We joked about fishermen's inherent tendencies to lie about length. Soon he began to bring in pictures of hefty rainbow trout he had caught in Alaska, boasting about his catches with broad grins.

While admiring his catches, I commented on how he seemed determined to secure me as a fishing buddy like his father, while at the same time putting me in a position of envying him (some of these fish were as long as a man's arm). Following these interchanges, our therapy sessions became warmer and more spontaneous. My hunch about increasing our frequency was paying off. *Getting me to envy him, was he also hinting at an underlying envy of me?*

A few sessions later he was fifteen minutes late. *Was he distancing from our recent intimacies around fishing? Perhaps provoking me to be critical?* I waited for him to begin. He opened with an apology and shared fantasies that I would be critical for his apparent lack of respect. He recounted defensively that he had gone overtime on an important phone conference with some colleagues. I empathized with the stressful and time-consuming nature of his work. He revealed how pressured he felt about meeting high standards of professionalism in his competitive work environment, fearing that he might lose some important clients. I wondered out loud if he was assuming I would hold him to the same high standards and find his lateness inexcusable. A long pause ensued in which he gazed at me with a faint, seductive smile.

I broke the silence with a conjecture. "I have a feeling you want something from me but are unable to express it. Let me venture a guess. How can you be acceptable to me as a hermaphrodite and to your colleagues as a professional? You're not even allowed to be late for an appointment with me without fear of judgment, expecting me to respond critically as your mother did. It is as if you have to be perfect for me and everyone else to be even minimally acceptable."

He responded by describing his latest dream:

I was in a locker room. I am lying down on a bench on my back. There is a hefty man there like I've fantasized before. He is in boxer shorts—I have no idea why. He took off his shorts and I noticed he had a small penis like mine. His testicles weren't visible.

I immediately recalled a Polaroid photo he had shown me in the first weeks of treatment showing his small penis, a slightly darker vulva, sparse pubic hair, and no testes. *Was I the man in the boxer shorts, or was it Andy, perhaps his stepfather, or all of the above???* I waited...

Andy had awakened anxiously from the dream and said he felt the scene from his dream had happened a long time ago. I asked him for his associations to the figure lying down on the bench. He felt he was in a feminine role on the bench, preparing for sex with the man in the boxer shorts.

I wondered: *Was this his experience of me in our sessions, like a woman on the examining table about to get a pelvic exam, or perhaps a man getting a rectal exam, or a man getting a pelvic?* My musings were disorienting, but I sensed we were getting closer to core issues. Perhaps my disorientation reflected his own.

Just then, I noticed that our time was up. I indicated that this was a very important dream and that we'd want to explore it further next time. As he got up to leave, Andy nearly fell off the couch, as if he'd fallen off the bench in his dream. Having recovered his stance, he blurted out, "If anything ever happens to my wife, I'd try to find an hermaphrodite partner."

Astonished, I exclaimed, "Really?"

"You seem surprised," he responded.

"You've never shared that fantasy before," I added.

"That's not much of a stretch," he retorted, implying any idiot could have grasped his point. We both chuckled as he walked out, saying, "Thank you Dr. Graves" in an annoyingly subservient tone. *Pretty formal for a guy who is seducing me,* I thought.

Andy opened our next session by saying that he had "forgotten" his dream. Before I was able to inquire about this, he launched into a proud recounting of his research regarding the details of corrective surgery for hypospadias at Johns Hopkins. I congratulated him on his courage, given that he had entered therapy terrified about having further surgery. His main motivation for surgery, he said, was that he was unable to urinate standing up, an impediment which made him feel "humiliated, impotent, and feminized," especially when fly fishing with his buddies.

I recalled the gay demonstrations outside the APA meetings in San Francisco. Here I was, twenty-five years later, working with a hermaphrodite with fluid gender identity who had repeatedly sought out ambisexual experiences in fantasy. I wondered: was I working on the side of liberation or of oppression? My doubts about the focus of our work sometimes haunted me. I would simply have to take my cues from him as to how to proceed.

I returned from these questions to the more concrete clinical issue before us and inquired, "Might your decision to explore surgery at this time in any way be related to our recent sessions and your recent dream?"

He immediately recalled his dream and said, "I just saw a tape of Drew Carey's jokes describing being molested by his uncle as a teenager and then attempting suicide."

"That doesn't sound like much of a joke," I commented. "You must have really empathized with the teenager on that tape. You've been yearning for empathy all your life from someone who could really understand your experiences."

"I thought the heavyset man in the dream could really empathize with me," he offered.

"It's interesting that in your dream the man you view as empathic is also apparently sexually interested in you," I conjectured. I wondered if he was talking about his stepfather or me, or perhaps both.

"I'm not attracted to men generally...I'm reluctant to believe I'm homosexual," he replied.

"This must have been a really uncomfortable dream for you to experience and share here," I said, thinking about his recent anxiety regarding our increased sessions.

"Yes it was...A few days ago I was watching portions of *The Exorcist* and I felt like electric shocks were going through my whole body."

"I wonder if you're suggesting that homosexual feelings make you feel devilish or wicked." I became aware that I, like Andy, tended to conflate meanings involving homosexuality with those involving the more complex web of ambisexuality experienced by hermaphrodites.

"It seems contrary to nature," he replied. "I spent my whole childhood thinking I was cursed. Being a hermaphrodite felt like a punishment."

"A punishment?"

"Yes, a punishment... for my mother's alcoholism."

"You were being punished for _her_ sins?"

"Yes, I would ask myself over and over, why _me_...why _me_?"

At this point he looked very sad, on the verge of tears. I reflected this back to him and we sat in silence for a while.

"Your whole childhood must have been horribly oppressive and lonely. What an awful legacy your mother left you with her devaluations. You continue to struggle to exorcise yourself of these feelings and negative attributes more than forty years later." Another long silence followed. This time his tears flowed copiously. I had an impulse to reach out and hug him.

Andy ended the pause by explaining that the boxer shorts in his dream reminded him of what doctors wear and that the locker room bench reminded him of an examining table. I wondered again if this reflected his experience of me in therapy. I asked, "I wonder how you feel about how I view you in these sessions?"

"The perfect situation," he said, "would be to have an hermaphrodite doctor." At first I was stunned, then the full import of what he was saying hit me.

"So you wish I were hermaphrodite like you so I could really empathize with you in our work together?"

"That's a tough one. I wouldn't want to put a curse on you. But it would be nice to have a mate who is also hermaphrodite. It would be kind of nice if she looked like Shania Twain, kind of a 'she-male.'"

Confused and awash with ambiguity, I ventured, "Suppose I was a hermaphrodite and didn't feel cursed. Then I would be able to help you be comfortable with both your anatomy and ultimately with your whole being." I realized that we were treading on complicated turf here, conflating sexual relationships with the need for a truly empathic therapist. Then I realized that he was expressing a wish for an identical twin, the ultimate doctor-mate and empathic partner. The fact that his wishes were sexualized was not the main issue. What was important was his increasing comfort with being open and sharing core fantasies about us in the present.

Andy had told me early on in therapy about a childhood friend, Chucky, who accepted him for who he was, without judgment. "Chucky," I said, "was a true friend. He treated you like a regular boy and taught you the ropes. You were comfortable talking with him about sex, like you're feeling more comfortable here speaking with me." Our session ended spontaneously. We arose and shook hands, this time without the "Dr. Graves" formality.

Over the next four years, Andy worked steadily in his twice weekly therapy. We ultimately were able to discuss, via his dreams and associations, his wishes to have sexual relations with me both as male and female with interchangeable roles for each of us. In listening to him and responding to his flirtations, I struggled to visualize myself as a female with male genitalia and *vice versa*. At times his fantasies were more conventionally gay, with me as his gay partner. At first I was uncomfortable with these "gender benders" and struggled with my own prudishness. I recalled that Plato, in his *Symposium,* had dealt with this issue some 2,400 years ago. In this essay on the varieties of love, Plato had described hermaphrodites as a third gender, apart from males and females:

"(There was) in those days, a being which was half male and half female…they actually tried…to scale the heights of heaven and set upon the gods…Zeus took counsel with the other gods and cut them all in half (leaving) each half with a desperate yearning for the other, and they ran together and flung their arms around each other's necks, and asked for nothing more than to be rolled into one. So you see, gentlemen, how far back we can trace our innate love for one another, and how this love is always trying to reintegrate our former nature, to make two into one, and to bridge the gulf between one human being and another" (11).

While I never shared this passage with Andy, Plato's recounting of Greek mythology grounded me with a better understanding of the intensity of Andy's isolated brokenness and yearnings for me as a full partner in becoming a whole person. His early experiences of denigration by his mother, his stepfather's molestation, his near-fatal surgical complications, and our pervasive cultural insistence on clear-cut binaries had sliced him in half emotionally. His very soul was bisected and bleeding. By learning to imagine multiple gender roles for myself, corresponding with his fantasies, I increased my empathic range regarding his complex sexuality and compelling search for wholeness. I was learning, as Plato wrote, "to bridge the gulf."

As we continued to address and empathize with his sense of isolation and estrangement as a complex sexual being, Andy began to report significant improvements in his sexual and emotional intimacy with his wife. Their sexual relationship became more spontaneous and less fraught with anxiety related to his former concerns about homosexuality, which he now saw as outmoded.

Andy went on to have corrective surgery repairing his hypospadias, thus enabling him for the first time as an adult to urinate standing up, proudly and forcefully, like the man he'd always hoped to be. Three months after he ended therapy, he called me and reported exuberantly that his marriage was in good shape and that he was doing well at work. I congratulated him on his progress. Then the punch line came: "Check out my trout pictures in the sporting magazine article." I already had. In the photos Andy was grinning ear to ear. He was holding a monster rainbow trout.

My therapy experience with Andy and a growing research literature on the biological bases of homosexuality in the 1990s (12, 13) helped prepare me for my later therapeutic encounters with gay and bisexual men. I also benefitted from reading the seminal work of Richard Isay, *Becoming Gay: The Journey to Self-Acceptance.* Isay, a divorced gay psychoanalyst, described his own odyssey of early homosexual attractions, retreat into heterosexual marriage, failed conversion therapy, and struggles with depression related to the suppression of his authentic self. Prompted by his own personal journey, he described the awkward process of coming out, wherein self-loathing is jettisoned:

"Coming out alleviates the anxiety and depression caused by the sense of inauthenticity that arises from hiding or disguising oneself" (14).

He was able to use his own personal experiences to enrich and inform his practice in working with homosexuals. The men he treated emerged from the shadow of depression by uniting, after decades of disconnection, their authentic selves in their new modes of gay relationships.

I also read the compelling, often wrenching biography of Leonard Bernstein describing how the renowned conductor-composer agonized in his sixties about time running out before he could live authentically (15). In his last few years, Bernstein ultimately separated from his wife and engaged in openly gay relationships, but at a significant emotional and physical (he became addicted to pain medications) cost to himself, his family, and friends. Reading this account helped me better empathize with the dilemmas of some of my older bisexual patients who continued to struggle with social stigma and the oppressive fixation on sexual binaries operating in American culture.

In working with Andy and with gay and bisexual men I realized, once again, what a privilege it is to be a therapist. These men taught me how to be more comfortable with my own loving feelings towards my men friends, especially those in my men's group where we have learned to be more openly affectionate. Now I can give and receive a full-bodied, two-armed hug with another man without tensing up. I can also admire other attractive men without feeling chagrin or questioning my own heterosexuality.

I learned that we all exist and live along a bisexual spectrum and that where we find ourselves often depends on social context as well as biology. The choices we make regarding the gender and orientation of our sexual partners are also dependent on our age, maturation level, and marital status. For example, married bisexuals in their late sixties with adult children and grandchildren most likely perceive a narrower range of viable sexual partners compared with divorced gay men in their forties.

In conducting these treatments, I was also able to broaden my perceptions of myself as a sexual being. I became increasingly comfortable imagining myself at various times as their homosexual lovers and, in the case of Andy, as his female/hermaphrodite lover. No longer bound to a repressive binary system, I came to accept a surprising degree of fluidity and ambiguity in myself. To paraphrase C.G. Jung: If we don't grow in the course of providing therapy, we probably haven't made a deep and helpful connection. We grow while helping others grow.

CHAPTER 13

CHANGES IN THE FIELD OF PSYCHIATRY

Psychiatric practice has changed dramatically since I began my training in 1972. The most significant change has involved an evolution from a pathological, concept-based theory of mental functioning, originating with Freud, to a more brain-based model, deriving from multiple domains of neuroscience research. New developments in brain scanning technology and neurophysiology gave birth to the field of cognitive neuroscience, which in turn allowed neuropsychologists and psychiatrists to ask and answer fundamental questions about the brain's processing of affects, traumatic stress, mood changes, and memory.

In parallel with these developments, there have been significant advances in psychodynamic therapies, psychopharmacology, and the development of cognitive behavioral (CBT) and dialectical behavioral therapy (DBT). Clinical research in the past fifteen years has increasingly focused on mechanisms of resilience and healthy adaptations to stress, a change which has recently been called "Positive Psychiatry," to distinguish it from its former focus on pathology.

More women have advanced to leadership positions in the field, improving the range of empathic understanding, as well as much needed

173

gender-based research involving major psychiatric disorders. An increasingly competitive health insurance industry and the creation of managed care practice monitoring has had significant impacts on my patients and practice, many of which have been stressful. Congruent with these changes, the nature of residency training and how psychiatrists are viewed have evolved in ways I could never have anticipated.

ADVANCES IN
PSYCHODYNAMIC THEORY AND PRACTICE:

During the 1970s and 80s a quiet revolution unfolded involving innovative concepts of psychoanalytic theory and technique. Heinz Kohut broke away from Freud's focus on sexual and aggressive drives and developed a new and cogent psychology of the self, based on the vicissitudes of parental empathy and how empathic deficits came to be played out in a variety of transferences seen in psychoanalysis (1). The patient's response to empathic failures by the therapist could now be used as leverage for healing early developmental deficits and traumas.

In Britain, Bowlby, Winnicott, Klein, and Fairbairn's clinical studies revealed that the fundamental need to attach oneself to a nurturing caretaker or friend took precedence over the libidinal drives which Freud had emphasized. A whole new landscape of psychotherapy techniques emerged from the fertile soil of these attachment and object-relations theories (2). With these developments, the focus of therapy expanded from Oedipal conflicts to the quality and consistency of empathic nurturing relationships, encompassing both conflicts and deficits. The real relationship between therapist and patient, along with the concept of a new developmental object relationship with one's therapist, became just as important to understand as classical transference phenomena (3).

A decade later, the works of Mardi Horowitz with traumatic war injuries (4) and Judith Herman with victims of physical and sexual abuse (5) provided practitioners for the first time with coherent models for understanding the whole spectrum of post-traumatic stress disorders, from acute brief stress reactions to profound, psychotic-level dissociative states and identity disorders. These advances enabled me to treat scores of individuals with more effective and focused dynamic therapy, many who had previously attained only modest gains with more generic versions.

I sought my own personal supervision on a monthly basis from more eclectic practitioners who helped me implement these new approaches. It was a relief to cast off the illusory veil of "analytic objectivity" and to relate to my patients in a more egalitarian, warm, and engaging manner. My professional identity became more congruent with who I am as a person. One of my patients, whom I had seen since I was a resident, said, "You seem so much more relaxed lately." Freed from analytic dogma in the 1980s, I felt I could truly enjoy my work.

In 1999 I decided that I needed to better integrate the newly emerging psychoanalytic theories and techniques into my practice. I enrolled in the Psychodynamic Psychotherapy Training Program offered by the Denver Institute for Psychoanalysis and taught by many of my colleagues. In this two-year program I took four hours of seminars per week and treated two intensive psychotherapy cases under supervision with successful outcomes. With it, I developed more confidence in the validity and relevance of psychodynamic therapy for my general practice. I learned that many of the difficulties I had experienced in my own psychoanalysis were based primarily on the misapplication of an outmoded theory of mind.

THE MOVEMENT FROM PATHOLOGY TO POSITIVE ADAPTATION:

Beginning in the 1950s, some of the best minds in American psychology and psychiatry began to transfer their focus of inquiry from psychopathology to processes of healthy adaptation. In 1954 the humanistic psychologist Abraham Maslow published a groundbreaking volume in which he described the Hierarchy of Needs, best remembered by a pyramid diagram with physiological needs at its base, rising upwards with layers of safety, love and belonging, esteem with self-actualization and self-transcendence at the apex (6). I became interested in Maslow's writings while I was at Union Seminary working on a term paper on the ego-ideal and self-actualization.

On a whim, I sent Maslow a draft of my paper and was delighted to receive a helpful handwritten critique within two weeks, encouraging further research in this area. Not long after receiving this, I decided to "self-actualize" by taking the MCATS and applying to Columbia University to complete my pre-medical studies. I was impressed not only by Maslow's accessibility, but also by the fact that he had focused on studying healthy, successful individuals such as Albert Einstein and Eleanor Roosevelt. His comment that "studying crippled specimens...can only yield a cripple psychology" left a lasting impression (6).

George Vaillant's participation in the Grant Study of Harvard undergraduates led to his developing a hierarchy of defenses arranged in sequence from least to most adaptive, including: psychotic, immature, intermediate, and mature. Examples of mature defenses include altruism, anticipation, humor, sublimation, and suppression. For Vaillant, defenses are dynamic and changeable over time and readily subject to modification in therapy (7). Using his perspectives, I found that my focus shifted from "looking down" to investigate maladaptive coping patterns, to joining the patient in "looking up" to review their most effective coping skills. I reframed my inquiries by asking what had interfered with their more adaptive skills recently. This had the effect of boosting their psychological resilience by reinforcing their inner strengths.

Recently, Dr. Dilip Jeste has described many of these developments as "Positive Psychiatry." Jeste traces how newer psychiatric treatment modalities emphasize maximizing wellbeing of body, mind, and spirit by focusing on resilience, adaptive coping, optimism, personal mastery, and developing a healthy spirituality (8). It has been gratifying to read his works and realize how they have validated my attempts to integrate spirituality and religious faith in therapy.

THE INTEGRATION OF CONCEPT-BASED PSYCHOLOGY WITH BRAIN-BASED PSYCHOLOGY:

In 1895, Freud wrote a letter to his friend Wilhelm Fliess outlining a "Project for a Scientific Psychology" in which he sought to integrate what he had learned about the human nervous system from fifteen years of basic research with his more recent discoveries regarding hysteria, including the mechanisms underlying repression, perception, memory, and consciousness (9). In what has remained an ongoing mystery in the history of science, Freud abandoned research in this area for the more pressing demands of his growing clinical practice. His "Project" remained an object of both titillation and hope among three generations of psychoanalysts who sought to buttress their "soft" psychological science with the "hard" findings of brain research.

These hopes were partially fulfilled a century later in the 1990s, "The Decade of the Brain," which was financially supported through a bipartisan resolution of Congress. Our former department chairman at the University of Colorado, Dr. Herbert Pardes, in his role as director of the National Institutes of Mental Health, coordinated dozens of public and private basic science research projects on the causes of brain and spinal cord diseases. By the end of the decade, substantial progress had been made in the development of functional MRI neural imaging and computational neuroscience; the understanding of neuroplasticity, critical periods of neural development, the neurophysiology of memory, second generation antidepressants and anti-psychotics, the neural pathways in alcoholism; and the discovery of genetic mutations responsible for Huntington's Disease, Amyotrophic Lateral Sclerosis, and Rhett Syndrome (10). Freud would have been pleased and excited by these developments.

Erik Kandel in his research on the giant sea snail elucidated the mechanisms of short and long-term memory and how the flow of information in the snail's neurons could be modified by learning. He was able to show that sensory neurons in the snail actually *grew new dendrites in response to repeated stimulation.* For these discoveries, Kandel, initially trained as an analyst, shared the Nobel Prize in Physiology or Medicine in 2000. He summarized his groundbreaking research:

"We three have taken the first steps in linking mind to molecules by determining how the biochemistry of signaling within and between nerve cells is related to mental processes and to mental disorders....The biology of mind bridges the sciences—concerned with the natural world—and the humanities—concerned with the meaning of human experience. Insights that come from this new synthesis will not only improve our understanding of psychiatric and neurological disorders, but will also lead to a deeper understanding of ourselves" (11).

It is hard to appreciate the contagious enthusiasm that these findings generated in both the scientific community as well in the lives of patients with neurologic diseases. Neurology, which had previously been viewed as a diagnostic specialty, now found itself on the cutting edge of new and exciting clinical research. The discovery of Brain Derived Neurotropic Factor (BDNF), a protein which has since been associated with neurogenesis and dendritic sprouting, generated further waves of excitement (12). The emerging concept of "neuroplasticity" (i.e., that nerve cells can grow new connections) offered a new sense of hope, even to patients who barely understood its scientific basis. Patients with brain injuries and serious mental illness could look forward, at last, to more hopeful treatment options.

Inspired by these findings, I took a position as consultant on the Closed Head Injury Unit at Craig Rehabilitation Hospital in Denver, where I worked from 1989 to 1993 with Dr. Alan Weintraub, a neuro-rehabilitation specialist, and a team of neurologists, neurosurgeons, and neuropsychologists associated with the Colorado Neurological Institute. I treated many young patients who had sustained acute brain injuries from falls, athletic traumas, and automobile accidents. In this setting, I assisted rehabilitation efforts by prescribing novel medications for agitation, anxiety, and depression. In addition I provided psycho-education with patients and their families and continued to treat some individuals for several years as outpatients. These were fascinating and challenging cases in which I was able to use a combination of cutting-edge neuroscience research along with supportive individual, couples, and family therapies.

EXPANDED OPTIONS IN PSYCHOPHARMACOGY

When I first began practice in 1975, psychiatrists had a small toolkit of medications consisting of four categories: antipsychotics, anti-anxiety and sedatives, antidepressants, and the recently discovered mood stabilizer, lithium carbonate. There were only three or four options to prescribe in each class of medications and many of them had severe side effects, making adherence a formidable obstacle. In med school our psychopharmacology professor admitted that little was known about the pathophysiology of mental disease or precisely how many of these drugs worked. The psychopharmacology sections in our text by Goodman and Gilman occupied less than a hundred pages (13). Today's leading text by Stephen Stahl includes over one thousand pages of detailed descriptions, including several categories of neurotransmitters, neuromodulators, transporters, receptors, ion channels, genetics, and the postulated neural circuitry of all the major psychiatric disorders (14). To keep abreast of this explosion of knowledge, I took 25 to 30 hours of psychopharmacology courses every two years for the past forty years.

A major breakthrough came with the introduction of Prozac (fluoxetine) by Eli Lilly in 1986. This new class of selective serotonin reuptake inhibitors (SSRIs) represented the first useful alternative to tricyclics and MAO inhibitors in decades for treating depression. Prozac had virtually no cardiac side effects compared with older antidepressants and was generally well-tolerated with initial low dosages. Within a few years it had replaced Valium as the most widely used psychiatric medication, with annual sales in the billions. Since the advent of Prozac, over a dozen serotonin receptor subtypes have been discovered, prompting development of five newer drugs in this category alone.

Peter Kramer's best-selling *Listening to Prozac (15)* summarized how its use may actually alter personality functioning in chronically depressed patients. I corroborated some of his findings in my own practice, where some individuals I had viewed as insecure, passive, or masochistic developed a more solid sense of self along with being more assertive in their relationships. For many, including myself, the liberation from chronic depression has been life-changing.

Beginning in 2000, innovations in brain scan technology revealed that unipolar and bipolar depressed patients had decreased volumes in their hippocampus, a seahorse-shaped temporal lobe brain region associated with encoding working memory. These changes probably occur under the influence of stress hormones (16). Significantly, the hippocampal volume loss increases in direct proportion to the length of untreated depression. This finding explains the short-term memory deficits seen in depressive episodes which lift as patients improve with antidepressants. We now understand the mechanism for this is related to medication effects which increase brain-derived neurotropic factor (BDNF), which facilitates the "sprouting" of dendrites (17).

These findings provided an excellent scientific rationale for encouraging my depressed patients to continue their antidepressants for extended periods rather than stopping after a few months of treating a single episode, with a high risk of recurrence. By explaining this process in detail, my patients' medication compliance improved along with their overall functioning and quality of life.

Following the introduction of lithium by Ronald Fieve in 1970 for the treatment of bipolar disorder, neurologists observed that some patients taking anticonvulsants for seizures who were also bipolar demonstrated noticeable decreases in their mood swings (18). Since several anticonvulsants worked by augmenting the action of the inhibitory neurotransmitter gamma amino butyric acid (GABA), it was postulated that these agents were dampening the "kindling" of excitable moods seen in manic episodes. Several anticonvulsants are currently in use for treating bipolar disorder, including carbamazepine

(Tegretol), sodium valproate (Depakote), and lamotrigine (Lamictal). Patients who previously were unable to tolerate the multiple serious side effects of lithium carbonate are now using these mood stabilizers, avoiding costly hospitalizations and leading more productive lives.

In the 1990s and early 2000s second and third generation "atypical" antipsychotic medications with complex dual actions of blocking dopamine receptors and partial activation of certain serotonin receptors have added significantly to the toolkit of medicines for both schizophrenia and bipolar disorder. While there is no "magic bullet" among these newer compounds, the greater number of choices offers hope for both psychiatrists and their patients for assuring more stable functioning, particularly for bipolar patients who have a mixture of depression *and* mania in the same episode and rapid cyclers with four or more mood episodes per year.

Psychiatrists now understand that prescriptions of carefully-dosed medication combinations can also be very helpful. For example, a combination of fluoxetine and olanzapine, Symbiax, was approved by the FDA for both bipolar disorder and treatment resistant depression in several dose combinations (19). Likewise, venlafaxine (Effexor), a dual-action medication acting on serotonin and norepinephrine receptors, has been quite effective in treating depression, generalized anxiety disorder, panic disorder, and social phobias.

As of this writing, one of the most exciting developments in antidepressant treatment involves ketamine, an N-methyl D-aspartate (NMDA) receptor antagonist (also used as an anesthetic) active in the medial prefrontal cortex. Clinical trials have demonstrated that this agent, used in conjunction with an oral antidepressant, can reduce suicidal symptoms within hours. Significant side effects include sedation and dissociation, requiring prescribing physicians to observe the patient for at least two hours following administration.

THE DEVELOPMENT OF
NEW TREATMENT MODALITIES: CBT AND DBT

Cognitive Behavioral Therapy (CBT) and Dialectical Behavior Therapy (DBT) are now such a standard part of therapeutic interventions that it is difficult to imagine a time when they did not exist. Both CBT and DBT were developed from philosophies and spiritual practices which have been known for centuries. The principles underlying

CBT derive from the ideas of Stoic Philosophy, beginning with the writings of the Roman slave, Epictetus (55-135 A.D.). Sharon Lebell's rendering of Epictetus' *Enchiridion*, contains many passages which seem strikingly modern:

"Things themselves don't hurt or hinder us. Nor do other people... it is our attitudes and reactions that give us trouble...We cannot choose our external circumstances, but we can always choose how we respond to them....By facing the realities of death, infirmity, loss, and disappointment, you free yourself of illusions and false hopes and you avoid miserable, envious thoughts" (20).

Dr. Aaron Beck, building on these foundations and the writings of Alfred Adler and Albert Ellis, originated the technique of cognitive behavioral therapy (CBT) which challenged the very foundations of psychoanalysis. Whereas classical analysis starts with the assumption that unconscious conflicts drive neurotic symptom-formation, cognitive psychology posits that one can alter the course of mental disorders by *changing the ways in which we think about ourselves*, our relationships, and our views of the future (21). CBT focuses on identifying and correcting irrational thought patterns, after which we are able to see our situations more realistically, thus enabling us to engage in more productive problem-solving.

I first read Beck's works in the mid-1980s when I saw several patients with intractable anxiety who arrived with histories of trying most of the tranquillizers in the PDR and some form of analytic therapy with little improvement. Many of these patients were immobilized by their view that that problems and solutions *came from outside themselves*. They sought a "magic cure" from prescription medicines and were inevitably disappointed. By helping them understand how irrational their thinking was, they began to use their own repertoire of adaptive coping skills and became noticeably less anxious.

The development of Dialectical Behavior Therapy (DBT) in the late 1980s by psychologist Marsha Linehan is a story of triumph over intense personal pain. Linehan described how a religious experience at age twenty-four transformed her life from multiple episodes of suicidal despair to the emergence of self-love and compassion. At age seventeen she was hospitalized in Hartford's Institute of Living for over two years. Misdiagnosed with schizophrenia, she was given Thorazine, ECT treatments, and psychoanalytic therapy for disorganized thinking, suicidal depression, and impulsive behavior, including head banging.

181

Following her discharge, she was diagnosed with Borderline Personality Disorder and sought out more helpful therapies.

While studying psychology at Loyola University she went to a Catholic chapel to pray. Suddenly the crucifix began to shimmer and she had a powerful revelation in which she found herself exclaiming, "*I love myself.*" In a *New York Times* interview she recalled, "I developed a therapy that provides the things I needed for so many years and never got" (22).

Whereas CBT focuses primarily on correcting cognitive distortions, DBT focuses on how overly intense emotional-reactivity can lead to self-destructive behavior. If one can accept and transform these negative feelings into positive ones by deliberate refocusing, the resulting negative behaviors can be replaced with deliberate "opposite actions." It was Linehan's genius to combine Buddhist loving-kindness meditation, the recognition and taming of overly intense feelings, practical problem-solving, cognitive behavioral therapy, and assertiveness training. Originally developed to treat individuals with borderline personality and chronic suicidality, DBT has since been applied successfully to treat PTSD, substance abuse, and bipolar spectrum disorders (23). Beginning with her own personal efforts at self-cure, Linehan has left a legacy of considerable value and hope for therapists and their patients.

ADVANCES OF WOMEN IN PSYCHIATRY:

Gender bias, until the late twentieth century, was as prevalent in psychiatry as it was in all the other medical specialties. I became aware of this early in my own practice when I treated a woman professional in her thirties. At one point I loaned her a book on psychotherapy practices. She graciously accepted the book and about three weeks later returned it with a sharp retort, "You *do* recall that all the chapters were written by *men.*" I was chagrined when I realized I'd never given it a thought. Her brief comment challenged my patriarchal assumptions head-on. I had read many groundbreaking articles and books by Anna Freud, Frieda Fromm-Reichmann, Melanie Klein, and Karen Horney, yet it had never occurred to me to recommend any of them to her.

Gender bias in medical practice and research has only recently been addressed by our profession. Mariette DiChristina, the first female editor-in-chief of *Scientific American,* published a special issue on sex and gender in September 2017 entitled, "This is not a Women's Issue: Why the New Science of Sex and Gender Matters for Everyone"

(24). Several articles in this issue describe how pervasive gender bias in animal and human research, including a predominance of male subjects, has resulted in negative treatment outcomes in women.

A glaring example of this is how the developers of zolpidem (Ambien) knew for years that side effects were much more prominent in women than men. Nevertheless, the initial marketing recommended equal starting doses for men and women with the result that some "5.7 million women reported driving impairment eight hours after taking the drug." It took several years of patient complaints before dosing recommendations were altered (25).

In my residency training class, there was one woman out of a total of fifteen trainees. During the last thirty years, recruiting efforts have led to gender equality in medical student classes and psychiatry residency programs. The content of my training in the early 1970s contained frequent gender biases, including the diagnosis of "hysterical neurosis" which equated "excessive emotionality" with being female, whereas traits of deception and aggression seen in anti-social personality were reserved primarily for men. We now know that both men and women can manifest these traits.

The presence of women in positions of leadership within psychiatry has been slowly increasing. Women did not attain the American Psychiatric Association (APA) presidency until 1985 when Dr. Carol Nadelson became the first to be elected. Since then there have been twelve other women presidents. Women currently comprise 11 out of 36 total active members of the editorial board of the *American Journal of Psychiatry*. Taking its cues from Dr. Nadelson's stellar career, there is no doubt that the next generation of psychiatrists will include more equal representation of women in leadership positions at all levels of training, professional associations, research, publications, and practice.

INSURANCE CHANGES AND MANAGED CARE

As a resident, I was taught that direct payment for my services was an important part of the therapeutic relationship and that difficulties with payment often reflected a variety of intra-psychic conflicts. Regular payment was viewed as evidence for my patient's commitment to making substantive changes. Many of my early patients paid me in full, as insurance coverage for mental health treatment was limited. During the first five years of my practice, I wrote my own statements and handed them to patients at the beginning of each month. Payments for the previous month's treatment were due in full on the fifteenth of the next month. If their income decreased for any reason, I asked patients to inform me as soon as possible so we could make adjustments. Patients were usually charged for non-cancelled appointments unless I was able to schedule someone else during their hour. These policies were given to patients in writing at the end of the first session and any questions regarding them were discussed in the second session. As long as I communicated clear expectations about payments and discussed them openly, my collection rate for services remained close to ninety-five percent. Since my training took place in an outpatient clinic serving an indigent population, I was accustomed to discounting my fees to enable motivated patients to initiate and continue treatment. During my first ten years of practice (1975-1985) my charges per 50-minute outpatient session doubled to $100. In the late 1980s it became clear that medical charges in many specialties were outpacing national inflation rates. The American Psychiatric Association, in response to these trends, strongly urged its members to curtail fee increases. I supported this policy and complied with it for many years.

Around the same time, health insurance companies, with intense pressure from patient advocacy groups, began to add mental health treatment to their covered services. Psychiatric disorders with a clear biologic basis were finally mandated for coverage by The Mental Health Parity Act in 1996, which required reimbursement at the same rate as other medical treatments (26). With this increase in coverage, many of my newer patients entered treatment with the expectation that their insurance would cover most of my charges. While some patients avoided insurance billing to protect confidential information, the majority asked me to bill their insurance companies for reimbursement.

These changes obviously benefited my patients but complicated my billing procedures significantly and added to my work stress. As a result, I hired a mental health billing specialist who understood the Byzantine details of diagnostic and therapy procedure codes. The issue of payments, which began as a direct doctor-patient interaction, had become a contractual agreement between myself, my patients, and six major insurance companies. I sometimes waited up to four months to get paid at a rate that was discounted by a third of what I had previously charged. I handled these changes by increasing my total number of patient hours and taking on more part-time consulting positions.

CHANGES IN THE FIELD OF PSYCHIATRY

Around 1990, my practice stress level was becoming intolerable. Part of this related to increased therapy hours with high-acuity patients. A larger portion involved the increased complexities of insurance billing with its demands to justify my services as reasonable and necessary, sometimes to Utilization Review (UR) specialists who had little or no clinical training. After discovering this, I refused to spend time reviewing cases with anyone except those with clinical training.

Just as I began to feel more adept at addressing these hurdles, "managed care" made its entry into the world of medical practice with its ten-page legal contracts, mounds of paperwork, legions of practice monitors, and even lower payments for services. None of the time spent in preparing four-page treatment updates for every eight sessions or speaking with UR persons was reimbursable. When some patients complained about the loss of confidentiality, I offered to complete the treatment update forms during sessions and attempted, reluctantly, to make it part of their therapy. We quickly learned that time spent justifying the therapy was detracting from doing the therapy.

Under managed care, prior authorizations for medications required up to twenty minutes of non-reimbursable phone time in which I had to repeat the same confidential information to two or three people before connecting with the pharmacist who made the final decision. Approval took up to seventy-two hours, sometimes resulting in missed doses and relapses.

As I struggled to cope with managed care, I became aware of more subtle changes going on with respect to my professional identity. I was now being described as a "provider," and my patients as "consumers" of care, not unlike a vacuum cleaner salesman and his customers. The doctor-patient relationship, once based on mutual trust and a long tradition of ethical professionalism, was being transformed into a contractual arrangement where market forces set the rules. In a fascinating study, William May contrasted the covenantal with the contractual relationship:

"The contractual approach tends to reduce professional obligation to self-interested minimalism, *quid pro quo*...Do no more for your patients than what the contract calls for...In spirit, contract and covenant differ markedly. Contracts are external; covenants are internal to the parties involved...Covenants cut deeper into personal identity" (27).

Reading this helped me better grasp the depths of my frustration. Managed care was not merely cumbersome and costly. It consist-

185

ently devalued my profession, my patients, and our treatment relationship. After discussing these issues in detail with several patients, I decided to terminate all my insurance and managed-care contracts.

Patients who needed both medications and psychotherapy had a difficult choice to make: find an available psychiatrist who also did psychotherapy, or split treatment between a master's level therapist and a psychiatrist "medication manager." The second option had its own set of inherent difficulties, since many psychiatrists, recently deprived of their dual roles, were reluctant to collaborate with professionals they viewed as less experienced competitors. Psychiatrists were also afraid of increased exposure to liability since they were still viewed by litigants and their attorneys as "captains of the treatment team" with deep pockets.

During this period, average hospital stays dwindled from two to three weeks per admission to three to five days. Hospitalization of acutely depressed, manic, or psychotic patients was focused mainly on rapid tranquillization, reduction of suicidal impulses, and delusional content. Hospitals began to pressure "providers" to discharge patients prematurely, including some with ongoing risk for suicide. Many of these patients were discharged to stressful environments unchanged from those existing at the time of admission. This put me and my colleagues in serious ethical, clinical, and legal binds. As a result, several psychiatrists I knew resigned from hospital medical staffs, handing over the care of their outpatients to a new class of professionals, the psychiatric "hospitalists."

Hospitalists, in my experience, fell into two categories: older, experienced psychiatrists who were burned out from struggling with managed care; and recent graduates from residency programs who needed steady income and enjoyed the challenge of working with high levels of acuity. As a whole, they were high-functioning practitioners who worked in pressure-cookers with rapidly revolving doors.

Since my training and treatment philosophy emphasized continuity of care, I often sought to visit my recently hospitalized patients as a "consultant." This was fine in principle. However, hospitalists who cared for my patients were often too busy to speak with me personally regarding pertinent clinical information. Because of these difficulties with continuity, I ultimately decided not to accept any new patients with histories of hospital treatment. Those patients I had seen for years who had required several hospitalizations I gradually transferred to other practitioners. My patients and I mourned the loss of continuity.

CHANGES IN RESIDENCY TRAINING
AND PROFESSIONAL IDENTITY

Beginning in the early 1980s I supervised third-and fourth-year psychiatry residents in the University of Colorado program on their inpatient, outpatient, individual, group and marital therapies. Their case presentations sounded familiar as they were grounded in psychoanalytic theory and treatment techniques. The resident's professional identity, like mine, was that of a medically trained dynamic psychotherapist who was also an expert in the fields of psychopharmacology, psychosomatic illnesses, and consultation-liaison psychiatry. Residents understood the concepts of therapeutic alliance, transference, countertransference and various levels of defenses and interpretive techniques at least on a theoretical level.

Over the years, changes in training and the economic factors discussed above have produced specialists in neuroscience who practice an eclectic array of brief psychotherapies such as CBT, DBT, or Interpersonal Therapy, depending on patients' presentations. More recent residents have only a superficial acquaintance with psychodynamic issues which, despite the fact that they are found in all psychotherapies, are now relegated to elective courses taken in the fourth year or via the post-graduate Psychodynamic Psychotherapy Training Program. Most of the residents I supervised in the last ten years of my practice participated in this program.

Due to federal funding cutbacks in residency training, residents now must carry much heavier caseloads generating billable hours to support their training stipends. This increase necessitates decreasing psychotherapy session length from forty-five to thirty minutes to allow for on-site faculty supervision. Medical record keeping is entirely computerized and often done during sessions, thus altering the whole ambience of face-to-face interactions and making it more difficult to observe and comment on subtle changes in patient dynamics and body language. Billing functions are performed by specialists who work in an office outside the clinic so residents gain little understanding of how economic issues impact their patients' treatment.

Because of the higher stress levels involved in providing services, residents struggle with insomnia, anxiety, and guilt about spending more time away from primary relationships, spouses, and children. In their supervision I found myself increasingly focused on

187

discussing burnout issues and strategies for increasing self-care. Many residents were anxious about paying off massive debts following graduation, which were equivalent to a second mortgage. Due to these multiple stressors, supervision sessions began to feel like doing therapy. Fortunately, I was able to make referrals to my colleagues when the need for treatment became apparent.

In recent years, fewer of my trainees saw themselves going into private practice, which they viewed as a continuation of the high stress levels they were already experiencing. To help them adapt, I often shared with them what I had learned about finding a balance between work, relationships, recreation, and the need for rejuvenating solitude. Many of their evaluations reflected a deep appreciation for revealing what I had learned from my own experiences.

My own identity as a psychiatrist changed to some degree, but not as drastically as the changes I witnessed in my supervisees over the years. My dual role as psychotherapist and medication prescriber was strengthened by the fact that many of my patients with chronic anxiety and mood disorders chose to stay in supportive therapy for several years, including a number of men who had participated in my groups.

I developed ways of integrating CBT, DBT, medication treatment, and psychodynamic therapy, using the newer modalities for symptom reduction at the outset of treatment, followed by psychodynamic approaches for those who wished to work on changes at a deeper level. The psychodynamic principles that I learned as a resident provided a strong foundation for dealing with fears of change and transference issues in all types of therapy and with non-adherence regarding prescriptions. I became eclectic in my choice of therapies and combined techniques from many modalities. After 44 years of practice, I felt I was a more versatile psychiatrist, capable of treating a wider spectrum of better informed, more complex patients. As my practice matured, I was thankful for the opportunity to refer more time-intensive patients to younger colleagues.

There were several other significant advances in my field which I mention briefly, since I didn't utilize them personally: eye movement desensitization and rehabilitation (EMDR) for specific traumas, transcranial magnetic stimulation (TMS) for treatment-resistant depression, neurosurgical approaches for severe obsessive compulsive disorders, and a number of innovative medications for schizophrenia. Many of these newer and promising treatment approaches are currently undergoing multicenter clinical trials.

As I conclude this review of advances in psychiatry, I am filled with gratitude for all that my patients have taught me about human resilience and courage, the multiple paths to health and wellness, the essential unity of mind, body, and spirit, and the unique pleasures of being a psychiatrist. Keeping up with the explosion of knowledge in brain science and specialized therapy techniques has been both challenging and stimulating.

One of the chief joys of doing psychiatry is that it taps into almost every known corner of the humanities and sciences. On any given day in practice I may have drawn on the wit and wisdom of Shakespeare, the *metta* meditations of Buddha, the "good enough mothering" of Winnicott, or the "dendritic sprouting" of Kandel. No other medical specialty, in my opinion, combines intellectual stimulation of this depth and breadth with the privilege of being in an intimate healing relationship.

CHAPTER 14

FUTURE TRENDS IN PSYCHIATRY

Y ogi Berra once said: "It's tough to make predictions, especially about the future." With all due respect to the Yankee sage, I'll advance some educated guesses based on my observations of trends unfolding during the last decade.

Innovations in psychiatric research, training, and practice in the mid 21st century will likely move faster and over a much wider terrain than those I experienced during my career. No longer confined to treating intra-psychic and interpersonal processes, psychiatry will need to expand its focus and scope to deal with national, global, environmental, social, and political phenomena which will generate high levels of stress and trauma, including a new set of phenomena which I call "Acceleration Anxieties," after Thomas Friedman's recent description of our era as "The Age of Accelerations."

Friedman cites Erik Teller's observation that when the human capacity of adaptation lags behind the rate of acceleration of change, people become anxious and disoriented, feeling out of control (1). Acceleration anxieties are already showing up in a wide variety of manifestations, both individual and social.

Psychiatrists, accustomed in the past to working in the more predictable, safe confines of the consultation room, hospital, or research lab, will find themselves struggling to handle many of the same

190

stressors as their patients. This leveling of the playing field will carry the risk of increased burnout among practitioners. On the other hand, it will also provide exciting opportunities for strengthening empathy, compassion, and resilience on both sides of the therapeutic partnership. In the future, concepts of acceleration anxieties, social anxieties, and "post-traumatic stress" will be balanced by new formulations of what it means to be resilient.

By mid-century, psychiatrists will have made significant advances in their understanding of how climate change affects biological, psychological, and social functioning. The advantages and liabilities of internet use will become clearer, allowing for more optimal use in early detection of mental illness and treatment interventions. The novel coronavirus pandemic will generate important innovations in telepsychiatry for those whose location, economic circumstances, or illnesses make face-to-face therapies difficult. Issues involving our aging population, gender differences in diagnosis and treatment, and internet addiction will become common currency in psychiatric practice.

Our specialty will become more attuned to racial and ethnic differences and will strive to better understand and confront the scourge of racism. New treatment techniques on the interface of neural circuitry, genomics, and cognitive science will address social and acceleration anxiety, depression, psychoses, interpersonal violence, and veterans' ailments. Population increases and the aggregate effects of climate change will impel humankind to return to Earth's moon, mine the asteroid belt, and perhaps colonize Mars. Psychiatry will expand its domain to include the challenges of space exploration.

If you doubt these assertions, observing a typical morning Starbucks scene will clarify what I am describing. As you approach the counter, a young barista promises to fill your orders *really fast.* Customers are engrossed with their cellphones and laptops, minimally interacting with their tablemates. Everyone is elsewhere, connected by a caffeination ritual, knees and ankles vibrating faster than a drummer doing his best licks. Hissing espresso-makers alternate with notification rings and in a microsecond you and other multi-taskers clutch and scan your cellphones in full FOMO mode. Streaming videos of the latest North Korean missile test and two tropical storm warnings appear in your digital news feed. Your jaw clenches and your Fit Bit tells you that your pulse has increased 15 bpm since you sat down. Your familiar dull headache, chest tightness, and dizziness return. You pause to take a few deep breaths and quietly exhale OM.......before rushing out to your smart car to brave the traffic jams on the way to your office. A line from "Stop the World—I Want to Get Off" suddenly intrudes and you find yourself humming it.

THE BENEFITS AND RISKS OF THE DIGITAL REVOLUTION

The instantaneous connections of the digital age, like the splitting of the atom, have the potential for unleashing an increasing number of constructive or destructive forces worldwide. On the one hand, families and friends separated by thousands of miles have been brought together by constantly improving technology.

Online educational ventures such as the Khan Academy have made hundreds of college level courses available to inhabitants of even remote villages in Mongolia (2).

The worldwide dissemination of medical research and new therapies has made it possible to intervene more quickly and successfully in large-scale epidemics such as Ebola and Zika. Whether or not this can be said regarding the novel coronavirus remains to be seen.

On the other hand, the capacity to instantly visualize increasing numbers of hurricanes, flooding, and fires related to climate change, pandemics, the bloody effects of local violence and international terrorism, increasingly hostile political debates, and renewed threats of nuclear war have thrust us into cycles of fear, outrage, numbness, and exhaustion. It is to these and other features of the Age of Acceleration that we now turn.

THE PSYCHOLOGICAL AND MEDICAL EFFECTS OF CLIMATE CHANGE

In the past several years the medical and psychiatric community has intensified research on the effects of climate change on physical and mental health.

The incidence of post-traumatic stress disorder and depression is likely to increase due to the effects of extreme weather events related to climate change. These adverse effects are anticipated to be most burdensome for minorities, the poor, children, the elderly, and others with limited immune responses and access to health care (3).

A landmark ruling in 2016 by an Oregon District Court laid down a core principle connecting climate and health: "The *right to a climate system capable of sustaining human life* (italics mine) is fundamental to a free and ordered society" (4).

Recent clinical research has observed correlations of high ozone levels and other air pollutants with inflammatory disease, increased risks of autism, brain inflammation, dementia, Parkinson's disease, and other neurodegenerative disorders. Prolonged high temperatures have been associated with increases of "assaults, murders, suicides, domestic violence, and child abuse" (5). According to a Harvard/SUNY indoor study, elevated CO_2 impairs cognition in the areas of strategic thinking, information processing, and crisis management (6). These alarming findings demonstrate a compelling need for further research by brain scientists.

In September 2005 I volunteered to triage and support refugees from Hurricane Katrina who were airlifted from New Orleans to Denver. These individuals were exhausted, grief-stricken, and disoriented by the flooding of their homes, the loss of family members, and the comforting support of neighbors.

Their distress appeared to be aggravated by their sudden displacement. Screening for acute stress reactions, depression, and psychosis, I found that many also suffered from a condition known as *solastalgia*, an acute "loss of connection to one's home environment" (7). While many survivors were supportive of each other and grateful for our services, others manifested their acute distress with sullen hostility, altercations with those of different ethnicity, and intense, often unrealistic, demands on caretakers. In cases where family members were separated and flown to separate camps, panic and outrage erupted. A teenage girl shrieked, *"What have they done with my little sister? Where did they take her?"*

These scenes are being played out internationally in refugee camps created in response to climate change, failed states, and civil wars. Some studies have estimated that, by 2050, climate change events will have caused the displacement of some 200 million people worldwide (7). Thus far, the majority of these displacements have occurred in far-away places. The increasing frequency of severe weather events striking our own shores, mountains, and prairies will likely lead to increased geographical displacement. As a result, "Disaster Psychiatry" will be forced to evolve from an adhocracy to an evidence-based practice specialty.

Psychiatrists, in response to these trends, have a clear and compelling responsibility to educate their patients and the general public about the medical and mental health risks of climate change. The legal right of all humans to a healthy life-sustaining climate set forth in the Oregon case will undoubtedly be tested in numerous class-action suits. Processes related to climate change and pandemics such as the novel coronavirus will have marked effects on our basic sense of security, our diets, living environments, recreational opportunities, and overall physical and mental health.

Maintaining resilience and hope in the face of these changes will create challenges for psychiatrists and their patients within the next decade.

GUN VIOLENCE: THE LEGACY OF OUR TRANSGENERATIONAL HISTORY

Americans are armed to the teeth, with many households harboring multiple firearms. According to Brady Campaign data, 1.7 million children live in a home with an *unlocked, loaded gun*. Moreover, 82 percent of adolescent firearm suicides involve a gun that belongs to a family member (8). These and other data encompass trends indicative of repeated tragedies across the nation.

The 2017 massacre at a concert in Las Vegas, New Mexico with 58 killed and 546 wounded currently stands as the largest single-event mass murder in U.S. history. Our flags continue to stand at half-mast in a numbing blur of ongoing tragedies. Most new gun control legislation has been stalled at the federal level since then. It would appear that Americans are *both* afraid of guns and feel they need them to protect themselves. These fears are not unfounded, given our transgenerational history, beginning with the settlers' genocide of indigenous peoples, the African slave trade, the Civil War, widespread violent urban uprisings during the Civil Rights movement, widely publicized police shootings, and more recently, fatal episodes of racial and religious hatred in our cities, churches, and schools.

Graphic visual images of violence and bloodshed are aired weekly by national and international news media covering mass shootings and terrorist attacks, reinforcing the perception that there are few safe places in the public realm. To their credit, several states have recently enacted Extreme Risk Protection Orders, allowing police or family to confiscate guns of those demonstrating violent impulses.

In our culture of violence, the differences between "social anxiety reactions," "social anxiety disorders," and post-traumatic stress disorder will become academic in the face of escalating real threats.

Trauma expert Bessel Van der Kolk stated recently:

"Traumatic experiences do leave traces...imperceptibly passed down through generations. They also leave traces on our minds and emotions, on our capacity for joy and intimacy, and even on our biology and immune systems" (9).

Concluding his study, he implored mental health professionals to make a connection between "psychic suffering and social conditions" (9). In my opinion, the phenomena of increased suicide rates, opiate overdoses, childhood obesity, pervasive loneliness on college campuses, and various forms of internet addiction and bullying are interrelated manifestations of a traumatized and demoralized society struggling to adapt to accelerating rates of change in the absence of strong leadership. Psychiatrists will be challenged to become activists in confronting social ills if they are to adequately address the widening panorama of private sufferings.

INTERNATIONAL VIOLENCE AND TERRORISM

In the weeks and months following the 9/11 attacks, I listened to dozens of patients who were experiencing intense feelings of loss, helplessness, and rage.

Many complained of feeling anxious and exhausted by watching endless replays of the Twin Towers collapsing, traumatized by each repeated viewing. It became clear that the technology of instant replay is the terrorist's greatest weapon. I counseled my patients to titrate and minimize their exposure and to use relaxation exercises before and after viewing the news.

In my own nightmares I joined firemen rescuing victims and struggled to subdue the terrorist pilots, steering the hijacked planes away from certain annihilation. I experienced a profound sadness as one woman wept about losing several of her colleagues who were incinerated and crushed in the South Tower.

My own empathic capacities began to feel like a personal liability. Fifteen years later I stood at the memorial fountains at Ground Zero, sobered by the realization that suicides and homicides, every month, claim as many lives as Islamic terrorists did on September 11. Psychiatrists will need to find innovative methods for self-soothing and meditation for themselves and their patients to cope with these ongoing traumas.

THE MANIFESTATIONS OF "ACCELERATION ANXIETY"

In the Age of Acceleration, numerous manifestations of Acceleration Anxiety have come to the fore. Millions of people are feeling increasingly anxious in a complex world which is changing too fast for them to understand, adapt to, or control. Anxiety can lead to either adaptive or maladaptive responses.

Adaptive responses serve to warn us about dangerous situations and help us mobilize our defenses. We use an "internal locus of control" to draw on the lessons of experience to assess strengths and weaknesses and solve problems collaboratively by considering alternatives.

Maladaptive responses to dangerous situations are characterized by inaccurate assessment of dangers, fear-based decision making, and high levels of denial and minimization. Thinking is dominated by "external locus of control" or the perception that outside forces are responsible for the crisis. Scapegoating of the "Evil Other" spreads rapidly. Extreme forms of this are found in paranoid delusions. Those who use these maladaptive responses ignore facts, view themselves as passive victims of conspiracies, and turn to demagogues who promise simple solutions in utopian uniformity. Demagogues derive their power from millions who fall prey to deep existential fears and utilize maladaptive responses.

Acceleration Anxieties are manifested by chronic insomnia, irritability, diffuse rage in search of a target, increased sensitivity to stimulation, decreased frustration tolerance, increased aches and pains, a feeling of chronic fatigue, and feelings of hopelessness, helplessness, and despair. It is not surprising that these symptoms are similar to those seen in combat veterans.

In the Age of Acceleration, Americans must find ways of revitalizing a society torn apart by fear-driven divisiveness. We must also do everything possible to honor our multicultural world with all of its creative diversity.

Psychiatry has an important mission in opposing tyranny in all of its forms. The starting point for this opposition is to maintain its commitment to personal truth, self-care, empathic listening and respectful communication, healthy, loving relationships, and nonviolent conflict resolution.

PERSONAL HEALTH AND THE INTERNET: GAINS AND LIABILITIES

The internet has produced both widespread gains as well as liabilities.

Medical institutions are providing useful, updated information regarding diagnosis and treatment of psychiatric disorders for anyone who is computer-literate and curious. Many patients are now better informed and arrive prepared with relevant questions. Others unfortunately experience increased anxiety following their involvement with online "chat rooms" rife with misinformation, frightening medication side-effects, and unethical treatment practices.

The increasing prevalence of internet addiction will command more attention by psychiatrists. This phenomenon shares many characteristics of "classical" addictions, such as excessive preoccupations and use; inability to reduce behavior after repeated attempts; depression, anxiety, and irritability when digital devices are removed; negative impacts on relationships; lying to cover one's habit; and involvement of the neural circuitry of dopamine reward systems (10, 11).

The curious paradox of being "friended" on social media sites while feeling increasingly isolated raises existential questions about the meaning of friendship and our needs for social and emotional intimacy. I recently saw a slender young woman walking across Harvard Yard, right hand outstretched palm-upward in front of her face, *sans cellphone*. Was this the sad, silent beckoning of a social media amputee, returning from her first internet addiction (IAD) meeting? As I watched, I was haunted by echoes of the Newark Airport cyber-orphan girl described in Chapter 5 on Listening and Empathy.

The use of digital technology in "cyber-therapy" holds great promise as well as significant caveats. Many of my colleagues are now using Skype and Zoom therapy sessions after initial face-to-face evaluations. Others, particularly those who practice psychodynamic psycho-therapy, argue that anonymous, digital text-based treatments tend to reinforce the loneliness and stigma associated with mental illness rather than mitigating it. For those who are most troubled with trauma in highly conflictive personal relationships, there is still no adequate substitute for face-to-face therapy and "having your pain witnessed and validated" (12).

The UK's National Health Service has recognized computerized cognitive behavior therapy as a preferred method of treatment for mild depression and anxiety. Using interactive programs, "Beating the Blues" and "Fear Fighter," patients view introductory videos and participate in eight one hour-sessions based on standard CBT methods.

Preliminary outcomes for the depressed group demonstrate at least 50 percent improvement of their symptoms after three months of treatment (13). Similar programs are already gaining increased acceptance in the U.S., targeting rural and aging populations with limited access to care.

In my home state, a National Mental Health Innovation Center was recently established at the University of Colorado with a mission to change how we think about mental health, redefine the workforce addressing mental illness and substance abuse, develop curricula for better self-care, and expand the use of digital technology to help millions deal with conflicts, anxiety, and depression. The Innovation Center is now using virtual reality goggles for the treatment of individuals suffering from a variety of specific phobias, veterans with PTSD, addictions, and pain management during medical procedures such as skin grafts (14). Increasing applications for these devices will be forthcoming.

One of the most promising, albeit controversial, uses of internet technology involves employing smartphone technology to detect early signs of mental illness.

Dr. Thomas Insel, a former director of the NIMH, has developed a cellphone application which can track daily behavior associated with the onset of depressive episodes. The application records the number of people spoken with and responded to, pace and volume of speech, size of vocabulary, proportion of time spent at home, and changes in sleep patterns. These data can be compared with the phone user's prior normative behavioral patterns and generate warnings about early onset depressive symptoms. Phone apps then refer the user to peer counselors or, if appropriate, to licensed professional therapists (15). If issues regarding security can be overcome, these innovative technologies may soon become available for millions of users worldwide.

In response to the devastating worldwide effects of the novel coronavirus pandemic, thousands of healthcare institutions and individual practitioners have now come to rely on telemedicine as a safe and efficient means of conducting selected evaluations and follow-ups. In March of 2020 as the pandemic gained momentum and stay at home orders were instituted in a majority of states, face-to-face psychotherapy sessions in the United States virtually disappeared. Mental health professionals flocked to online webinars on how to provide online therapy from the safety of their and their patients' homes.

Early reports indicate that some populations, particularly adolescents who are already more comfortable using What's App and social media, find video sessions less anxiety-provoking. The American Psychiatric Association's Committee on Telepsychiatry successfully lobbied Medicare and Medicaid as well as some private health insurers to reimburse home video therapies and in some cases reduce or eliminate copays. It is likely that these trends will have major and permanent impacts on the practice of medicine and psychiatry in the future (16).

PROBLEMS OF AGING AND GENERATION GAPS

My work with senior citizens has included some of the most gratifying experiences of my practice. As I aged along with my patients, I increasingly viewed them as "my people" and identified with them in their empty nests, downsizing, physical decline, retirement, loss of friends, spouses, and parents, intensification of spiritual issues, and contemplating mortality. My parents' longevity provided me with excellent models for aging gracefully. I was able to use their examples, along with a selective use of self-disclosure, to help my patients negotiate their own autumn years. During my last years of practice I visited disabled patients at home, in the hospital, and in hospice, sitting quietly beside them in their recliners and beds, communicating with few words and brief touches on their hands or shoulders. They were grateful for my presence and I for the privilege of being with them in their final passages.

Psychiatrists in the next generation will be treating increasing numbers of patients over 65 who will number 82 million by 2040 (17). On an interpersonal level, the management of conflicts with aging children and grandchildren, and the complexities involving elder dating, second and third marriages, and multiple stepfamily relationships will come to the fore. There is now a growing literature on the complexities of caring for aging parents (18) as well as dealing with the alienation of adult children from their elderly parents for a variety of reasons (19).

Social anxiety disorders will expand to include stress reactions of those being replaced by robots and other forms of AI. Human/robot relationships will demand new conceptualizations of relationship therapies, as demonstrated by the fascinating movie *Her*, starring Joaquin Phoenix and Scarlett Johansson in 2014.

An aging population will wonder why these conflicts are so central for their children and grandchildren, even as they struggle to master their new digital devices in their downsized modular homes.

In the last ten years of my practice I discovered that millennials typically did not make or return phone calls or emails regarding scheduling appointments or renewing prescriptions. For them, it was texting, social media, or nothing. Some wanted to use texting to deal with treatment issues, which, for me, was unacceptable. Others simply disappeared into cyberspace, unwilling to respond to my attempts at follow-up. These kinds of generational disconnects are now occurring with increasing frequency in the workplace, where older managers who schedule face-to-face meetings are frustrated by young workers for whom "give me a shout" means texting from their local coffee shops. It is likely that today's teenagers and millennials will continue to insist on more therapy being conducted digitally. For this to be successful, privacy and security concerns will need to be addressed more aggressively by internet service providers.

Several colleges have expanded their *in loco parentis* functions by creating "safe spaces" to protect their more fragile students from purported triggers of psychic harm. In a world of iPhones, social media, and digital magnification of conflict, post-traumatic stress clouds frequently darken the landscape. The development of intimate sexual relationships on campuses is now complicated by legalistic guidelines which attempt to delineate the meaning and gradations of mutual consent. Equalizing due process for victims and perpetrators of sexual aggression on campus is now commanding legal attention.

Media reports are emerging involving teenagers pushed to suicide by the online complicity or urgings of their peers, whose parents are now beginning to press homicide charges (20). Forensic psychiatrists will increasingly be called upon to evaluate victims' families and alleged perpetrators to determine levels of both psychic harm and legal culpability.

With increasing longevity, cancer diagnoses are expected to proliferate, leaving those with limited means unable to afford expensive new therapies. Psychiatrists will increasingly be called upon to evaluate those who wish to use physician-assisted dying and expensive neurosurgical techniques such as deep brain stimulation for intractable Parkinson's disease, depression, and obsessive compulsive disorder.

OPIOID ADDICTIONS:
A NEW FORM OF DOMESTIC TERROR

The current opioid addiction epidemic, like social anxiety and traumatic stress syndromes, should be viewed more broadly as symptomatic of socio-economic distress. Physicians, taken in by false safety claims of Big Pharma, have been over-prescribing now for decades. Following a minimally invasive spine surgery in 2011, I was given 60 Percodan by my surgeon, of which I used a mere handful before switching to Tylenol.

Many of my patients and friends have described similar experiences. My emergency physician colleagues describe how difficult it is to turn away throngs of patients complaining of "chronic pain" and demanding "just a few more" opioids. Opioid overdoses now claim the lives of over 100 Americans daily. Librarians, social workers, EMTs, and firemen are now injecting the opioid antagonist Naloxone to save the lives of homeless opioid users. Insurance company actuaries estimate that the economic value of opioid-related (intentional or accidental overdoses) deaths alone is between a $100 and $150 billion in lost wages and tax income (21).

Recent studies indicate that non-prescription pain medications and newer treatment modalities may be as effective as the opioids. This constitutes a tragic footnote for those who have perished but offers hope for those embarking on newer interventions. These findings do not begin to do justice to the widespread mourning in extended families and friends of overdose victims, many of whom will find their way into the offices of family practitioners and psychiatrists with their own addictions, depression, and anxiety problems.

While the neural, genetic, and behavioral pathways for addiction are well-researched, the socio-economic and racial pathways are complex and poorly documented. Increased funding for rehabilitation programs, newer therapies, and addiction-specific medications will do little to stem the tide if socio-economic issues are not addressed. Psychiatric addiction specialists will need to collaborate with public health professionals, elected officials, and citizen advocacy groups to intervene in this more subtle form of domestic terror.

DISABLED VETERANS: THE IMMENSE COSTS OF ENDLESS WARS

Since the terrorist attacks of September 2001, U.S. armed forces have been engaged in Afghanistan, Iraq, and Syria. U.S. military are also engaged in numerous other high-risk covert military operations around the world in endless "wars on terror." The triad of PTSD, depression, and traumatic brain injury secondary to Incendiary Explosive Devices in returning veterans has been reported in multiple medical journals as well as by public media. Suicide rates in returning veterans, particularly those with multiple deployments, are significantly higher than in non-combat adult populations. The widespread traumatic effects in family members and friends of these combat-related casualties are immeasurable and will occupy the attention of psychiatrists until mid-century.

THE THREAT OF NUCLEAR ANNIHILATION: COLD WAR 2.0

One of my earliest memories of kindergarten was of our petite teacher, Miss Portley, calmly instructing us to crouch under our desks during air raid drills. Striding up and down the aisles, she made sure that we 25 roly-polies were positioned according to protocol. I wondered why Miss Portley never hid under *her* desk. Maybe she had invisible armor. There was a prolonged silence, punctuated by nervous giggles, as we struggled to maintain our positions. The ear-splitting bell over the blackboard signaled the end of the drill and we crawled back up into our seats. The next morning we sang "America the Beautiful" louder than ever and pledged allegiance to the Flag, adding "under God," President Eisenhower's assurance that we would survive, whatever happened.

Thanks to increased nationalist isolationism in the U.S., bomb-angst regarding Iran and North Korea is now back with a vengeance and it is not likely to go away any time soon. As the saying goes, "when a gun appears in Act One, someone will get shot by the end of Act Two." In addition, we now face the specter of rogue terrorist groups obtaining nuclear weapons. Psychiatrists and other mental health professionals find themselves in a situation where they and their patients will be struggling to adapt to the very same survival threats. In this context, optimal management of chronic stress syndromes with resilience enhancement techniques will become increasingly important. Flexibility and creativity will be essential skills for managing treatments in this challenging environment. Psychiatrists will need, more than ever, to monitor their own emotions, thoughts, and behaviors as they struggle to stay attuned to various forms of their patients' Acceleration Anxieties and to maintain their own sense of meaning and hope.

THE BRAVE NEW WORLD OF
PSYCHIATRIC TRAINING AND PRACTICE

To help their patients deal with these challenges, young practitioners will require training that is more attractive, efficient, and broadly-based. We will need, due to shortages, to attract more highly motivated medical students to our specialty. Men and women who are proficient in psychiatry will continue to need a highly developed combination of empathic listening, communication, and therapeutic technical skills in addition to being proficient with all the latest digital technology. They will be on the forefront of developing new models of integrated and preventative care involving state-of-the-art online practices of meditation, stress reduction, and physical and emotional wellbeing.

Psychiatric training, in order to meet evolving social needs, will likely evolve in the direction of more subspecialties. Dr. Steven Sharfstein, former APA president, foresees a four-fold specialization emerging in the fields of neuroscience, medical psychiatry, psychotherapy, and social psychiatry. According to Sharfstein, most of the neuroscience specialists will be M.D-PhDs with special expertise in genetics, brain imaging, magnetic stimulation, and psychosurgery. Due to their prolonged training, they will be the highest paid psychiatrists.

Medical psychiatrists will still practice within more traditional models with child, adolescent, adult, and geriatric caseloads in addition to treating addictions. Their practices will be increasingly integrated with family practice, pediatrics, and internists in outpatient clinics and hospital settings. Psychiatric geriatricians will treat a growing population of individuals living beyond age 100. Psychiatrists specializing in psychotherapy will have integrated study programs including theology, psychology, education, and the humanities (22).

Recertification and CME requirements will be stricter and more frequently monitored, with online testing offering immediate feedback regarding areas needing improvement. A significant part of training will include a wide spectrum of face-to-face and digital communication skills with patients and colleagues in integrated care systems.

Increasingly, psychotherapy approaches will be selected and targeted with algorithms based on disease-specific biologic markers and brain scanning techniques identifying vulnerable neurocircuitry and neurochemistry. Patients will be increasingly involved in the diagnostic and treatment process through the use of handheld and implanted digital devices measuring parameters involving psychiatric illness.

Following the chaotic developments in Trump's presidency, future U.S. presidents will, in my opinion, need to have detailed neuropsychiatric evaluations alongside the more traditional and time-honored examinations by their internists (23). The selection of the specialists assigned to perform these duties will likely be the subject of intense debate.

PSYCHIATRISTS AS
ACTIVIST WITNESSING PROFESSIONALS

Given the expansion of social anxieties, multiple "traumatic traces," and widespread manifestations of acceleration anxieties, it is reasonable to ask whether and to what extent the responsibilities of psychiatrists and other mental health professionals should be extended beyond the boundaries of the consultation room. This question has become more relevant in the context of a U.S. presidency characterized by divisiveness, racism, shameless propagation of falsehoods, and provocations of violence. As psychiatrists we must attend to individuals within our professional skillset, but we do them a disservice if we isolate them from their social and political contexts. According to my colleagues, increasing numbers of patients are presenting with deep feelings of demoralization, hopelessness, and social despair since the 2016 election. For many, these feelings are exacerbating preexisting psychiatric disorders.

Psychiatrists have always had a commitment to help their patients develop autonomy and assertiveness in order to realize their full potential. Without imposing our own beliefs, we can support individuals, couples, and families to become more active in their churches, synagogues, and mosques, to spend time volunteering at shelters, and to become more involved in addressing public issues in their home towns. We can teach our patients about non-violent means of conflict resolution and support the development of these skills as key elements of elementary and secondary education. We can discuss the risks of handgun possession, provide data on homicide and suicide rates, and encourage patients to familiarize themselves with gun safety procedures. We can discuss the health benefits of giving up resentments and pursuing a path of forgiveness. For many individuals who are immobilized by depression, anxiety, and a variety of addictions, developing a commitment to these kinds of activities can be an integral part of their recovery.

Robert J. Lifton recently described an expanded role for psychiatrists and other mental health professionals in what he calls "The Activist Witnessing Professional" who confronts situations where there is a clear adaptation to and normalization of evil. Lifton, who evaluated the doctors who were involved in Nazi genocide, defined a limited activist role:

"...a disciplined professional approach with the ethical requirements of committed witness, combining scholarship with activism...This requires us to be disciplined about what we believe we know, while refraining from holding forth on what we do not know" (24).

Lifton wisely abstains from offering diagnostic opinions regarding the president. He "witnesses" by calling our attention to the fact that frequently our president's words and actions are both evil and congruent with the behaviors of previous tyrannical leaders. His views echo those of Hannah Arendt on totalitarianism, written almost sixty years previously (24, 25).

Lifton's writings suggest a professional *educational role* which is designed to focus the attention and awareness of all citizens who wish to confront tyranny and preserve democratic values and human decency. Psychiatrists in the 21st century will need to make their own moral decisions regarding the extent to which they choose to involve themselves in the political arena on behalf of their patients. One thing is clear at this point: to remain silent is to countenance more divisiveness, chaos, and suffering.

With the rapid developments in digital technology, our field will become more responsive to acceleration anxieties related to the changes I have described. Future practitioners will do well to keep in mind that their most valuable tool remains their capacity to develop an empathic, non-judgmental, and trusting relationship, whether it takes place in the comfortable confines of their offices or via the convenience of a secure home digital network.

CHAPTER 15

RETIREMENT

For several years before I retired, I knew that I wanted to stop working when I was near the top of my game. I had seen several colleagues continue to work with increasing disabilities and it wasn't pretty. One of them, well known for taking on difficult cases, died suddenly of a heart attack. The psychiatrist who took over his office space had debilitating back pain and spent his last years in practice attempting to treat patients while *he* lay on his back on a custom-designed couch. He was continuing to treat a few patients in his home shortly before he died. Hearing this, I vowed not to follow suit.

HOW I DECIDED TO RETIRE

My first step was to set an approximate timeframe for ending my practice. This decision came after conferring with my accountant and financial advisor to determine if my plans were realistic. With some modifications to my retirement portfolio and by paying off my townhome for future use as a rental property, I was assured of a reasonably comfortable financial future. While these deliberations were going on, I was fortunate to find a romantic partner with whom I now live. I felt confident that I could retire comfortably between the ages of 71 and 74.

Rather than choose an arbitrary date, I decided to allow my intuition and careful self-monitoring to be my guides. I began by resigning from a very stressful consulting position in an intensive outpatient program, which served as a step-down unit for hospital patients, many of whom had recently been suicidal. My immense relief after quitting this position validated the appropriateness of my decision. Soon thereafter, I decided not to take any more new patients and to allow my practice to diminish organically as patients completed their therapies. My demeanor must have revealed my plans, as several patients began to inquire if I was thinking about retirement! I responded by being open regarding my overall timeframe. Our sessions began to focus on the issue of ending treatment versus continuing with another therapist. Many patients began to focus on their own losses, which initiated a parallel process of mourning my work and my relationships with them.

This process took a painful turn when I lost two patients by suicide within a two-month period. As I began to mourn these individuals with my mentor and consultation group, I realized that I had been carrying a heavy *cumulative bereavement burden,* which included the patients who had suicided, plus countless other emotionally intimate treatment relationships which had ended over the years. I was approaching a critical mass and resolved to trust that I would know when I reached it.

Shortly after I turned seventy, I began to notice several changes in how I functioned with patients. Conducting my four and five o'clock sessions began to feel like running the last few miles of a marathon. Staying focused and connecting empathically became increasingly difficult. Even with my hearing aids turned up, I felt I was missing nuances in vocal tone and losing my empathic edge. Intensely emotional interactions left me feeling depleted and distracted with carryover into my next patient sessions. I handled this by cutting back to three days per week, which meant that my leisure time now exceeded my work time, making work a lower priority. I began to introduce myself as John, rather than Dr. Graves, reflecting the subtle shifts taking place in my sense of self. When my retired colleagues and friends spoke about how relieved they were to be done with work, I noticed I was becoming envious.

Like many practitioners my age, I had some "senior moments" in the office. I began to take more notes in sessions, fearing I would miss something important. This began to interfere with more empathic communication, so I backed off. I tested my short-term memory and determined my decline was normal for my age. When mid-afternoon patients canceled, I set my alarm and took thirty minute naps. I awoke feeling invigorated enough to see one or two more patients.

A louder alarm sounded when, in a session following a two-week vacation, I suggested to a patient that we ought to consider starting Wellbutrin for his depression. He responded, "But Dr. Graves, you started me on it *three weeks ago!*" I was mortified by my lapse and apologized profusely. Then and there I decided it was time to set a definite retirement date.

Once I made my decision, I experienced a palpable sense of relief. I began to inform patients a year in advance of my target date, which I set for January 2016. This provided more than enough time for long-term patients to either end treatment or to find a new therapist. I told those who opted for ongoing therapy that I would assist them in their search, but that they needed to take the initiative and do the bulk of the work of exploring their options. Rather than stringing out requests for treatment summaries following retirement, I informed everyone that I would prepare a one to two-page summary for them prior to our last session, which they could use at their own discretion.

I reviewed these summaries in sessions to confirm that I had covered everything they deemed essential. Our reviews triggered some meaningful discussions about the differences between what I and my patients felt were the most important gains or limitations of their therapy. In talking about these discrepancies, I was amazed to learn how some interventions I had considered to be trivial were actually highly significant for them. In these cases I revised my summaries to reflect more accurately what had led to their improvements.

Writing these sixty-five summaries over a period of several months intensified my own mourning process which, in turn, helped me be more open with each person about how I appreciated working with them. I look careful notes on these discussions, including direct quotes about what they felt was most helpful in their treatments. I include a list of these in Appendix Two. Most of my patients' graduations from treatment and transfers went well.

I spent a few months deliberating on whether to continue my active medical license, which was scheduled to expire one year after I closed my office. I inquired about an inactive status but this required maintaining expensive liability coverage. The right decision, I felt, would emerge in due time if I was patient. I awakened one morning with my decision made: I would allow my license to lapse entirely.

The full impact of my decision came unexpectedly when I got a call requesting a refill from a former patient. Returning his call, I began to inquire about dosing details. I caught myself, chagrined, in mid-sentence. "I'm really sorry. I can't prescribe this for you—I'm no longer licensed to practice." Hearing myself make this simple declaration for the first time was an important marker which had the effect of sealing my fate. I still had my medical degree but I could no longer legally treat patients with written prescriptions.

After ending the conversation, I began reminiscing about a singular event in my third year of medical school. I was in the busy cafeteria lunch line at Jacobi Hospital in the Bronx. My classmates and I were all tricked out with our short white coats, new pagers, and black leather medical bags (our first bribe from Eli Lilly). We had just filled our bags with ophthalmoscopes, otoscopes, stethoscopes, reflex hammers, tuning forks, rubber tourniquets, gauze 4x4s from the nursing station, and the *Washington Manual*—the quintessential tools of the trade. Many of us were on our first clinical rotations in medicine or surgery.

"Paging Doctor Graves for extension 4-3-8-1" rang out loud and clear twice over the PA system. At first I was a bit startled. Then I realized the page was for *me*. I called the extension and my friend Betty picked up the phone. "Just checking to see if you were paying attention," she chuckled. She had done me the honor of marking this momentous transition with what felt like a mini Bar Mitzvah. A few minutes later I paged her to return the favor. In another two years we would be fully-licensed physicians, with all the responsibilities, privileges, respect, and trepidation this entailed. My new identity had commenced with a page and ended with declining a prescription request. I had to admit my doctoring days were over.

HANDLING PATIENTS' DEATHS
FOLLOWING THE END OF TREATMENT

Within two months of closing down my office, two of my patients died within a five-day period and a third passed away a month later. I had told each of them in our final sessions that, due to their frail conditions, I would appreciate hearing how they were doing in the weeks and months ahead. Under the circumstances, I felt that these post-treatment contact offers were clearly indicated. Friendships don't end by punching out on a clock. The deep emotional connections in therapeutic relationships are no different.

Doug, in his mid-50s, had sought help for depression and concerns about a disabled daughter. During the last year of our treatment relationship, his daughter died unexpectedly and Doug developed severe pneumonia. Shortly thereafter he was diagnosed with metastatic cancer, necessitating his taking an early retirement. We discussed the painful ramifications of his cancer diagnosis in our remaining office appointments. He became so debilitated that we transitioned to scheduled phone sessions and impromptu ones whenever he needed them. My retirement date couldn't have come at a worse time for him. Since I didn't want to extend my office closing just for him, I offered to make a few home "social visits" without charge following my retirement.

During these visits we discussed the unfairness of his life being cut short just when he was beginning to feel better about himself. He wept about not being able to see his son play freshman football and thanked me for my support in the aftermath of his daughter's death. Our meetings in his bedroom ended abruptly when he developed coughing fits. As he was gasping for air, I said goodbye and promised to see him the following week. Four days later, I read his obituary in *The Denver Post*. When his wife called to inform me of his death, I asked if it would be helpful if I came to his memorial service and she immediately accepted my offer.

I had never attended an open casket service before. This one included a Roman Catholic Rosary with a receiving line for family members. After greeting them and expressing my condolences, I took a seat in the back row. As I prayed, the soft words of the Rosary provided a soothing accompaniment. This was followed by the Lord's Prayer, which my mother had taught me as a child. I felt comforted by joining in the unison of communal prayer. For a moment I slipped into a meditative state and nearly dozed off. During a pause, the man seated next to me asked me how I knew Doug. I was one of his doctors, I replied. So was I, he said.

When my turn came to approach Doug's casket, I felt faint. What should I say? There was no protocol in the psychiatry texts covering this situation. I yearned to speak with him and to finish our work together. It was not to be. What remained of Doug appeared serene and Buddha-like. He was wearing a sport coat I recognized from our office sessions.

I searched for words and none came.... Time stopped.... I had no idea how long I stood there. Something moved me to touch my heart and to place my right hand on his chest. It felt cold and hard.... I finally managed to whisper, "Goodbye Doug, I've enjoyed working with you." As I drove home in the wet April snowstorm, I was glad I had come. I felt a bittersweet sadness, realizing I had done all I could. My cheeks moistened and I let the tears flow.

A NIGHTMARE
ANNOUNCES AN EXISTENTIAL CRISIS

Shortly after attending Doug's Rosary service, I was awakened by a nightmare which shook me to the core:

I was driving home with two members of my men's group. Suddenly a four-story high wall of trash and some coffin-shaped items loomed up in front of me. Out of the rearview mirror I noticed a similar wall of trash and coffins closing in from behind. I and my friends were about to be crushed in a giant trash compacter. I looked to my left and saw three men sitting at a high counter at the controls of the compacter. I jumped out of the car and yelled STOP! STOP! at the top of my lungs. The menacing trash came to rest, teetering above me. I awakened, tense and breathless.

Was I trash, about to be relegated to a landfill, of no use anymore to society? I was horrified. What about those coffins? Whose were they? I'd gone to memorials for a half dozen older colleagues in the previous two years. A patient I was devoted to had just died. Death seemed to be closing in all around me. Would I get depressed like some of my retired colleagues? I was obviously concerned about how to maintain a sense of meaning and usefulness in my retirement and I refused to believe I was trash. This was an archetypal dream about retirement and the death of part of myself. What part of me had just died?

I recalled a book I had recently read by Richard Rohr, a Franciscan priest whose essay on preparing for the "second half of life" helped clarify my dream. In it, Rohr had addressed my situation with uncanny accuracy:

"When you first discharge your loyal soldier, it will feel like a loss of faith or loss of self. But it is only the loss of the false self and is very often the birth of the soul. Instead of being ego-driven you will begin to be soul drawn" (1).

I intuitively grasped that "my loyal soldier" referred to the focus and discipline I had maintained along the path of getting married and raising a family, training in medicine and psychiatry, making money and gaining the approval of others. In my strivings to attain all these things I had been successful, but in the process I had created a "false self" (similar to the Greek mask, or *persona*) involving my identity as a physician. Maintaining my false self as "Dr. Graves" had formed the core of my self-esteem, the major thrust of my motivations, and the foundation for many of my closest friendships. My nightmare was telling me that my false self must die before my true self as "John" could be born.

Like the two manifestations of the goddess Shakti in Hindu mythology, a complex dance of destruction (Kali) and creation (Durga) was taking place in my unconscious. I had feared that in giving up my identity as a physician, or "discharging my loyal soldier," I would actually die. I felt relieved when I realized that the *dramatis personae* in my dream, including the compactor-operators, represented parts of myself as well as a representation of my solidarity with my two retired friends. I was not alone. Together, we would weather the turbulent transitions we were undergoing.

A month after this dream I received calls from relatives of two other patients who had recently died. Janice had shared premonitions of death as she mourned the loss of her husband during our brief treatment. After ending treatment with her, I visited her in the hospital and finally in hospice two days before her death. I said goodbye and wished her well on her journey.

I had treated Robert, a Korean War veteran, for over twenty-five years. Both Janice and Robert's family members invited me to their funerals. Coming so close on the heels of Doug's memorial service, I was overwhelmed with sadness. I had to make a cleaner break from my work, so I declined their invitations and instead sent sympathy cards, describing how much I had valued working with their loved ones. I believe what I did in maintaining these contacts was as much for me as for my patients. Their deaths gave me an opportunity to more fully appreciate my other losses and to accept the reality that I had entered an entirely new phase of my life.

Several months later my closest friend Geoff, my sister-in law Joann, and my brother Tom died within a period of three months. I had assisted hundreds of patients with their mourning over the years. Now it was my turn to get help. I enrolled in six sessions of support groups sponsored by the Denver Hospice. Our groups huddled together with pictures and mementos of our relationships to concretize our feelings of loss. I brought a beat-up leather briefcase my friend had given me 30 years before, symbolizing both our friendship and my career.

It was very comforting to know that I was by no means alone in struggling with multiple losses. I was able to use these groups to put my staggering grief into words. Our support groups ended just before the 2016 Winter Solstice. In the last group we enjoyed a potluck meal and went our separate ways. As I walked to my car, the words of Isaiah suddenly came to me: "The people who walked in darkness have seen a great light." My heart lightened and in ten days I began the New Year with a glimmer of hope.

DON'T JUST FADE AWAY... THROW A PARTY

Many psychiatrists who are in private practice seem content to close their offices without marking the occasion in any public way, allowing themselves to just fade away. I'm a strong believer in rituals to mark important passages. Perhaps it's my upbringing as an Episcopalian. When my father retired after thirty-eight years as an engineer with the phone company, he was feted at a luncheon in his office building which included brief laudatory remarks by senior management, a brass plaque commemorating his years of service, and a round of hearty handshakes beneath flickering fluorescent lights. I don't recall my father having much, if any, input into the design of the proceedings. The whole sterile affair must have been scripted by someone in corporate headquarters.

I decided to do mine differently. I would like to have invited many of my patients who, after all, were truly my "co-workers," but this would have been awkward and a clear ethical violation. I invited my closest friends and colleagues, all the members of my men's group and their spouses. In addition, I invited one person from each decade of my professional life along with their spouses or partners. Forty of us enjoyed a gourmet luncheon with wine at Cucina Colore, one of Denver's popular Italian restaurants. My romantic partner read a summary describing the arc of my career. I recognized everyone and thanked them for their friendships, referrals, and emotional support over the years. A few of my close friends responded with kind remarks. It was a jolly, heartwarming party and immensely helpful for my transition.

FROM LOYAL SOLDIER TO WILLING SERVANT

Many people view retirement as "what happens after you stop working." In doing so, they are adhering to a centuries-old work ethic which entails a sharp demarcation between work and play, in which it is assumed that the retiree will simply play more now that (s)he has more free time. For me, retirement thus far has involved a more subtle movement from active professional pursuits to more time nourishing my inner world and prioritizing service activities which are both gratifying and meaningful. Reminiscences of my professional activities flood my awareness even as I remove their trappings (books, diplomas, and professional awards) from their former places of prominence to storage in my basement. My office "uniforms" (ties and sports coats), save for a select few for church, weddings, and funerals, have found their new owners through Goodwill.

Occasionally, I retrieve my tattered leather briefcase for trips to the library. The sweat-stained handle fits my hand perfectly and I notice that walking with it provides a comforting connection to my former life. As I ascend the library steps, I am reminded of my colleague Peter Mayerson's apt description of his retirement: "It's like removing a seventy-five pound pack...you don't know how heavy it's been until you take it off." My briefcase feels lighter than ever now.

My initial concerns about getting depressed and disoriented haven't materialized. In fact, since I've retired I've experienced virtually no signs of my former recurrent depressions or hypomanic behavior. I know I still carry genetic vulnerabilities and because of this I am careful in managing my stress levels. I can't wait to get up in the morning, make my coffee, read the paper, and get moving in a variety of activities.

The need to be involved in socially useful activities has not disappeared with the closing of my practice. In the last presidential election, I did voter registration. In 2018 I became more focused with canvassing to maximize voter turnout among registered Democrats. I've also become more active in writing letters to the editor on gun violence, the health effects of environmental degradation, and the divisiveness of current social and political discourse. All of these activities in some way reflect and are enhanced by my past professional experiences.

215

In working with homeless women at my church, my tasks are more hands-on. With a team of several others, I set up cots and blankets, greet and sign the women in at the door, serve dinner and do cleanup. I try not to intrude on the women, as they are generally exhausted after a long day on the streets. Recently, something very heartwarming happened. I was taking a break after dinner and an African American woman in her early forties sat down next to me. She introduced herself and immediately asked if I knew the meaning of her name in Hebrew. I told her I wasn't a student of Hebrew but that I'd be glad to help her find out.

We Googled her first and last names on my phone and immediately found the information she requested. It turned out that her first name means "noble" or "protected by God." Her last name derives from the yew tree, which was used to make hunting bows and weapons. When I shared this information with her she became animated, telling several others what she had just learned. "I'm noble and I'm protected by God and I have a weapon to protect me!" She spoke confidently, standing up a little taller. What a blessing.

As the suicide rate and serious drug addiction has been escalating in Colorado, I felt a need to use my training to address these issues in a meaningful way. Shortly after I retired, I became involved in volunteering for Mental Health Colorado, a non-governmental organization involved in lobbying, public education, and support for increasing accessibility of mental health services throughout the state. I helped them design their Mental Health Toolkit for use in all 178 of Colorado's school districts. The Toolkit, which was published in 2018, promotes wellness programs and assists each district in utilizing best practices for assessing children at risk for developing mental health and substance abuse problems (2).

THE INGREDIENTS OF A POSITIVE TRANSITION

I believe there are several reasons for my generally positive transition. First, I have made a conscientious attempt throughout my work life to maintain a balance between my work and other activities. This was absolutely necessary to combat burnout and minimize triggers for my mood disorder. I made a point of taking Wednesday afternoons off for piano lessons, fly fishing, skiing, or hiking, depending on the season. I took vacations with my family and rarely combined them with professional conferences. I took my emotional pulse regularly and got therapy and consultation when I sensed I was overburdened. I kept my hospital practice to a minimum to lessen the inevitable 2:00 a.m. emergency calls. I evaluated patients carefully on the phone, referring often to colleagues if I felt anxious or ambivalent about accepting them into treatment.

I deliberately varied my practice to include one or two consultation positions in a variety of public and private settings. These positions challenged me to learn new skills, provided important gratifications of working with many stimulating colleagues, and led to a steady flow of interesting referrals. Cultivating a general practice helped me avoid getting stuck in the boring rut of specialization and more frequent burnout cycles.

My mantra regarding clinical and consultation work was: "If you don't love what you're doing, give it up and try something else." During the course of my practice, I made healthy retreats from doing adolescent treatment when I became frustrated with parents unwilling to change their own destructive behaviors; forensic evaluations when I came to understand that the legal process was more about winning at all costs than striving for justice; medical management when I realized that my temperament was ill-suited for a hospital director's job; and couples therapy when the conflicts in my own marriages interfered with maintaining objectivity with my patients. In each case, I found significant relief by prioritizing my own mental health over pushing on at all costs.

While I attended regular continuing education courses, I preferred ones that were offered locally, intentionally avoiding long "working vacations" out of state. During my first few years of practice, I made myself available by phone to patients who were in crisis when I was away on vacation. Gradually, I put an end to this by making it clear that they would need to rely on the colleagues covering my practice. This not only addressed the issue of excessive dependency but also provided an opportunity for my patients to become more flexible in their adaptations. My vacations became more enjoyable and allowed me to devote more time and attention to my family.

THE VALUE OF POSITIVE RETIREMENT MODELS

Each of my parents provided excellent templates for how to flourish in retirement. My mother, who quit college after her sophomore year to elope with my father, committed herself to taking a full spectrum of adult education courses, culminating in a rigorous study of Hebrew in her early seventies. She became an avid biblical scholar and traveled to Israel several times with a few close women friends. My father, who worked as an engineer, had originally wanted to be a marine architect, but was forced to begin his career as a telephone line man during the Great Depression. He had already built several small sailboats by the time he retired at age sixty-two when I finished college. Soon thereafter, he made a careful study of ship models and took great joy in creating over a dozen scaled replicas of various sailing vessels, including those he owned, all meticulously crafted from original blueprints and materials.

My parents, who had prevailed over several rocky episodes in their marriage, each described their retirement years as the most rewarding of their life together. They sailed together on their Alden schooner, "Samantha," and later bought a forty-foot ketch, "Explorer," on which they cruised with their many friends for over ten summers on Lake Ontario and around the Thousand Islands of the Saint Lawrence River. When they no longer had the physical stamina to sail on their own, they sold the "Explorer" and continued sailing with friends in the Caribbean on chartered vessels.

When I asked Pop once how he managed to stay married for 63 years, his reply was terse and telling: "Stubbornness and good manners." My mother attributed their longevity to joining together in worship at their little Episcopal church and befriending several couples near the ages of their three sons. Their friendships with the younger generation kept them young and vigorous in many of their pursuits. Pop fly fished with friends in his canoe well into his mid-eighties and walked a mile a day, making rounds and greeting all of his younger neighbors.

Together with my brother Charles, he developed a detailed genealogy which culminated in a trip to Derbyshire and Yorkshire in north central England where several of our ancestors on both sides had worked as farmers and craftsmen in the seventeenth century. These researches solidified his sense of identity and brought him closer to Charles, from whom he had been estranged for many years. My mother taught Sunday school into her mid-eighties and was by far the oldest member of her congregation when she died at age 101. It is no accident that two of my initial projects following retirement have included building an eight-foot, two-piece bamboo fly rod and volunteering to serve homeless women in our Episcopal church.

WRITING AS RETIREMENT THERAPY

There is no doubt that the process of writing this book has played a key role in helping me manage and mourn the profound changes encompassing my retirement. Writing, like the mythical ferryman Charon, has enabled me to navigate some turbulent waters on my journey to the far shore. For most of my life, I have used writing to help me through complex, daunting experiences. During my analysis I kept a regular dream journal. Occasionally, my entries evolved into brief essays on how I was experiencing treatment both as patient and as a newly-minted therapist.

Writing articles about bipolar disorder helped me deal with the onset and setbacks with my own variations of this illness. Following my article on Robert Schumann (3), I wrote a poem on Schumann's tragic demise in a mental hospital. I wept when I set down my pen. I was mourning my intense identification with Schumann and also how my own experiences with bipolar disorder had caused conflicts and pain in my marriages and family. In the mid-2000s I corresponded almost daily by email with a high school classmate who lived in France. During my regular self-reflections with Penny, I created rough sketches for materials which later formed the backbone of this memoir.

A key part of writing anything, I had learned, was to select a title. I meditated on what formed the core of my life and work—it was, quite simply, the nourishment and maintenance of hope. My title came to me in a flash. I would call it *Lessons on the Road to Hope: A Psychiatrist's Journey*. I discovered that much of what I have written concerns not just hope, but the relationship between mourning and hope. As a young practitioner, struggling with my own losses, I did extensive research on bereavement, wrote articles on it and consulted with the Denver Grief Education Institute, where I participated in public seminars. I learned that as I and others endured the process of acute grief and managed the longer task of mourning, we tended to gain energy and clarity, often through writing.

I discovered that there are interesting paradoxes inherent in hope and mourning. What often begins with shock and despair can, with regular support, evolve into increased vitality, the release of creative energies, and a deepening of spirituality. The best example of this is found in Victor Frankl's *Man's Search for Meaning* (4). In the history of memoirs, there is no better portrayal of how a thoughtful psychiatrist managed to save his own life and those of countless others through his dogged determination to find meaning and purpose amidst the suffering of the Nazi death camps. His creation of logotherapy is a remarkable demonstration how traumatic life experiences can be creatively transformed to foster innovations which reduce the sufferings of others.

In his memoir, Frankl demonstrates how writing itself can give form to chaos, darkness, and despair. What is terrifying can be transformed by a process in which inner becomes outer. Writing and the spoken word (*logos*, from the Greek) create new potent realities. Events become more real and concrete in our minds when we set them to print. In writing and creating our own narratives, we assert a modicum of control over events which threaten to hold us captive. Anecdotes become antidotes.

In writing I acknowledge my deep connection with my patients and with the rest of humanity, thus I am not alone with my uncertainties about the future. I resurrect those I have lost and the pains of loss are overcome by the pleasures of recollection with enhanced meaning.

ALTERATIONS OF TIME-SENSE

Since retiring, I've often been surprised by alterations in my sense of time. Over many decades of training and practice, I have had to keep a strict calendar, often dividing each work day into multiples of fifteen-minute segments. Getting more than fifteen minutes behind often disrupted my appointment schedule for the entire day, forcing me to skimp on lunch or exercise breaks. As much as I prioritized seeing patients on time, I had to accept the reality that their (and my) intense emotional experiences could not be parceled into neat forty-five or sixty-minute quanta.

Patients who have been traumatized often share powerful narratives in which time becomes warped or even stops. In these situations, I found that bringing patients back to the here and now proved to be the best approach, for them and for myself. I was reminded of Einstein's thought experiments in the early 1900s when he predicted that clocks would slow down in the presence of intense gravitational fields. I wondered whether his model might also apply to the intense emotional force-fields of traumatic memories, where stress hormones and disruptions of circadian rhythms induce a sense of timelessness or time-stopping.

When I was seeing a large number of traumatized individuals, my altered time sense would frequently linger for considerable periods after I left my office, leaving me absent-minded in the presence of my family and friends. The demanding work ethic of patients before self frequently threatened to override my own circadian rhythms. To compensate for this, I deliberately sought refuge in the wilderness; hiking, climbing mountains, or wading trout streams to re-equilibrate. There I found peace in reconnecting with natural cycles, sunsets, moon rises, and the predictable march of the constellations as the seasons progressed. Realigning myself with the natural world brought me back to reality and restored my sense of order and my sanity.

Playing classical piano helped me deal with the disorganizing emotional intensity of seeing patients. Musical compositions, with their time signatures and repeated rhythmic patterns, helped me organize time and provided a safe container for the frequently chaotic emotions embedded in my patients' stories. When I carried a heavy clinical caseload and neglected my keyboard time, my hands began to ache and I recognized that my life was out of balance. During the stress of helping patients deal with the 2001 terrorist attacks, I suspended my piano playing for several weeks. Realizing what I was missing, I wrote this poem to my piano:

> Your voice stilled,
> the curve of your back
> recalling moments of calm
> when you responded faithfully
> to the nuances of my touch
> on the white surface of your eager face.

Allowing my body and mind to fall more into sync with natural cycles, I generally wake up shortly after sunrise, take naps in the afternoon if I'm tired, and retire in the evenings when I feel the urge. I try to avoid lengthy exposure to my laptop or disturbing news media in the evening. Since I am most alert and energetic in the morning hours, I typically do most of my writing and piano playing then. I continue to use a written weekly calendar for social events and to avoid being overbooked.

If I feel too tired, I cancel engagements. I'm less compulsive about returning phone calls, emails, or text messages, annoying some of my friends. I am on time for most appointments and give myself more than enough time to get where I am going. If I happen to be late, that's OK. I haven't gotten any speeding tickets since I closed my office. When I make a to do list in the morning, I try to keep it short and manageable, with the understanding that I may not complete all the tasks. It is exhilarating to discover that there are actually very few things that must be done *today*.

I find, much to my surprise, that I actually enjoy "passing the time" with bank tellers, shoe repairmen, and fellow parishioners after church services, all luxuries I rarely allowed myself while I was working. I have given up trying to multitask, which I never did well anyway.

Reminiscence, more intense and frequent that I have ever known, seems to pervade my existence to a degree that I never anticipated. Whether it represents a summing-up or a catching-up, or simply a reminder that I have more time behind me than ahead of me, I cannot say. Perhaps it is a kind of defragmentation of my cortical computer, compressing megabits of professional and personal memories into more compact storage, allowing my own lived experiences to come to the fore in surprising bursts. When people ask me what I miss about my practice, I respond by saying, "I miss my patients, not the work."

RETIREMENT'S IMPACT ON MY RELATIONSHIPS

Because I am less depleted and tired, I've been gratified by being able to spend more time with my friends, many of whom are also retired. Several of my men's group members and I enjoy regular Wednesday and Saturday morning breakfasts followed by leisurely walks through Denver's picturesque parks, where we delight in the antics of Canada Geese, soaring red-tailed hawks, and the playful giggles of children. With my newfound energy, I am more available and flexible to engage in spontaneous activities such as a hiking or catching a late afternoon movie, jazz, or dance concert with my partner.

I can plan vacations now without the arduous process of signing off to other psychiatrists covering my practice or warding off the dark undertow of depressed patients. Before I retired, my longest time away from my practice was eighteen days. In the past two years I've traveled abroad in Europe for periods of nearly six weeks.

RETIREMENT

I continue to enjoy my men's group and my men's reading group, and recently provided fly fishing classes for members of my church who contributed by bidding in our annual fundraising auction. Once apprehensive about inviting visitors in our home due to my need for solitude, I now enjoy hosting young leaders from around the world for periods of three weeks sponsored by World Denver and the U.S. State Department.

As a psychiatrist, I have devoted most of my adult life to helping others identify motivations and solve conflicts. It is only natural that I would carry my helper impulses over into my personal relationships. Since retirement, I am learning that it is best that I simply listen to others empathically, rather than trying to plumb their feelings or engage in problem-solving. Like many in my profession, I know that my urge to help is often combined with needs for admiration, respect, and gratitude. In retiring, I lost the steady stream of these reinforcements that came from my patients and colleagues, many of which have been interwoven with my identity as a physician.

Initially, I found myself becoming defensive when I experienced devaluation or snubs from friends. Now I view these experiences as indicators of my vulnerability as I continue to let go of my professional persona.

In one of my recent men's groups, my friends confronted me for trying to problem-solve with another physician member who was struggling to help a family member who was ill. It was as if I was back in my men's therapy group giving a patient a homework assignment. I apologized to my friend in the group. Identifying with my friend's helper-instincts, I had been foisting mine on him. It's hard to teach old docs new tricks.

At age seventy-one, Erik Erikson delivered the Jefferson Lectures, describing how our third president, in retirement, went on to remodel his beloved Monticello, assembled a massive library, founded the University of Virginia, and continued his prodigious output of writings and inventions. Erikson had, a quarter century earlier, described generativity vs. stagnation as one of the seminal challenges of advanced age (5). In his essay on Jefferson, he recognized how generativity ultimately springs from our growing awareness of finitude:

"One pole of any identity, in any historical period, relates man to what is forever contemporary, namely, eternity....this pole of identity deals with the awareness of death" (6).

223

In closing my practice and negotiating the first few years of retirement, I am beginning to appreciate Erikson's wisdom. Aging, mourning the loss of my patients, my practice, my friends, and some family members have made me aware that my time is limited. I am grateful for the support of my family, my teachers, my friends, and all that I have learned from my patients. I look forward to continuing my journey on the road to hope and to passing on what I have learned to future generations.

Loving, playing, creating, I dream of spring as time's shadow lengthens.

Men's group: Left to right: David Gies, Paul Walker, Dan Foss, Ed Ladon, Mel Grusing, John Cooper, Erwin Moser, Larry Englander, and George Hartlaub, Denver, Colorado, 2020

APPENDIX ONE
Ten Maxims Which Have Guided My Practice

1. I will view my patients, as did Maimonides, as none other than fellow creatures in human suffering.

2. It is our relationship, not my theory of mind or technique, which heals.

3. I will do my best to support my patients' strengths and natural healing processes.

4. I will commit myself to a lifetime of learning about my vocation and myself from my patients, colleagues and, when needed, from my own therapy.

5. I will nourish my tolerance for uncertainty and ambiguity, for the complexity of the human soul is infinite.

6. My work requires that I listen compassionately to stories of horror, grief, and despair without being overcome by them. To do this, I will take adequate time away from my work to restore myself.

7. I will seek out consultation and supervision from trusted colleagues and be as honest as I can with them to learn from my mistakes.

8. I will strive to be aware of my own limitations and those of my patients so I can set realistic goals for treatment.

9. I will address my own personal needs outside of treatment relationships so that I do not use my patients to fulfill these needs.

10. As no treatment is removed from my own or my patients' values and beliefs, I will strive to appreciate how these affect our work.

APPENDIX TWO
Words of Appreciation from my Patients

Thank you for all of your support and help over the years. I truly appreciate you and count you as one of the many blessings I've been given.

Thank you for being there for me always and for believing in me. You have the gift of a loving heart.

I am always grateful for your support, kindness, and belief in me. I relied on you totally. Now I can stand on my own two feet.

You saved my life.

You helped me getting older. You helped me with anxiety—the black spot of my life. I would not have made it without you…You have a good ear and a soft shoulder.

I got my life back. I have more self-confidence than I ever had. When I talk my colleagues listen. I am very grateful. My boys have a better dad.

You saved my life.

You helped me get over hurdles and I'm not going back. Therapy improved my health.

You guided things well in therapy. You never let me take over. You viewed me as an equal. My life is more balanced now.

I've come a long way this last year. I'm more optimistic, less scared. You encouraged my creativity. Now I can even make small talk.

This shit (addiction) caused me to have a heart attack. Your willingness to accept my lying and take me back as a patient really helped me.

I've grown up quite a bit and I'm not as vulnerable to the machinations of my own brain.

I've become very self-aware, especially about my depression and its insidious onset. Now I know when it's coming and can put it into words. My mood holds up well, even under stress.

You've been a real rock. My life is better for our work together.

Now I think before I speak.

I'm better focused on task. I learned a lot about empathy as a therapist. The group gave me a new toolbox with better tools.

Now I can put myself first and not feel selfish. You've taken me from the darkness into the light.

I wish there were another Dr. G. Your support during my daughter's rehab was really helpful.

You were a blessing with your knowledge (of my faith). Now I can be responsible in very difficult conflicts. You should be proud of all the people you have helped. You have also given me the skills to "rock on."

You've been a father figure I could trust. You have no agenda except getting me to care for myself. You offered me some forgiveness when I wasn't able to forgive myself... I believed in you as much as you always believed in and hoped for me.

You helped me let go of shame about what happened in my family. Now I have a good foundation for dealing with stress. I can accept and manage my depression and temper. I can break out of isolation and loneliness.

I'm less sensitive to changes. I can take care of myself now and take care of others better. Your availability on the phone really meant a lot. You've helped me live with a lifelong illness.

WORDS OF APPRECIATION FROM MY PATIENTS

I have more energy now and can tolerate my stepdaughters, who used to drive me crazy.

You listened. You were non-dictatorial. We had an ally-ship.

You accepted me in spite of my dishonesty (about addiction). You didn't tell me what to do. I've learned to listen with my heart and to trust God.

You've been great on the medical part. You helped me delve deep and release old issues. I was so disconnected and you helped me get ignited to re-engage. You've provided a different lens to look at things.

You've helped me with aging and dealing with my surgery. Now I can say no to the helper/pleaser part of me.

You had clear boundaries. I'm much more focused and less depressed.

Now I have twenty-two years of sobriety. I'm more involved with parenting.

Your more structured sessions were very helpful. Now, when I look in the mirror, I see a person who is kind, not ugly, and more pleasant.

I'm more assertive about my needs. You really helped me by grounding and reframing my thoughts about my ex, my father, and my boyfriend.

I'm more accepting of my husband's religious faith. I appreciate your ability to deconstruct and help me be rational rather than emotional. You've been my rock.

You saw me through many losses (head injury, job, marriage). I can just be me now.

Author's note: Many of these quotations came near the end of treatment when I asked specifically what they felt they had learned from therapy. A few of them came from emails and cards I received after I retired.

CHAPTER NOTES

Chapter 1: Born to Listen

1. Pasternak, Boris. *Doctor Zhivago*, Pantheon Press, 1958, 542.

Chapter 2: The Making of a Wounded Healer

1. Kesey, Kenneth, *One Flew Over the Cuckoo's Nest*, Penguin, Toronto, 1962.
2. Freud, Sigmund (1917). Mourning and Melancholia, in Vol. IV, *The Collected Papers of Sigmund Freud*, Institute for Psychoanalysis and Hogarth Press, London, 1924.
3. Kazantzakis, Nikos, *The Last Temptation of Christ*, Bantam Books, New York, 1961.
4. Calvin, John, *The Institutes of the Christian Religion*, 2 vols, John T. McNeill, ed., F.W. Battles, trans., Westminster Press, Philadelphia, 1960.
5. *Ethical Writings of Maimonides*, Raymond Weiss and Charles Butterworth, eds., New York University Press, 1975, 129-154.
6. Kovel, Joel, *White Racism: A Psychohistory*, Pantheon Books, New York, 1970.

Chapter 3: Training and Early Practice Years

1. Medical Oath from the *Declaration of Geneva*, 1948.
2. Wallerstein, Judith and Blakeslee, Sandra, *The Good Marriage*, Houghton Mifflin Harcourt, Boston, 1995.
3. Graves, John (1976). On Becoming a Psychiatrist: Or, Adolescence Revisited, *Psychiatric Annals*, 4:100-108.
4. Yalom, Irvin, *Existential Psychotherapy*, Basic Books, New York, 1980.

Chapter 4: Managing the Stresses of Practice

1. MacDonald, John, *Psychiatry and the Criminal*, 3rd. ed., Charles C. Thomas Publishers, Springfield, 1976.

2. Charles, S.C. (1985). Physicians on Trial: Sued and Non-Sued Physicians Self-Reported Reactions of Malpractice Litigation, *Am. J. of Psychiatry,* 142: 437-440.

3. Ofri, Danielle, *What Doctors Feel,* Beacon Press, Boston, 2013.

4. Kantrowitz, Judith, *The Patient's Impact on the Analyst,* Analytic Press, London, 1996.

5. Herman, Judith, *Trauma and Recovery,* Basic Books, New York, 1992.

6. Graves, John (1993). Living with Mania: A Study of Outpatient Group Psychotherapy for Bipolar Patients, *Am. J. Psychotherapy,* 47:1,113-126.

7. Jamison, Kay Redfield, *An Unquiet Mind: A Memoir of Moods and Madness,* Vintage Books, New York, 1995.

8. Guy, James, *The Personal Life of the Psychotherapist: The Impact of Clinical Practice on the Therapist's Intimate Relationships and Emotional Well-being,* John Wiley and Sons, New York, 1987.

Chapter 5: Listening and Empathy

1. Jamison, Kay Redfield, *Touched With Fire: Manic Depressive Illness and the Artistic Temperament,* Free Press, New York, 1993.

2. Reik, Theodore, *Listening With the Third Ear,* Garden City Books, New York, 1948.

3. Cage, John, *Silence,* Wesleyan University Press, Middletown, 1961, 13-14.

4. Nhat Hanh, Thich, *The Long Road Leads to Joy: A Guide to Walking Meditation,* Parallax Press, Berkeley, 1996.

5. Winnicott, D.W., *Boundary and Space: An Introduction to the Works of D.W. Winnicott,* M. Davis and D. Wallbridge, eds., Bruner Mazel, New York, 1981, 99-102.

6. Nouwen, Henri, *The Wounded Healer: Ministry in Contemporary Society,* Image Books, Doubleday, New York, 1990, 91-92.

7. Kohut, Heinz (1959). Introspection, Empathy and Psychoanalysis, *J. Am. Psychoanalytic Assoc.,* 7:459-483.

8. Greenson, Ralph, Empathy and Its Vicissitudes, in *Explorations in Psychoanalysis,* International University Press, New York, 1978.

9. Herman, Judith, *Trauma and Recovery,* Basic Books, New York, 1992.

10. Sacks, Oliver, *Musicophilia: Tales of Music and the Brain,* Vintage PB, New York, 2007.

11. Schwartz-Salant, Nathan, *Narcissism and Character Transformation: The Study of Narcissistic Character Disorders*, Inner City Books, Toronto, 1982.

12. Rizzolati, G. and Craighero, L. (2004). The Mirror Neuron System, *Annual Review of Neuroscience*, 27: 169-192.

13. Keysers, Christian, *The Empathic Brain*, Christian Keysers, Lexington, KY 2011.

14. Buzan, R., Kupfer, J., Eastridge, D. and Lema-Hincape, L. (2004). Philosophy of Mind: Coming to Terms with Traumatic Brain Injury, *Neurorehabilitation*, 34: 601-611.

15. Coleman, Joshua, *When Parents Hurt: Compassionate Strategies When You and Your Grown Child Don't' Get Along*, William Morrow, New York 2008.

16. Dowrick, Stephanie, *Intimacy and Solitude: Balancing Closeness and Independence*, W.W. Norton, New York, 1991.

17. Krause, Bernie, *The Great Animal Orchestra: Finding the Origins of Music in the World's Wild Places*, Little Brown, New York, 2012.

Chapter 6: Integrating Spirituality, Religious Faith, and Therapy

1. Geoffrey, Lloyd, ed., *Hippocratic Writings*, 2nd ed., Penguin Books, London, 1983.

2. Miller, William, *Integrating Spirituality into Treatment: Resources for Practitioners*, American Psychological Association Press, Washington, D.C., 1999.

3. James, William, *The Varieties of Religious Experience: A Study in Human Nature*, First Collier Books Edition, New York, 1961, 377. Originally published in 1900.

4. *The Gift: Poems by Hafiz, The Great Sufi Master*, Daniel Ladinsky, trans., Penguin Compass, New York, 1999.

5. The Gospel of Thomas, Thomas O. Lambdin, trans., in *The Nag Hammadi Library*, James Robinson, ed., Harper Collins, San Francisco, 1990.

6. Borg, Marcus, *Meeting Jesus Again for the First Time: The Historical Jesus and the Heart of Contemporary Faith*, Harper Collins, New York, 1994.

7. Pagels, Elaine, *The Gnostic Gospels*, Vintage Books, New York, 1979.

8. Nouwen, Henri, *The Return of the Prodigal Son: A Story of Homecoming*, Image Books, Doubleday Press, New York, 1992.

9. Tillich, Paul, *The Courage to Be*, Yale University Press, New Haven, 1962.
10. Miller, William, *op. cit.*
11. My recommendations for patients (especially Roman Catholics) to listen to Gregorian Chants came from my own experience and from reading Katherine Le Mee's *Chant: The Origins, Form, Practice and Healing Power of Gregorian Chants*, Bell Tower, New York, 1994.

Le Mee summarizes the therapeutic power of chant as follows:

> "The effect of chant is to balance the mind, emotions and body. Singing or simply actively listening to chant with directed attention, we feel whole and part of a greater whole. It is precisely this integrating tendency that constitutes healing." (140)

12. Jung, C. G., *Psychology and Religion: West and East,* R.F.C. Hull, trans., Bollingen Series, Vol. 11, Pantheon Books, New York, 1958.

Chapter 7: Forgiveness

1. Arendt, Hannah., *The Human Condition*, University of Chicago Press, Chicago, 1958, 214.
2. *The Book of Common Prayer*, Seabury Press, New York, 1979, 449-452. Originally drafted by the American Anglican Church in 1789.
3. Nouwen, Henri, *The Return of the Prodigal Son: A Story of Homecoming*, Image Books, New York, 1995.
4. Giridharadas, Anand, *The True American: Murder and Mercy in Texas*, W.W. Norton, New York, 2014.
5. Ludin, Rafaat and Loopesko, Windham, *And the Sun Will Rise from the West: The Predicament of "Islamic Terrorism" and the Way Out*, X Libris, 2016, 34-40.
6. *The Bhagavad Gita: A New Translation* by Stephen Mitchell, Harper Collins, New York, 1988, 169-170.
7. Erikson, Erik, *Gandhi's Truth*, W.W. Norton, New York, 1969, 41.
8. Dalai Lama and Victor Chan, *The Wisdom of Forgiveness: Intimate Conversations and Journeys*, Penguin Press, New York, 2004, 234.
9. *Exploring Forgiveness*, R.B. Enright and J. North, eds., University of Wisconsin Press, Madison, 1998.
10. Fitzgibbons, Richard, Anger and the Healing Power of Forgiveness: A Psychiatrist's View, in Enright and North, 71.
11. Fitzgibbons, in Enright and North, 65.

12. Potter-Effron, R.T. and Potter-Effron, P.S., *Letting Go of Anger*, 2nd ed., New Harbinger Publications, Oakland, 2006.
13. Fitzgibbons, in Enright and North, 79.
14. Luskin, Fred, *Forgive for Good: A Proven Prescription for Health and Happiness*, Harper Collins, San Francisco, 2002.
15. Elkins, Dov Peretz, *Rosh Hashanah Readings*, Jewish Lights Publications, Woodstock Vermont, 2006.
16. Keating, Thomas, *Intimacy with God: An Introduction to Centering Prayer*, Crossroad Publications, New York, 2009.

Chapter 8: Boundaries

1. Epstein, R.S. and Simon, R.I. (1990). The Exploitation Index: An early warning indicator of boundary violations in psychotherapy, *Bull. of the Menninger Clinic*, 54:4, 450-465.
2. Martinez, Richard (2000). A Model for Boundary Dilemmas: Ethical Decision-Making in the Patient Professional Relationship, in *Ethical Human Sciences and Services*, 2:1, 43-61.
3. Roughton, Ralph (1992). Useful Aspects of Acting Out: Repetition, Enactment and Actualization, *J. of the Amer. Psychoanalytic Assoc.*, 41:2, 13-34.
4. Blum, H.P. (1973). The Concept of the Erotized Transference, *J. of the Amer. Psychoanalytic Assoc.*, 21:61-76.
5. Gabbard, Glen (1989). Patients Who Hate, *Psychiatry*, 52:2, 86-96.
6. Kelly, John and Olsen, Homer, The Therapist as a New Developmental Object, unpublished MS, ca. 1976.
7. Gabbard, Glen (1995). Transference and Counter-transference in the Psychotherapy of Therapists Charged with Sexual Misconduct, Psychiatric Annals, 25:2, 100-105.
8. Herman, Judith, *Trauma and Recovery*, Basic Books, New York, 1992.
9. Naht Hanh, Thich, *The Miracle of Mindfulness*, Beacon Press, Boston, 1987.

Chapter 9: Depression, Suicide and the Dialectics of Hope

1. Graves, J.S. (1978). Adolescents and Their Psychiatrist's Suicide; A Study of Shared Grief and Mourning, *J. of the Amer. Acad. Of Child Psychiatry*, 17:3, 521-532.
2. Rogers, M.L., Galynker, I., Yaseen, Z., *et. al.* (2007). An overview and Comparison of Two Proposed Suicide-Specific Diagnoses:

Acute Suicidal Affective Disturbance and Suicide-Crisis Syndrome, *Psychiatric Annals*, 47:8, 416-420.

3. Baumeister, Roy, *Escaping the Self: Alcoholism, Spirituality, Masochism and Other Flights from the Burden of Selfhood*, Basic Books, New York, 1990.

4. Schneidman, Edward, *Suicide as Psychache: A Clinical Approach to Self-Destructive Behavior*, Jason Aronson Press, published by Rowman and Littlefield, Lanham, MD, 1993.

5. Zero Suicide Website: www.zerosuicide.sprc.org, accessed August 20, 2017.

6. Heron, Joan Carroll. Suicide-Specific Treatments: How Evidence-Based Research and the Zero Suicide Movement Contribute to the Understanding and Treatment of the Suicidal Patient. Lecture to the Denver Society for Psychoanalysis, September 22, 2017.

7. Real, Terrence, *I Don't Want to Talk About It: Overcoming the Secret Legacy of Male Depression*, Scribner Press, New York, 1997.

8. Goodwin, Frederick and Jamison, Kay R., *Manic Depressive Illness*, Oxford University Press, New York, 1990.

9. Rostila, M., Saarel, J., Kawachi, I. (2013). Suicide Following the Death of a Sibling: A Nationwide Follow-up Study from Sweden, *Br. Medical Journal,* open2013, e002618,doi10.1136/bmjopen, accessed January 18, 2018.

10. Dinwiddie, Stephen (2017). Thinking About the Assessment of Risk, *Psychiatric Annals*, 47:9, 440.

11. Simon, O.R., Swann, A.C., Powel, K.E., et. al., (2001). Characteristics of Impulsive Suicide Attempts and Attempters, *Suicide and Life-Threatening Behavior*, 32: 49-59.

12. Marcus, M.B. (2015). More Attention Urged to Decrease Medical Trainee's Suicide Risk, *Psychiatric News, 50:*8, 9-10.

13. Shea, Shawn C. (2017). Uncovering a Patient's Hidden Method of Choice for Suicide: Insights from the Chronological Assessment of Suicide Events Approach, *Psychiatric Annals*, 47:8, 421-427.

14. Groopman, Jerome, *The Anatomy of Hope: How People Prevail in the Face of Illness*, Random House, New York, 2004.

Chapter 10: Group Therapy and Consultations

1. Yalom, Irvin, *The Theory and Practice of Group Psychotherapy*, Basic Books, New York, 1970.

2. Yalom, Irvin., *Inpatient Group Psychotherapy*, Basic Books, New York, 1983.

3. Yalom, 1970, 305-306.

4. Duke, Patty and Hochman, Gloria, *A Brilliant Madness: Living with Manic Depressive Illness*, Bantam Books, New York, 1992, 179.

5. This discussion is a modification of a previously published article by the author: Graves, J.S. (1993). Living with Mania: A Study of Outpatient Group Therapy for Bipolar Patients, *Amer. J. of Psychotherapy*, 47:1, 113-126.

6. Kohut, Heinz (1972). Thoughts on Narcissism and Narcissistic Rage, in *The Search for the Self,* P.H. Ornstein, ed., Vol. 2, International Universities Press, New York, 615-658.

7. Ewing, W., Lindsey M. and Pomeranz, J., *Battering: An AMEND Manual for Helpers*, AMEND and Loretto Heights College, Denver, 1984.

8. Shapiro, Joan, *Men: A Translation for Women*, Dutton/Penguin, New York, 1992.

9. Herman, Judith, *Trauma and Recovery*, Basic Books, New York, 1992.

Paul Walker and I used the following resources in conceptualizing our interventions in our men's psychotherapy group. In some cases, we recommended that group members read and discuss some of these in group sessions:

10. Bly, Robert, *Iron John: A Book About Men*, Addison Wesley Press, New York, 1990.

11. Bolen, Jean Shinoda, *Gods in Everyman: A New Psychology of Men's Lives and Loves*, Harper and Row, New York, 1989.

12. Duvall, Jeffrey and Churches, James, *Stories of Men, Meaning and Prayer: The Reconciliation of Heart and Soul in Modern Manhood*, Four Directions Press, Nederland, CO, 2001.

13. Faludi, Susan, *Stiffed: The Betrayal of the American Man*, William Morrow Press, New York, 1999.

14. Glover, Robert, *No More Mr. Nice Guy: A Proven Path for Getting What You Want in Sex, Love and Life*, Running Press, Philadelphia, 2003.

15. Johnson, Robert, *He: Understanding Male Psychology*, Harper and Row, Perennial Library, New York, 1997.

16. Keen, Sam, *Fire in the Belly: On Being a Man*, Bantam Press, New York, 1992.

17. Levenson, Daniel, *The Seasons of a Man's Life*, Ballantine PB, New York, 1978.

18. Moore, Robert and Gillette, Douglas, *King, Warrior, Magician, Lover: Rediscovering Archetypes of the Mature Masculine*, Harper, San Francisco, 1990.

Chapter 11: Treating Physicians. An annotated bibliography

1. Myers, Michael and Gabbard Glen, *The Physician as Patient: A Handbook for Mental Health Clinicians*, American Psychiatric Association Press, Washington, D.C., 2008, p. 33. This volume expands Klitzman's findings to include physicians in psychotherapy and is particularly helpful with its discussion of how doctors handle the predicament of role-reversal. My chapter exemplifies Myers' and Gabbard's concepts with detailed case descriptions.

2. Klitzman, Robert, *When Doctors Become Patients*, Oxford University Press, New York, 2008. Klitzman, a psychiatrist at Columbia University, provides a useful description of the psychological issues seen in doctors who are in treatment for serious, life-threatening illnesses. His discussion of the processes of collusion to deny and minimize the severity of illness helped me conceptualize how mutual idealization and admiration can interfere with accurate diagnosis and with providing the most effective psychiatric care.

3. Alexander, Eben, *Proof of Heaven: A Neurosurgeon's Journey into the Afterlife*, Simon and Schuster, New York, 2011. Alexander describes his near-death experiences while in a coma from a fulminant *E. coli* meningitis. His integration of a strong religious faith with the hard science of neurophysiology provided a useful model for my own work as a psychiatrist.

4. Groopman, Jerome, *The Anatomy of Hope: How People Prevail in the Face of Illness*, Random House, New York, 2004. Groopman's distinctions between true and false hope proved invaluable for my work with suicidal and terminally ill patients, particularly regarding treatment decisions which maximize control and autonomy for the individual.

5. Groopman, Jerome, *How Doctors Think,* Houghton Mifflin, Boston, 2008. A brilliant discussion of the cognitive errors made by physicians in five categories: representativeness, attribution, affect, anchoring and availability. Applying Groopman's analysis to my own practice, I was able to review some of my own diagnostic cognitive errors in ways which improved the course of several treatments.

6.   Holt Terrence, *Internal Medicine, A Doctor's Stories*, Liveright Publishing, W.W. Norton, New York, 2013. In this description of the "harrowing crucible of medical residency," Holt highlights the importance of the capacity to compartmentalize and forget some of the horrific experiences encountered in training and practice. Reading Holt's memoir penetrated my amnesia about painful practice experiences and sharpened my focus in writing about them.

7.   Marsh, Henry, *Do No Harm: Stories of Life, Death and Brain Surgery*, St. Martin's Press, New York, 2014. Marsh, a British neurosurgeon, reveals how he struggled with guilt and shame in cases involving fatal or debilitating operative results. His keen scalpel dissects away his own *hubris*, revealing intense fears of failure and disgrace. Reading Marsh's work helped me console myself and family members of two patients who suicided and also to apologize to other patients where I missed the correct diagnosis at the outset of treatment.

8.   Nuland, Sherwin, *The Uncertain Art: Thoughts on a Life in Medicine*, Random House, New York, 2008. Nuland's work uses an aphorism attributed to Hippocrates to make an impassioned plea for humility in medical practice, thereby providing an antidote for the perfectionism and excessive certainty implied in today's "evidence-based" treatments.

9.   Ofri, Danielle, *What Doctors Feel: How Emotions Affect the Practice of Medicine*, Beacon Press, New York, 2013. Expanding on Groopman's work, Ofri anchors her discussion with a focus on a patient who was initially denied a heart transplant based on her status as an undocumented immigrant. Her descriptions of her own anger, frustration, guilt, shame and helpless bewilderment gives permission to all who practice medicine to normalize and discuss these inevitable feelings. She also argues convincingly for a less exhausting, more empathic and humane training experience.

10.   Weisman, Jamie, *As I Live and Breathe: Notes of a Patient-Doctor*, Farrer, Strauss and Giroux, New York, 2002. Weisman's experience with a rare immune deficiency disease led to her decision to become a doctor and enriched her ability to more fully empathize with her patients. Her writings validated my own use of self-disclosure with a variety of patients, including physicians, regarding my adaptations to chronic back pain.

11.   Yalom, Irvin, *The Gift of Therapy: An Open Letter to a New Generation of Therapists and Their Patients*, Harper Collins, New York, 2002. In this valedictory, Yalom offers 85 maxims for therapists. In a chapter

on occupational hazards, he describes how important his own professional support groups have been for him in dealing with painful practice experiences. His openness encouraged me to become more transparent in my own support groups, thus decreasing my practice stress.

Chapter 12: Hermaphrodites, Gays and Bisexuals

1. *Diagnostic and Statistical Manual of Mental Disorders, DSM-II,* American Psychiatric Association Press, Washington, D.C., 1968.
2. Socarides, Charles, Homosexuality, Jason Aronson, New York, 1978.
3. *Diagnostic and Statistical Manual of Mental Disorders,* DSM-III, American Psychiatric Association Press, Washington, D.C. 1980.
4. Hickey, Philip, Homosexuality: The Mental Illness That Went Away, Internet Blog Posting, October 8, 2011, accessed October 14, 2017.
5. *Diagnostic and Statistical Manual of Mental Disorders, DSM-IV,* American Psychiatric Association Press, Washington, D.C., 1994.
6. *Diagnostic and Statistical Manual of Mental Disorders, DSM-5,* American Psychiatric Association Press, Washington, D.C., 2013, 215.
7. Carmel, T.C. and Erikson-Schroth, L. (2016). Know Your Rights: Transgender People and the Law, *Psychiatric Annals*, 46:6, 346-349.
8. Gorton, N. and Grubb, H., General, Sexual and Reproductive Health, in Erikson-Schroth, Laura, ed., *Trans Bodies, Trans Selves: A Resource By and For the Transgender Community*, Oxford University Press, 2014, 215-240.
9. Pula, Jack (2016). The Role of the Psychiatrist Working with Transgender Patients, *Psychiatric Annals*, 46:6, 340-345.
10. Leuze, Robert, Baritone and Bassi, James, Pianist in performance on the CD: *Songs of Our Lives: Operatic and Contemporary Selections that Reflect the Gay Experience*, Calvero Productions, New York, 1998.
11. Plato, *Collected Dialogues*, Edith Hamilton and Huntington Cairns, eds., chapter on Plato's *Symposium*, Michael Joyce, trans., Bollingen Series, Vol. LXXI, Pantheon Books, New York, 1964, 542-545.
12. Le Vay, Simon (1991). A Difference in Hypothalamic Structure Between Heterosexual and Homosexual Men, *Science*, 253: 1034-1037.
13. Baily, J.M. and Pillard, R. (1991). A Genetic Study of Male Sexual Orientation, *Arch. General Psychiatry*, 48: 1089-93.
14. Isay, Richard, *Becoming Gay: A Journal of Self-Acceptance*, Holt PB, New York, 1997, 8.

15.	Burton, Humphrey, *Leonard Bernstein*, Doubleday Publishers, New York, 1994.

Chapter 13: Changes in the Field of Psychiatry

1.	Kohut, Heinz, *The Analysis of the Self*, International Universities Press, New York, 1971.

2.	Greenburg, Jay and Mitchell, Stephen, *Object Relations in Psychoanalytic Theory*, Harvard University Press, Cambridge, 1983.

3.	Kelly, John and Olsen, Homer. The Therapist as a New Developmental Object, unpublished MS, ca. 1976.

4.	Horowitz, Mardi, *Stress Response Syndromes*, Jason Aronson, Northvale, NJ, 1986.

5.	Herman, Judith, *Trauma and Recovery*, Basic Books, New York, 1992.

6.	Maslow, Abraham, *Motivation and Personality*, Harper Press, New York, 1954.

7.	Vaillant, George, *Ego Mechanisms of Defense: A Guide for Clinicians and Researchers*, American Psychiatric Association Press, Washington, D.C., 1992.

8.	Jeste, Dilip, *Positive Psychiatry: A Clinical Handbook*, American Psychiatric Publishing, Washington, D.C., 2016.

9.	Freud, Sigmund, Project for a Scientific Psychology, Letter to Wilhelm Fleiss, 1895, commentary by Frank Sulloway in *Freud: Biologist of the Mind*, Basic Books, New York, 1979, 113-131.

10.	Jones, Edward G. and Mendel, Lorne (1999). Assessing the Decade of the Brain, *Science*, 284:739-41.

11.	Kandel, Eric, *In Search of Memory: The Emergence of a New Science of Mind*, W.W. Norton, New York, 2006, 403-404.

12.	Jones, K.R. and Reichart, L.F. (1990). Molecular Cloning of a Human Gene that is a Member of the Nerve Growth Family, *Proceedings of the National Academy of Sciences*, 87:20, 8060-8064.

13.	Goodman, Louis and Gilman, Alfred.,ch. 12 by Murray Jarvik, Drugs Used in the Treatment of Psychiatric Disorders, in *The Pharmacologic Basis of Therapeutics*, 3rd ed., MacMillan Publishers, New York, 1967.

14.	Stahl, Stephen, *Stahl's Essential Psychopharmacology: Neuroscientific Basis and Practical Applications*, 3rd ed., Cambridge University Press, New York, 2008.

15.	Kramer, Peter, *Listening to Prozac*, Penguin Books, New York, 1981.

16. Bremner, J. Douglas, *Brain Imaging Handbook*, W.W. Norton, New York, 2005, 98.

17. Duman, R.S. (2002). Structural Alterations in Depression: Cellular Mechanisms Underlying Pathology and Treatment of Mood Disorders, *CNS Spectrums*, 7: 140-147.

18. Okuma, T. and Kishimoto, A. (1998) A History of Investigation on the Mood Stabilizing Effect of Carbamazepine in Japan, *Psychiatry and Clinical Neuroscience*, 52:1, 3-12.

19. Symbiax Prescribing Information Pamphlet, Eli Lilly Pharmaceutical Company, 2010.

20. Lebell, Sharon, *The Art of Living: The Classical Manual on Virtue, Happiness and Effectiveness of Epictetus*, Harper Collins, San Francisco, 1995, 10-28.

21. Hollon, S.D. and Beck A.T., ch. 11, Cognitive Behavioral Therapies, in *Handbook of Psychotherapy and Behavior Change*, 6th ed., M.J. Lambert, ed., John Wiley and Sons, Hoboken, 2013.

22. Cary, Benedict, Expert on Mental Illness Reveals Her Own Fight, *The New York Times*, June 23, 2011.

23. Linehan, Marsha, *Cognitive Behavior Therapy of Borderline Personality Disorder*, Guilford Press, New York, 1993.

24. Di Cristina, Mariette (2017). This is Not a Woman's Issue: Why the New Science of Sex and Gender Matters for Everyone, *Scientific American*, 317: 3, 52.

25. Stefanik, Marcia (2017). Not Just for Men, *Scientific American*, 317:3, 52-57.

26. Barry, Colleen, et. al. (2010). The Mental Health Parity Act of 1996: A Political History of Federal Mental Health and Addiction Insurance, *Millbank Quarterly*, 88:3, 404-433.

27. May William. *The Physician's Covenant*, Westminster Press, Philadelphia, 1983, 118-119.

Chapter 14: Future Trends in Psychiatry

1. Freidman, Thomas L. *Thank You For Being Late: An Optimist's Guide to Thriving in the Age of Accelerations*, Farrer, Strauss and Giroux, New York, 2017, 28-32.

2. Kahn, Salman, Address to the Aspen Institute, Aspen, August 2015.

3. Watts, Vabrien. APA On Tour to Examine Link Between Climate Change and Mental Health, *Psychiatric News*, September 2, 2016, 22-23.

CHAPTER NOTES

4. Judge Ann Aiken. Opinion in *Kelsey Cascadia Rose v. United States of America*, Oregon District Court, 2016.

5. Van Susteren, Lise (2017). Hold Your Breath, *Clinical Psychiatry News*, 5:10-11.

6. Allen, Joe and Spengler, John (2016). *Environmental Health Perspectives*, 124:6, 805-812.

7. Albrecht, G., Kelly, B., et.al. (2007). Solastalgia; the Distress Caused by Environmental Change, *Australian Psychiatry*, 15: Supplement 1, S91-S98.

8. Brady Campaign Newsletter, September 2017.

9. Van der Kolk, Bessel, *The Body Keeps the Score: Brain, Mind and Body in the Healing of Trauma*, Penguin Books, New York, 2015, 1-9, 350.

10. Saison, J., Smith, M, et.al., Internet Use and Addiction: Signs, Symptoms and Treatment, adapted from *Harvard Health Publications* in www.Helpguide.org, updated December 2013, accessed August 22, 2017.

11. Malenka, R.C., Nestler, E.J., and Hyman, S.E., Reinforcement and Addictive Disorders, in *Molecular Neuropharmacology: A Foundation for Clinical Neuroscience*, 2nd ed., McGraw Hill Medical, New York 2009, 376.

12. Charatan, Dana, *The Denver Psychoanalytic Society Newsletter*, October 2018.

13. Barnett, David, Computerized CBT for Depression and Anxiety, *United Kingdom National Health Service Report*, updated May 2013, summarized in www.nice.org.uk, accessed 12 September 2017.

14. Vogel, Matt, Transforming Mental Health Through Innovation. Public lecture to the University of Colorado Advocates, Denver, September 23, 2018.

15. Dobbs, David, The Smartphone Psychiatrist, *The Atlantic Monthly*, July 2017.

16. Petersen, Andrea, Your Video Therapist Will See You Now, *The Wall Street Journal*, April 27, 2020, A11.

17. U.S. Census Bureau Website: Projections of the Size and Composition of the U.S. Population, 2014-2060, S.L. Colby and J. M. Ortman, eds. https://www.census.gov/content/dam/Census/Library/publications/2015/demo/25110-43, accessed September 22, 2017.

18. Jacobs, Barry, *The Emotional Survival Guide for Caregivers*, Guilford Press, New York, 2006.

19. Coleman, Joshua. *When Parents Hurt: Compassionate Strategies When You and Your Grown Child Don't Get Along,* William Morrow PB, New York, 2008.

20. Pilkington, Alexis. Facebook Horror! Cyber-Bullies Harass Teen Even After Suicide, www.huffingtonpost.com, May 25, 2011, accessed December 29, 2017.

21. Kohlhatkar, Sheelah, The Cost of the Opioid Crisis, *The New Yorker Magazine*, September 18, 2017, 21.

22. Sharfstein, Steven, The Psychiatric Care System of the Future, *Clinical Psychiatry News*, 2017, 5: 4-5.

23. Herb, James A., Donald J. Trump, Alleged Incapacitated Person: Mental Incapacity, the Electoral College, and the Twenty Fifth Amendment, in *The Dangerous Case of Donald J. Trump: 27 Psychiatrists and Mental Health Experts Assess a President,* Bandy Lee, ed., St. Martin's Press, New York, 2017, 136-147.

24. Lifton, Robert J., Our Witness to Malignant Normality, in Forward to *The Dangerous Case of Donald J. Trump, op.cit.*, 136-147.

25. Arendt, Hannah, *The Origins of Totalitarianism*, Meridian Books, World Publishing Co., New York, 1958.

Chapter 15: Retirement

1. Rohr, Richard, *Falling Upward: A Spirituality for the Two Halves of Life,* Jossey Bass, San Francisco, 2011, 50.

2. School Mental Health Toolkit for Colorado, published by Mental Health Colorado and the Western Interstate Commission for Higher Education Mental Health Program, 2018. See digital access at www.mentalhealthcolorado.org/schooltoolkit.

3. Graves, John (2005). Composition and Adaptation in the Life of Robert Schumann, *Bulletin of the Menninger Clinic,* 69:4, 313-330.

4. Frankl, Victor, *Man's Search for Meaning,* Beacon Press, Boston, 2006.

5. Erikson, Erik, *Childhood and Society,* W.W. Norton, New York, 1950.

6. Erikson, Erik, *Dimensions of a New Identity,* W.W. Norton, New York, 1974.

ACKNOWLEDGMENTS

Writing this memoir has been my way of saying goodbye to my patients and practice. I wish I could acknowledge each of them personally and the many ways in which they have taught me about hope and resilience in the face of daunting obstacles. I am deeply grateful for all who were willing to revisit our work together and to make constructive comments regarding the case studies included in this memoir. Speaking with them after so many years was very enlightening and gratifying.

I have benefited from the expertise of two able editors. Emily Wood helped me organize my discussion of early family and learning experiences and how these led me to choose psychiatry as a specialty. With her guidance, I was able to give form, substance, and flow to what emerged initially as a series of disconnected memories.

David Milofsky kept me on focus as to audience and tone and provided helpful suggestions from his personal knowledge of the mental health professions and the genre of medical memoirs. His insistence on brevity and precision led to further insights which propelled me forward with each new draft. I learned from David that a good editor, like a good therapist, helps liberate meaning from the shackles of confusing, sometimes overwrought narratives.

Many colleagues and friends have been immensely supportive during my practice years and especially during periods of uncertainty regarding what to include in this memoir. Dr. Peter Mayerson, my practice consultant and mentor, has been an enthusiastic supporter of my writing efforts for many years and offered ongoing encouragement during many phases of this memoir.

My late friend and colleague, Dr. Geoffrey Heron, walked with me through difficult dilemmas involving several of the treatments I discuss. I deeply miss his sense of humor, compassionate insights, and unique ability to grasp essential clinical themes.

My ex-wives, Ellen Graves and Nancy Bell supported me through my training, in co-parenting, and for significant periods of my practice. Nancy facilitated my getting back into treatment when I was experiencing my most severe depression. I remain deeply grateful to each of them for their support.

Several therapists and teachers have assisted me during my career, including the first four who have since passed away:

Dr. Joan Fleming encouraged me to write about the painful experience of losing two colleagues during my training years. Thanks to her, I have used writing throughout my practice to understand and master many challenging experiences.

Dr. Homer Olsen provided an empathic context for my understanding and adapting to the stresses of psychiatric training.

Dr. John Kelly led by example with his warmth and compassionate self-disclosure and taught me the value of the therapist as a "new developmental object."

Dr. Richard Vanden Bergh helped me survive and even thrive following the most painful of my depressions and often frightening transitions into hypomania.

Dr. David Hurst helped me clarify some of my personal relationship issues and made helpful comments on my chapters on treating physicians, gays, and bisexuals.

My piano teacher, the late Anne Pap, during nearly a quarter century of lessons, taught me to listen carefully to the music I was making and, by extension, to the tonal nuances of my patients. In many ways, studying and playing piano with Anne was my best therapy.

The Reverend Elizabeth Randall, with her gentle spiritual counseling, helped me reconnect with my own spiritual self and Episcopal traditions, broadening the scope of my treatment endeavors through enhancing my own forgiveness work.

Several friends and colleagues were helpful in providing critiques of specific chapters, including: Randall Buzan on Listening and

ACKNOWLEDGMENTS

Empathy (Chapter 5), Fred Luskin, Rafaat Ludin, and the late Ronald Young on Forgiveness (Chapter 7), William Van Doorninck on Spiritualty and Religious Faith (Chapter 6), and Future Trends (Chapter 14), Richard Martinez on Boundaries (Chapter 8) and confidentiality issues, Roy Lowenstein and Joan Carroll Heron on Depression and Suicide (Chapter 9), Woody Emlen and Sarah Patten on Treating Physicians (Chapter 11), Peter Mayerson and Ted Levin on Retirement (Chapter 15), Paul Walker on Men's Group Therapy (Chapter 10) and Morey Wolfson and Erwin Mozer on Future Trends (Chapter 14).

Joan Carroll Heron, LCSW, listened empathically as I described the painful experiences of losing four patients who took their own lives and also my own experience of a suicidal depression. Joan helped me reformulate what my patients were telling me and how I could have been more helpful to them.

Dr. George Hartlaub deserves special mention. A superb listener, George has an uncanny way of fertilizing new ideas which have been lying dormant. During our many morning walks around Denver's parks, I found myself articulating major themes for whole chapters for the first time. He and his wife, Dr. Joan Shapiro, graciously allowed me to enjoy the solitude of their Colorado mountain home as I composed and revised several chapters.

My brother Charles read the entire manuscript and provided helpful comments on my discussions of early developmental issues, family history, and my treatment of spiritual and religious issues. Having known me since I was born, his insights and support have been invaluable.

My late cousin, Robert Leuze, an operatic baritone, helped elucidate my work with gays and bisexuals. Discussions with Robert enabled me to become more comfortable examining certain elements of my own homophobic upbringing.

Jan Marie Pilcher also read the entire manuscript and helped me strike a better balance between personal and professional disclosures. Lila Pilcher, RN, offered helpful suggestions regarding my Introduction.

Members of my men's group, many of whom I have known for over 40 years, have been consistently empathic and supportive of my efforts as a therapist and writer. They include: John Cooper, Larry Englander, Daniel Foss, David Gies, Mel Grusing, George Hartlaub, Ed Ladon, Erwin Mozer and Paul Walker. These men, like brothers, helped me take my own emotional pulse and discern when I needed to lessen my load and, ultimately, when it was time to retire. Dr. Ed Ladon was always available for technical assistance when my laptop decided to abscond into cyberspace with carefully-fashioned documents.

Finally, I wish to thank my publishers at Stillwater River Publications, Dawn and Steven Porter, for their patience and steadiness in guiding me through the rigors of creating my first full-length book.

John S. Graves, M.D
Denver, Colorado
August 2020

AUTHOR BIOGRAPHY

Dr. John S. Graves recently retired after forty-four years of practicing psychiatry in Colorado. He completed his undergraduate studies in history and religion at Wesleyan University and attended Union Theological Seminary's interdisciplinary program in Psychiatry and Religion. Following pre-medical studies at Columbia University, he attended the Albert Einstein College of Medicine where he graduated with honors in 1971. He completed his psychiatry residency at the University of Colorado Health Sciences Center where he served for thirty-five years on the Volunteer Clinical Psychiatry Faculty.

His primary clinical interests and publications include managing practice stress, complicated bereavement, individual and group therapy for patients with bipolar disorder and the creative process. He is Board Certified in Psychiatry and Neurology and a Distinguished Life Fellow of the American Psychiatric Association. Following his retirement he has enjoyed doing volunteer work through his church with homeless women and for Mental Health Colorado. An avid hiker, fly fisherman, and classical pianist, he lives with his loving companion in Denver, Colorado.

Made in the USA
Coppell, TX
24 January 2021